D1231615

R 20 1990

The Holocaust Conspiracy

Other books by William R. Perl

Operation Action

The Four Front War

The Holocaust Conspiracy:

An International Policy of Genocide

By William R. Perl

Shapolsky Publishers
New York

For additional information, contact:
Shapolsky Publishers, Inc.
136 W. 22nd St., New York, NY 10011
212/633-2022   FAX 212/633-2123

10 9 8 7 6 5 4 3 2 1

Library of Congress Cataloging-in-Publication Data

Perl, William R.
   The holocaust conspiracy: an international policy of genocide - 1st ed.

1. Holocaust, Jewish (1939-1945)-Causes.
2. Refugees, Jewish - Government policy.
3. World War, 1939-1945 - Diplomatic History.
I. Title

940.53'1503924-dc19   D804.3.p47 1988   CIP 88-29526

ISBN 0-944007-24-4

Manufactured in the United States of America

TABLE OF CONTENTS

Notes On The Holocaust Conspiracy

Even a close study of the Holocaust material accumulated and published so far leaves the scholar, as well as the public, wondering how all this could happen, how was such a collapse of value systems possible? These crucial questions have not yet been fully answered.

Historians are geared by their training to investigate *what* happened and *how*, and the excellent work done so far is naturally centered around these questions. This author is a psychologist who in this book examines the *why*, utilizing and combining data largely unearthed and meticulously documented by historians. Why could humans act in such ways against their fellow humans?

The facts are well known, but their meaning has not been fully explored. This work is unique for several reasons. Its investigation leads to a result shattering in its impact.

By pulling together scattered findings as well as using his own research, Dr. Perl documents that the Holocaust and the frightful effectiveness of the Final Solution program were not simply the outcome of German planning accompanied by the passivity of the rest of the world. By extensive documentation from widely divergent sources, the author demonstrates and substantiates that plots and actions of the powers of the world so effectively supported the German genocide program, that they amounted to active cooperations and complicity in the Holocaust.

Acknowledgments

My first tribute of thanks goes to Charles Goolsby and Reuven Schlenker who in our regular Sunday morning sessions were a source of inspiration and who provided documentation for the subjects discussed.

At any time of day or evening I could-and did-call on Richard Greenfield of the Library of Congress. He responded by sending complete data, not only on the topic requested, but also on closely related subjects. Often this additional evidence contained unexpected valuable information.

Claude Furman was my research assistant who classified and organized the, especially in the early stages, overwhelming mass of intelligence.

Winnie Meiselman encouraged me decisively to start the actual work on this book which for a long time I had wanted to write. When I was seeking connections that would provide hard to obtain evidence, as well as on numerous other occasions she was most supportive of the task.

Dr. Liliana Picciotto—Faragan of the Milan based Centro di Documentazione Ebraica Contemporanea was most helpful in the research connected with Italy and the Vatican.

My thanks go also to Rozanne McKnew who typed the manuscript from the first draft to the final form and made many valuable suggestions.

Special thanks go to Maureen Berge for suggesting the cover design.

Finally, Lore, my wife, must accept expression of my gratitude here, too. She did not only help by her unending patience and emotional support. She assisted and worked with me on every phase of this book and shared to the full the labor, the frustration and the gratification of writing it.

Foreword

The history of mankind is wrought with tragedies but none so great as that of the Holocaust. The horrors of that dark period were unprecedented in magnitude and nature. Deportation trains, death camps, gas chambers, and the brutal and cold blooded murder of six million Jews by Nazi soldiers in pursuit of the "Final Solution" are constant reminders of man's inhumanity to man and his capacity to be cruel.

As the forces of evil were unleashed against the unsuspecting Jews of Europe, the so-called "civilized" nations of the Western world stood by and watched in silence. Respect for human life and dignity, the essence of civilized societies, eroded, only to be replaced by inertia or worse, indifference. The United States, a nation founded on the principles of liberty and equality for all human beings, allowed its commitment to these cherished principles to waive and made little effort to rescue the victims of Nazi oppression.

In my view, just about every Jew who was killed could have been saved if the governments of the Allied powers had provided timely refuge to European Jews who lived in countries coming under the control of Hitler's forces. Increasingly, their failure to do so is being recognized as a "conspiracy of silence." William Perl supports this thesis with comprehensive research and thought provoking analysis of the evidence. His book, which I urge every American to read, enlarges on that sad page in history when the United States and its allies turned a blind eye to the agony and terror of the Jews. It is an important contribution to the literature and the lessons of the tragedy of the Holocaust.

Claiborne Pell
Chairman
United States Senate
Committee on Foreign Relations

Conspiracy   Combination of persons for an evil or unlawful purpose.

The Oxford English Dictionary Corrected Re-Issue. (The philosophical Society, Oxford)

Conspiracy   A striking concurrence of tendencies, circumstances or phenomena as though in planned accord.

Webster's New International Dictionary of the English Language. Unabridged. A Merriam Webster. (G & C. Merriam Company, Springfield, Massachusetts.)

Conspiracy   A combination of persons for a secret, unlawful or evil purpose.

The Random House Dictionary of the English Language. Unabridged. (Random House, New York)

Chapter 1
CONSPIRACY
The Psychosocial Context

No contemporary historical event has been as thoroughly researched as the Holocaust. Literally hundreds of books, monographs and shorter studies have been published, and TV documentaries and movies added their versions. The Library of Congress has more than 1,300 titles catalogued as dealing with the subject. Why then still another book?

Certainly, countless details are known as to *what* happened, but there is only scarce information as to: *how could it all happen*? Data are widely scattered, and one seeking a comprehensive view has to obtain it from many sources. There is thus less need for even more data than for providing a global perspective for a wide readership.

Presenting brand new data together with extensive information from previous sources, this book performs a unique, radically different function. By collating, combining and synthesizing known elements with new ones, it establishes a completely new thesis. The conclusion becomes inescapable that it was not apathetic *inaction*, but that deliberate *action*, that conspiracies within individual governments and between governments produced a synergy of forces which—as planned—made escape impossible for the targeted victims.

New also is the treatment in detail—and the inclusion all in one volume—of the Holocaust policies practiced by countries hitherto relatively neglected by Holocaust research: Switzerland, Latin America, the Soviet Union, as well as those of the International Red Cross.

The probing of the basic relationship between the Holocaust and today's international terrorism, their *relationship in ideology, methodology and practice*, constitutes still another new element in the herewith presented work.

* * *

The Holocaust is a crucial issue for present political developments. Its tenets and the methods by which they are applied are alive today. Nowadays they threaten far more than a relatively small segment of the world's population. Aggressively on the offensive, these principles endanger today the social fibre upon which civilization and particularly the political existence of the world's democracies is built.

In several ways, Nazism and the Holocaust must be recognized as working models of modern terrorism. Let us look at the persons who played a major part in the ultimate phase of the Holocaust.

Hitler attracted attention first when he called for terrorist acts against the young German republic. On August 5, 1921, he founded the "storm units" for the admitted purpose of terrorizing his political opponents. Members were easily recruited from the numerous *Freikorps* fanatics, operating freely throughout Germany. These were terrorist organizations which, following World War I, committed numerous murders and acts of sabotage against the newly created German republic. In generally law-abiding Germany, three hundred seventy political murders were commited between 1919-1922, including the murder of the Foreign Minister, Walter Rathenau.[1]

Herman Rauschnig in his *Gespraeche mit Hitler*, Zurich, 1940, quoted Hitler as saying: "Cruelty impresses. People need a good scare. They want to be afraid of something. They want someone to make them afraid, someone to whom they can submit with shudder. Haven't you noticed after a brawl at a meeting, that the ones who got beaten up are the first ones to apply for membership in the party? What is this rot you talk about violence and how shocked you are about torture? The masses want that, they need something to dread."

Hitler's own lenient treatment after his abortive *putsch* and the outpouring of public sympathy strengthened his determination to do away with the German democracy. It revealed to him a spiritually weak system, no longer willing to defend itself.

Heinrich Himmler, next to Hitler the most powerful man in Germany, started his political career in the *Freikorps*. He continued, as supreme chief of the German police authorities, including the *Gestapo*, to adhere to the same principles of terror he had practiced during the moves to destabilize the young republic.

Martin Borman who in time became Hitler's personal secretary and therefore, extremely powerful, had come from the *Freikorps*. He had murdered his elementary school teacher and had been briefly jailed by the Weimar Government.

Ernst Roehm, who made his way to become commander of the *Sturmabteilungen* and who was assassinated by Hitler's orders, had also come from the terrorist *Freikorps*.

Rudolph Hoess, the commander of the Auschwitz extermination camp, was, while a member of the *Freikorps*, involved in a brutal political murder. He was convicted and sentenced to ten years in prison, but after serving five years was released by a weak government, only to resume at once his terrorist activities.

SS Lt. General Theodor Eicke, the first National Inspector of Concentration Camps, also came from the *Freikorps* organization, where he had become one of the leaders. He succeeded in evading arrest and was sentenced—in absentia—to death for his terrorist activities. He hid in Italy until 1928 when he returned to Germany and joined the SS. He is also known as the founder of the SS Totenkopfbrigade (Death Skull Brigade) which was to "guard" the concentration camps. Sections of the Totenkopfbrigade played appropriate parts when German troops invaded their eastern neighbors. Eicke was succeeded as National Inspector of Concentration Camps by SS Major General Richard Gluecks. Gluecks, too, had been a member of the *Freikorps* before the rise of the Nazi party. Interestingly, Gluecks, the master of all concentration camps, is described by Rudolph Hoess in that man's autobiography as being "good natured" and possessing "an unquenchable Rhenisch humor and he saw the funny side of everything. He made the most serious matters sound comic and he laughed about them." Eichman came straight to the Nazi party and the SS. He was too young to join the *Freikorps* in its time.

This "goodnaturedness" and the "unquenchable Rhenisch humor" of the National Inspector of Concentration Camps brings to the fore another element of ideology and attitude mutual to Nazism and the terrorism we are confronting today. It is the principle that the aim fully justifies any means, however barbaric they may be. Thus, the martyrdom of Robert Stetham, a young American seaman kidnapped with a TWA plane in June 1985. He was bound and gagged; had his knee caps and legs broken; was beaten so that every rib in his body was broken before, in the execution style practiced also by the SS, he was shot from the rear into the small of his neck (Genickschuss); and his body was dumped without identification on the tarmac of the Beirut airport by his Shiite hijackers who demonstrated the bestiality so typical of the Holocaust. And, after dumping the mutilated body and closing the door of the aircraft, the murderer is reported to have laughed— unquenchable humor.

There is still another element that Nazism shares with today's terrorists. Nazism with its final aim of world domination, used anti-Semitism, which was endemic in many parts of the world, as an effective entering wedge to introduce its other theories, to gain sympathy, and to demoralize the nations targeted for takeover. This practice goes hand in hand with the endeavor to achieve publicity for the terrorist's professed political aims. The intent: To further divide the victims and to pervert their value system. The terrorists seek sympathy— and often succeed in finding it. Thus the *Freikorps* claimed that it was fighting for a noble cause; all it wanted was fairness for Germany, including the right to defend itself, a right possessed by every other nation. The German disarmament as agreed to by Germany in the peace treaty of Versailles was thus "morally wrong." Secretly, the German militarists were rearming anyhow, and it is well known what happened once Germany felt she had enough weapons to start another war. Today's terrorists similarly seek opportunities for publicizing an image of being underdogs, of being treated unfairly, while brutal aggression and domination hide behind that underdog facade.

The claim that one's deeds, however horrifying, are justified, even demanded by God himself, is another element common to modern and Holocaust terrorism. Recent acts of terror are committed by groups that purport to fulfill the will of Allah: *Jihad* (Holy War), Hesbollah (Party of God), etc. And Hitler referred on numerous occasions to his acting on behalf of God. Specifically, as to the Holocaust he stated that "by destroying the Jews I am doing the will of God."

Today's terrorists are equipped not only with machine guns; they also possess and use rockets, anti-tank weapons, and powerful explosives. It is only a question of time until they obtain atomic weapons, either directly by theft and bribery, or even from one of the countries that uses terrorism for its own purposes. Our authorities could quite casually one day receive a message that suicide truck bombers are poised in New York, Washington, Chicago, Los Angeles and/or some other major cities and that, unless we surrender unconditionally to some very major demands, the truck bombs will be detonated. All our efforts to secure this country's safety by having sophisticated missiles, long-range bombers, aircraft carriers, and nuclear submarines would then be of no avail.

The striking parallel outlined above makes a book such as this, probing into the details of the international interplay and support which made the plan to carry out the Holocaust so frighteningly effective, a necessity for today. But even more pressing is the rapidly accelerating use of terror to shape international policies.

Holocaust research was valuably aided by the tens of thousands of pages accumulated in the course of the various war crimes trials. Pretrial investigators, prosecutors and defense attorneys often arranged their data in well-organized summaries, and these usually name the source of the statements and of the conclusions either to be announced in the trial or to have it all ready when and if the occasion arises.

The history of Holocaust research shows an interesting pattern of development. It was eight years after the end of World War II before the first major works— Gerald Reitlinger's *The Final Solution* and sixteen years before Raul Hilberg's *The Destruction of the European Jews*—was published. They were the first of a rapidly increasing number of studies.

Possibly influenced by the availability of data from the war crimes trials and maybe by the trials themselves, the earlier works dealt entirely with the actions perpetrated against the Jews by the Germans and their collaborators. The question of responsibility of others was rarely even touched. The sole responsibility of the Germans, who, after all, developed the plan and put it into action, was more or less assumed to be a matter of course. It took time to break away from that assumption and to arrive at the conclusion that other factors contributed to the extent to which the German plan was successful. It took even *more* time to announce it.

At that point, thoroughly documented books began to appear, which revealed the guilt of nations that were found not to have done enough to rescue those fleeing for their lives.[2] However, as scrupulously documented and well written as these studies are, they have a common limitation: they more or less confine their focus to specific areas (as often indicated by their titles).

It has taken more than a generation to have wide-scale acknowledgement of other nations' guilt in the Final Solution and to let the realization that the Germans were not the only ones responsible for the horror begin to sink into the public psyche. The fact that most of the "civilized" world closed its shores to the desperate victims when there was still a chance to rescue them is now well established by the documents of those very countries. It is time now to take the next step that the voluminous evidence makes all but inevitable: the conclusion that it was not only neglect, carelessness, ignorance or a host of other excuses, familiar to us all, that made the German "solution" so effective. The facts assembled in this book will fully support the finding that a virtual conspiracy existed among the Allies (and many others) which prevented the escape of millions from the Nazi death machine.

Action on the part of those who held the power of rescue played a decisive role in obstructing any major rescue effort. There were *deliberate, concerted steps to thwart rescue actions,* such steps decided upon not only by individuals in power, but by governments. De facto measures thus amounted to cooperation, collaboration, and collusion with the German genocide plan.

What the Germans planned and committed is hard to believe. That the world "failed to rescue" is even harder to accept. The conclusion that this failure to rescue was much more than a simple lack of action, but rather part of a deliberate, and not always concealed, set of actions bound to insure the success of the German annihilation plans seems unbelievable. However, the multitude of documents and records available today makes this conclusion not only logical, but inescapable.

To mention one example of this conspiracy, we refer to arrangement between Germany and a country widely viewed as a standard-bearer of humanitarian principles: Switzerland.

On June 24, 1938, the Chief of the Swiss Federal Police, Dr. Heinrich Rothmund, informed the German Legation in Bern that steps would have to be taken against what Dr. Rothmund called the "inundation" of Switzerland by Viennese Jews for whom, he assured the German Minister, Switzerland had no more use than Germany.[3]

On August 10th, the Swiss Minister to Germany called on the Chief of the Political Division of the German Foreign Office in his office in Berlin. He stated that the entrance of Jews into Switzerland had reached "extraordinary proportions," that on one day alone 47 Jews had arrived in Basel, and that the Swiss government was firmly determined to prevent a "Verjudung" (Judaification, a word straight from the Nazi vocabulary) of their country. He concluded with the demand that the so-far visaless entry of Germans into Switzerland would have to be stopped.[4] There was, however, one condition under which Switzerland would abstain from such revocation. This was, if the Germans would agree to mark all passports of all Jews (not only of those traveling to Switzerland) distinctly, so that the Jews should be pointed out as such. On September 29, 1938, a formal treaty was signed in which Germany obliged itself to mark all passports of its Jews, whether they were traveling to Switzerland or not.[5] The Germans then ordered, in accordance with the treaty, all passports of Jews to be identified as such by a large— 3 centimeters— red "J" that was to be placed next to the name of the bearer.

Within a few days, on October 4, the Swiss Bundesrat briefly debated and then ratified the agreement, and the ratified documents were exchanged November 11, 1938. Thus, the infamous Jewish passport was born, a measure that made it incomparably more difficult for Jews to pass any frontier anywhere.

Evidence of such conspiracies to keep the Jews bottled up in German-controlled territories abounds. This particular example was chosen for the Introduction because Switzerland has, for centuries, held a unique place in the spectrum of nations, as an independent state offering refuge in one form or another to the persecuted. Of all nations, Switzerland would be the last to be expected to have suggested and signed a treaty with Nazi Germany which could only contribute to the utter demolishment of a people.

That the question of global guilt due to active global involvement in the Holocaust was not probed from the beginning, is partly due to the misunderstanding of the initial German plans for the "solution of the Jewish Problem." Again and again, survivors are asked: "How did you succeed in getting out?" This very question shows the abyss of misunderstanding of the actual situation at the time of the Holocaust. Except for the very last years of the Nazi regime, the question was not at all how to get *out*, but rather where to go.

The Germans were not only ready, they were eager to get the Jews out of territories under German control. It was the combination of German determination to make Europe "Judenrein" (pure of Jews) and the refusal of the world to save those lives which still could have been saved, that resulted in the mass murders. Because the decision to rid Europe of Jews was final and irrevocable, the refusal of the outside world to accept any sizable number of Jews amounted to death sentences. The nature of the German determination to rid Europe of all Jews was made clear again and again to the outside world, epitomized in the nationwide pogrom of Krystallnacht (Crystal Night) on November 9-10, 1938. This would be the fate of all Jews if they did not leave. The world's refusal to open the doors to the desperate was further underlined by increasingly restrictive immigration policies imposed by the United States and Great Britain, among others. They made it clear to the Germans that the fate of millions was a matter of indifference to those countries. Thus, the automation of elimination became a goal, and one that acquired its own momentum and ghastly efficiency.

There can be no reduction in German guilt, but for nine years after Hitler came to power, his party pushed the emigration program while at the same time leaving no doubt of what would happen if the world refused to admit those who were otherwise lost. Many thousands of refugees left between 1938 and 1940 on ships flying the Nazi flag, river boats that brought them down the Danube, all the way, passing Czechoslovakia, Hungary, Yugoslavia, Bulgaria, and Rumania, to the Black Sea. There they were transferred to sea-going ships trying to smuggle them past the British blockade to Palestine.

As the situation became increasingly clear, the Allies felt it necessary to hold an international conference on the fate of the refugees. This was the Evian Conference held July 6–15, 1938. Thirty-two countries participated. It was watched with great interest, not only by those unfortunates whose fate was literally being decided in those rooms, but also by the German High Command, because the decisions made there would clearly indicate what the world was prepared to do to save the targets of Nazi wrath. The answer was clear: Nothing.

The good conference that had been a beacon of hope to millions had been called by the Americans and British. But from the beginning it had also been engineered by these same nations in such a way that it was bound to fail.

After the Evian conference the Germans undertook to make the finality of their decision even clearer to the world. Crystal Night was already mentioned. But lest there remain any doubt, Hitler himself in a major speech delivered in the Reichstag on the anniversary of his coming to power, on January 30, 1939, stated that in case of war— generally viewed as unavoidable by then— "there will be annihilation of the Jewish race in Europe." This announcement was immediately followed up by a circular that went out the day after Hitler's announcement, January 31, and which consisted of a cable by the German Foreign Office sent to all German diplomatic representatives abroad. It accused the Jews of not wanting to emigrate and announced that "Germany will therefore herself take the initiative in finding ways and means and the destination for emigration of the Jews from Germany." The Fuehrer's talk the day before had made it clear enough what that destination was.[6]

So confident were the Germans that the Crystal Night events would cause the world to open its gates, that they prepared to open the concentration camps for those Jews who had obtained an entrance visa to anywhere. Four days after the Crystal Night, on November 14, 1938, SS General Reinhard Heydrich, National Commander of the GESTAPO, sent a Blitz (highest priority) telegram to the Inspectorate of Concentration Camps and also to every concentration camp commander ordering the release of Jews who could emigrate within three weeks.[7]

What was the reaction of the civilized world to that threat of annihilation unless the Jews found new places to which to immigrate? The answer was organized intensification of immigration restrictions. One illustration of the collective obstruction of rescue efforts in the wake of these German announcements and of the Crystal Night will serve to demonstrate the deliberate, organized nature of these decisions and will underline again our thesis that it was not "merely" inaction, but was, in fact, a conspiracy of individuals and governments that helped bring the planned genocide so perilously close to complete success. This example takes us from Switzerland to the other side of the Atlantic.

Stimulated by the events of Crystal Night, on February 9, 1939, Senator Robert Wagner of New York and Representative Edith Rogers of Massachusetts introduced identical bills in their respective houses of Congress to admit by special action 10,000 refugee children under 14 years of age, in 1939 and another 10,000 in 1940. To avoid labor opposition, the bill provided that the children would not be permitted to work and would join their parents as soon as safety elsewhere was assured. The American Friends Service Committee, which volunteered their services, would organize the children's movements to the United States as well as their placement. Within 24 hours after the plan had become known, 4,000 American families had offered their homes to these children. Radio stations and newspapers were swamped with even more offers.

But a powerful group of isolationists and anti-Semites banded together and planned their strategy to prevent these bills from becoming law. By April, when the Congressional hearing started, the conspirators against the Children's Rescue Bill were well organized. Francis H. Kinnicutt represented thirty "patriotic organizations united in the Allied Patriotic Societies"[8] of which he was president! These included the Veterans of Foreign Wars, the American Legion, the Society of Mayflower Descendants, the Daughters of the American Revolution, the Lord's Day Alliance of the United States, the Daughters of the Confederacy, and other isolationist organizations.

Mr. Kinnicutt spoke up quite openly, "...this is just part of a drive to go back to the condition when we were flooded with foreigners who tried to run the country on different lines from those laid down by the old stock...Strictly speaking, it is not a refugee bill at all, for by the nature of the case most of those to admitted would be of the Jewish race." There was of course more activity on the part of those united to prevent the bill from becoming law. There was heavy lobbying in Congress. Colonel John Taylor lobbied for the American Legion against the bill and in support of a bill by North Carolina Senator Robert Reynolds which would abolish all immigration to the United States for the next ten years. Mrs. Agnes Waters, representing, as she claimed, the Widows of World War I Veterans, testified, that if the Children's Rescue Bill should pass, the United States "would be made helpless to guarantee our children their rights under the Constitution to life, liberty and the pursuit of happiness... if this country is going to become the dumping ground for the persecuted minorities of Europe. The refugees...can never become loyal Americans."

Because the lobbying in Congress was going well, those who supported the bill hoped that the President might make his influence felt. Congresswoman O'Day of New York wrote to Mr. Roosevelt hoping to obtain a statement in favor of the bill. But the President refused to become involved in a subject opposed not only by many Republicans but bitterly resented by the conservative Democrats of the solid South. O'Day's letter forwarded to Mr. Roosevelt by his secretary carries on the margin in his own handwriting the notation: "File-No action."[9]

In Washington, more issues are often revealed and decided at diplomatic cocktail parties than at formal meetings. Mr. Pierrepoint Moffat, chief of the State Department's Division of European Affairs, reports in his diary, now in the National Archives, about such a cocktail party which points out clearer than the official debates the true nature of the attitude of the insiders toward this rescue attempt. Mrs. James Hougheling, wife of the all powerful Commissioner of Immigration said: "The trouble with the Wagner-Rogers bill was that 20,000 children would all too soon grow up into 20,000 ugly adults."[10]

Well, the bills never left the committee. The conspiracy of anti-Semites and isolationists succeeded in torpedoing the rescue bills and the children did not grow up into any kind of adults.

This was early in 1939. Five years and more that three million dead Jews later, the flames that were consuming European Jewry were being fed effectively from both sides of the Atlantic. The Germans had added scientific extermination methods as well as modern industrial principles to their murder tools. And on the other side, the countries of possible escape had tightened their measures preventing rescue, thus making certain that the voracious death factories did not run out of supplies. We will now present one last example in this initial chapter of what we mean when we charge conspiracy.

The U.S. Treasury, which was in charge of Foreign Funds Control, had been involved in various rescue plans. Officials in the Treasury had, by the end of 1943, come to suspect obstruction by the State Department in such attempts at rescue. After one such particularly blatant instance, the Secretary of the Treasury, Mr. Henry Morgenthau Jr., asked the Treasury's General Counsel, Randolph Paul, to look into the matter and to provide him with a report. Paul enlisted the help of his assistant General Counsel, Josiah E. Du Bois Jr. As the task was both delicate and complex, still another high ranking official was added to the team: John Pehle of the Foreign Funds Division. Their findings were so incriminating that Paul, a lawyer and the highest ranking legal officer in the Treasury, must have read and studied the report more than once before he put his signature on it. But he did.

The report is eighteen pages long. Prepared by three high government officials, all of them Protestants, it is titled REPORT TO THE SECRETARY ON THE ACQUIESCENCE OF THE GOVERN-

MENT IN THE MURDER OF JEWS. Its conclusions speak for themselves:

These State Department officials are guilty of the following:

1. They have not only failed to use the Governmental machinery at their disposal to rescue Jews from Hitler, but they have even gone so far as to use the government machinery to prevent the rescue of these Jews.

2. They have not only failed to cooperate with private organizations in the efforts of these organizations to work out individual programs of their own, but have taken steps designed to prevent these programs from being put into effect.

3. They have not only failed to facilitate the obtaining of information concerning Hitler's plans to exterminate the Jews of Europe, but in their official capacity have gone so far as to surreptitiously attempt to stop the obtaining of information concerning the murder of the Jewish population of Europe.

4. They have tried to cover up their guilt by:

a) concealment and misrepresentation.

b) the giving of false and misleading explanations for their failures to act and their attempts to prevent action; and

c) the issuance of false and misleading statements concerning the "action" which they have taken to date.[11]

The Result of this report will be discussed in a later chapter. One must, of course, not look at the happenings of the Holocaust without viewing them in the context of the overall sociological and psychological framework within which they occurred. Surveying overall conditions existing at that time, we find especially that the combination of two factors heavily contributed to the Holocaust's birth, continuing spread, and altogether to its horrifying success. These two major contributing factors are psychologically deeply rooted, widespread anti-Semitism which operated in a world which saw much of its value system come crashing down. This loss of values had started prior to World War I and continued and worsened thereafter. The mixing of vehement anti-Semitism with the desire to find simple answers in a deteriorating world was a major factor in that cataclysmic explosion of all human values: The Holocaust.

No human trait has brought more suffering and destruction to humankind than the hatred of one group against another, especially religious, racial, and national hatred. Since the days that one group of primitive man clashed with another group, hatred of "the others" has taken a tremendous toll in lives, property, and the ability to enjoy a harmonious, peaceful life.

Anti-Semitism is the oldest and most persistent hatred in the world. Numerous scholars, among them historians, sociologists, theologians, and psychologists have given thought to the causes of the phenomenon of anti-Semitism. To approach this subject in any kind of detailed report would fill at least one full volume and anything approaching such an analysis is outside the scope of this book. Yet, we cannot deal with issues of the Final Solution without at least summarizing what is known about the sources of anti-Semitism.

Four main groups of causes are adduced for the existence of anti-Semitism and for its stubborn persistence in a world that is thought to be increasingly enlightened. They are: theological causes, psychological reasons, sociological factors and finally, economic conditions. Of course, none of these operates within a vacuum, and innumerable combinations of these four categories may be found leading to the end result of hatred as it has existed historically and as it persists today.

We believe that one very basic psychological element should be given more prominence than is generally attributed to it. It is the primordial development of primitive man's need and subsequent necessity to differentiate between what is good for him and what is bad. It was good to approach certain animals while it was bad or outright dangerous to be near others. It was bad to drop a rock on one's foot but good to hurl it at an opponent, animal or human.

Happenings outside man's control were, understandably, attributed to powers superior to his own: to good spirits or gods when the occurrence was a desired one. Unwanted or catastrophic events were seen as caused by bad, evil forces.

With the fervor of religious feelings sweeping the western world as Christianity spread, the need for a negative power, for the concept of a devil who threatened everything that was good was a parallel development. Historical conditions existing in the early years of Christianity lead it to cast the Jews into the role of satanic counterplayers of God, a role that was for almost two millenia, wherever Christianity penetrated, impressed upon the mind of man.

A look at the history of the time helps to explain the direction of such developments. The very early church stood up against anti-Jewish feelings. In his epistle to the Romans, Paul says, "they are beloved for the sake of their forefathers"[12] and "I myself am an Israelite, a descendant of Abraham, a member of the tribe of Benjamin."[13] However historical events, especially as they related to the Romans, soon influenced the new faith to distance itself from the one from which it had sprung and of which Christ himself had been a member. At the time of Christ, the Roman Empire comprised most of what was considered the civilized world. Roman rule had never been accepted in ancient Israel, and there were constant rumblings of revolt. Suspected leaders of insurrections or disturbances often met the same fate as criminals under Roman law— crucifixion. Just after Christ had been crucified, the Roman role in this horrific act was, for good reasons, downplayed in the subsequent Gospels. In the span of years between the crucifixion and the writing of the Gospels, yet another Jewish revolt had broken out against Roman rule. This one was particularly viciously fought by both sides, with the Romans finally victorious. Anger at the Jews accompanied this conflict and it must have seemed only prudent to the early Church fathers to distance themsleves as much as possible from their forebears.

This factor coupled with the firm desire to convert the Romans to the new religion made such rejection almost inevitable. Man's early fears of forces beyond his control, and his attribution of benevolence or evil to these forces became a necessary and soon prevailing factor in the hatred of the Jews. Early Christian teachings make a sharp division between the forces of good and evil. Because of Christ, the new Christians placed themselves on the side of good. The side of evil was reserved for nonbelievers, especially those who did not accept Jesus as the Messiah, the Jews.

In order to reinforce this idea and to strengthen the faith, early Christians were told that the Jews were the personifications of evil, cohorts with the devil, a group to be hated and persecuted. The religious fervor of the times (there had been dozens of self-proclaimed Messiahs in the two centuries surrounding Christ's life span) was fomented by the desperate uncertainties and turmoil of everyday life. It had made the need for an earthly scapegoat prominent. Christ offered hope in a seemingly hopeless world, but the persistence of evil long after his execution demanded an explanation. The devil was the known antagonist, but he was somewhat abstract. An earthly group that could be associated with the devil fulfilled several needs at once: the battle against evil could be expressed in direct acts; the scapegoat group could then be rejected, often killed or robbed, and otherwise brought to see the error of their ways— and all this in the name of God. At the same time, such a division served to differentiate Christianity from Judaism and to proselytize the new faith and people.

The most powerful preachers of Christianity subscribed to these beliefs, and their preachings were increasingly filled with incitement to hatred and slaughter.

From thousands of pulpits, as religion spread, anti-Jewish feeling became engraved and gave rise to myths of irrational hatreds that persist to this day. The Jews, it was claimed, had murdered Christ and had by that act made themselves cursed forever. They had become God's counter-players, devilish, satanic.

It was particularly John Chrysotom (347–407), the Church Father who earned high recognition by becoming the patriarch of Constantinople, who conducted a vehement campaign of Jew-hatred. He was a powerful speaker and an impressive writer and thus quite influential in forming public opinion. How his words were appreciated by his contemporaries is shown by the name with which they honored him. (Greek: chrysos-gold; tom-mouth.) He was made a saint in 438.

John Chrysotom thought that the Jews were "the plague of the universe...possessed by the devil...They kill and maim each other...They murder their offspring and offer themselves to the devil." He describes the synagogue as a "whorehouse" and a home for the devil. They had hatefully assassinated Christ, a crime for which there could never be an expiation. Christians who fraternized with Jews were "dancing with the devil"; the Jews were "fit for slaughter."

John Chrysotom's teachings became a model for teaching in Catholic seminaries. This was at a time in which the educational system inherited from the Romans and the Greeks had broken down, and the Church provided practically the only education available. As Christianity spread rapidly across Europe, so did its teachings and , with it, anti-Semitism. And the darker the Dark Ages became, the darker became the lives of the Jews.

One of the most pernicious myths has been that of Christian blood being demanded in the making of the flat Passover bread, matzoh. The primitive satanic elements of this blood libel myth, combined with the heightened religious tensions of the Easter-Passover season, were often enough to whip up the population into a frenzy of hate and destruction against the Jews. Again and again such outbreaks occurred all over Europe from early in the Middle Ages to almost the present day.

To mention just a few, in 1475 in Trent, Italy following a Lenten sermon by the fanatical Franciscan monk Bernadino de Feltre in which he described vividly the sufferings of Christ and announced that the Jews must suffer for their sins and that this would soon be manifested, a little boy disappeared. His body was found soon after. The charge of ritual murder arose, and all members of the Jewish community were arrested, including women and children. Seventeen of them had "confessed" after fifteen days of torturing. One died in prison; six were burned at the stake in a festive public ceremony. Two who had converted had earned the right not to die at the stake— they were strangled.[14] A similar picture repeats itself in Troyes, France (1171) where following a blood libel, thirteen Jews were burned at the stake. In Lincoln, England, (1235) the blood libel resulted in eighteen Jews being burned; in Fulda, Germany, (1235) four were burned, and the tragedies continued.

As the ritual murder charges increased, strongest in Germany and France, Popes Gregory IX and Innocent IV spoke out against the blood libel, but that myth was too deeply impressed upon the feeling and thinking of the Christian masses to permit the Popes' exhortation to have a major effect. Particularly in Eastern Europe— Poland and Russia— ritual murder trials multiplied, so that in 1759 Pope Clement XIV took a firm stand against the ritual murder myth. Yet as recent as in the late nineteenth century a murder trial was conducted in Hungary and in Russia. Even at the beginning of the twentieth century, one such trial took place in Austria. The rural jury convicted the accused, and he was sentenced to death; but the Emperor commuted the sentence, and some years later the man was quietly released.

During the early crusades, tens of thousands of Jews were massacred as the crusaders, on their way to the Holy Land, practiced their martial arts on the defenseless Jews. During the Black Death, the great plague that convulsed Europe, the Jews were accused of having been responsible for the disease's outbreak, and again thousands were slaughtered for their "crime." The claim at that time was that the wells had been poisoned to decimate the Christian population and thus assure domination of the world by Satan and the Jews. It is interesting to note that the much later anti-Semitic claim, made in the nineteenth century in the so-called *Protocols of the Elders of Zion* continues a similar myth.

The coming of Protestantism and of the Reformation had little influence on the phenomenon of Jew hatred. Martin Luther could not free himself from the mythological image of the Jew as representing Satan of this earth. He published and distributed several anti-Semitic pamphlets, and in one of them[15] he summarizes into nine points the way one should deal with Jews. "1...their synagogues or churches should be set on fire. 2. Their houses should likewise be broken and destroyed. 3. They should be deprived of their prayer books and Talmuds. 4. Their rabbis must be forbidden under threat of death to teach any more..." The pamphlet continues in that vein.

While the theological element is paramount in the creation and persistence as well as in the vehemence of anti-Semitism, it is not the only factor. Economic conditions, too, are responsible. In The Dark and Middle ages, until well into modern times, most occupations were closed to the Jews. They were not permitted to own land, and most economic life was organized into guilds from which Jews were excluded. There was one occupation open— that is, reserved for them. The Church forbade Christians to take interest. As the economy of Europe outgrew a primitive state and required the use of credit, the occupation of moneylender was one which the Jews filled. Moneylenders are not loved anywhere, and the Jews as moneylender perfected the image of the hated instrument of the devil.

In the late nineteenth and early twentieth centuries, literature appeared which gave national and racial reasons for anti-Semitism. The national socialist theory of anti-Semitism is based on the principle of race. Yet, at closer look, little that would be really new was added. Jew hatred had always been directed against the entire Jewish people— or Jewish race if one wants to call it that, yet the basic reason remained the same: the image of the Jews as satanic, which filled the human need to differentiate between good and evil, and simplified and reduced issues to the difference between the good guys and the bad ones. The emphasis on nationality and race just served to provide a "reason" for those Jew haters who themselves were not religious but who carried this religion-born devil image within.

Christian Clerics do in increasing numbers recognize the part which Christian teaching played in preparing the ground for the Holocaust. It is for good reason that a highly respected Church of England Bishop, one of the leading theologians, John Baker, Bishop of Salisbury, in an article entitled *Racism and the Bible* states that "Christianity must take a major share of the blame for Nazi genocide and also for the earlier pogroms in Russia. Anti-Judaism did not start out as racist, but in alliance with cultural forces it became racist." He states that the teachings of the New Testament had been distorted and demands that these distorted features be disowned. Christianity, he writes, has "spewed out" anti-Semitism from the earliest times.[16]

There is still another relatively recent driving force in anti-Semitism. To serve Anti-Semitic purposes and to give Jew hatred a more worldly basis, a historical forgery was committed. A political pamphlet directed by its author Maurice Joly against Napoleon III, attributing to him ambitions of world domination, was transformed in France by an unidentified author who worked for the *Okhrana*, the Russian secret police, into one which changes the villain in the forgery, to— the Jews. He added some "Jewish" features and claims that the Jews were striving to dominate the world under the cloak of democracy. It purported to be the secret protocol of a meeting of the Jewish governing body aspiring world domination. He called his forgery "The Elders of Zion. Protocols of the Learned." The Czar, Nicholas II, was handed this fabrication as a possible means of fighting democratic tendencies by proving that they were Jewish. Though impressionable and anti-Semitic, he was aware of the fraud, wrote on the margin of the manuscript "One does not defend a worthy cause by vile means." Interestingly for our subject, it was the members of the German *Freikorps* who first brought that forgery into mass circulation although copies of it had been circulated during the Russian civil war. The troops fighting the communists used the Protocols to show that the "democracy" which the bolshevists claimed to represent was actually a Jewish contrivance. Translated copies distributed by the *Freikorps* and its supporters even reached the United States where they found— up to 1927— a believer and promoter in Henry Ford. During the Nazi era the Protocols became a standard tool to be distributed to the countries that were on the intended victims list in order to sow the seeds of distrust and disunity into democracies. Although the very fact of the Holocaust disproves the whole existence of international Jewish power, the Protocols have recently assumed a very major role in promoting anti-Semitism. The Soviet Union has printed and distributed tens of thousands of its copies, and Soviet papers repeatedly quote this forgery. Arab countries, too, use this canard for inciting Jew-haters among their own populations as well as internationally.

Interestingly there was in the Orient none of the anti-Semitism to be found in Christian countries. Where some mild animosity against the Jews there showed up, it was just part of the general phenomenon of xenophobia. The Japanese had become familiar with the Protocols prior to World War II. Believing them to be genuine, they assumed that the Jews actually constituted a clandestine world power and thought of gaining in the Jews possible friends and allies. The total worldwide impotence of Jews in the face of German persecutions soon showed the Japanese that this pamphlet could not be genuine. Thus, Japan opened wide the gates of Shanghai (then Japanese-controlled) to Jewish refugees and 25,000, mostly from Germany, found a safe haven there. Before their ties to Germany grew very close, the Japanese even intended to befriend the Jews.

Altogether, the ground had been well prepared for the possibility of a disaster of the form and magnitude of the Holocaust.

The tremendous power born out of the human need to contrast black with white, God with the devil, combined with the primitive urge to hate, attack, and destroy, was ready to be directed against the Jews.

However, all the anti-Semitic happenings prior to the Holocaust do not justify the opinion that it was merely or largely a question of quantity of victims or of better organization which makes the Holocaust different from other persecutions. (The word Holocaust was specially formed from the Greek *holos*, total, and *caust*, burning, to define that singular happening.) It has elements that differentiate it sharply from any other mass killings. There is just one Holocaust. The tragedy that befell the Armenians at the hands of the Turks between 1915 and 1922, the mass murder of gypsies during World War II, the bestial killing of Cambodians following the American exodus from Southeast Asia, are most shameful events, but for reasons that we will shortly outline they differ from the Holocaust.

There are at least five factors that set the Holocaust apart from any other mass persecution or genocidal attempt.

1. Goal. 2. Organization. 3. Location. 4.Results. 5. International cooperation.

The goal was the total annihilation of the Jewish people— men, women, and children—wherever they lived. The fate of the Gypsies under German rule was horrifyingly tragic. It is estimated that 250,000 out of a total of one million gypsies who were in the Germans' grasp were murdered, most of them in Auschwitz. But not only did three fourths of the gypsies under German rule survive, there was no plan to murder all gypsies. The Germans differentiated between gypsies who lived in Germany and had lived there for centuries, and those of other counties; they treated differently those who were productive members of the community and those whom they considered antisocial vagrants and thieves. Native gypsies were those who had resided in Germany since the fifteenth century. They were viewed as citizens and entitled to the protection offered by German law. Gypsies were persecuted and murdered as "useless" because they were seen by the Germans as antisocial elements. Even as late as 1943 in the territories of the East, Himmler excluded from the fate assigned to the "vagrant" ones, those gypsies who were not nomadic and were engaged in useful occupations. Jews, to the contrary were all, without exception, to be annihilated— whether one had served in World War I with highest distinction and earned coveted decorations, or whether one came, as many did, from a family that had resided in Germany since the times of the Romans: no difference. There were no mitigating factors. Not for what a Jew did or did not do, but for what he or she was, Jews were destined for extermination. No exception whatsoever.

The Armenians certainly suffered terribly at the hands of the Turks. Mobs as well as military units engaged in the massacres. There was government collusion, but there was no organized plan designed and executed at great government expense to murder all Armenians, wherever they lived. Let us not forget that the list made up at the infamous Wannsee conference[17] includes the Jews of the entire world, those in Britain as well as those in the United States, Latin America, etc..

The element of *organization and magnitude* makes the Holocaust unique but does so more in combination with the other factors described here. Let us first note that the Holocaust was not a byproduct of the war. It was organized and started before the start of World War II and was not conducted to further the war aims. In fact, it seriously impeded the war effort. Part of the man power which was so short in Germany was diverted to murdering the Jews.

Separate military units, the *Einsatzgruppen*, were formed with the assignments of massacring Jews. In a time of critical shortages of fuel and vehicles, hundreds of trucks brought Jews to the collection centers, and hundreds of trucks were in use for the personnel at the various centers. From all over Europe, trains crisscrossed the lands bringing Jews to the slaughter places. Six major death factories were built: Auschwitz is the one best known, but the Germans constructed five more murder plants at which, using modern industrial methods, the slaughter was performed in an assembly line manner. These other five plants: Majdanek, Treblinka, Sobibor, Chelmno and Belzec too, required not only the use of military personnel, of which Germany was so short, but also the involvement of the German chemical industry for the production of the gas used for the mass murders.

Besides, a net was thrown all over Europe to make the manhunt one hundred percent effective. Civilian authorities everywhere, Germans as well as local ones— who could have otherwise been utilized for different purposes— were working on the huge extermination process. Unique is also the organized commercial profit which the German Government tried to derive from the Holocaust undertaking. Golden teeth broken out from the bodies of the victims were forwarded to the German Treasury, the hair of women was sent to Germany for use there.

Also the *geographical location* sets the Holocaust apart from other massacres with a genocidal element. The center of this total genocide activity was not in far away Anatolia, not in the jungles of Southeast Asia. It was in the heart of Europe. Hundreds of correspondents and diplomatic representatives, ambassadors, consuls and their often large staffs were at the seat of the openly announced master plan and were with their own eyes witnesses to ruthless persecution and murder. Up to World War II, Germany was considered by many as a model of scientific advancement. German scientists and physicians were called upon to aid in the cultural and scientific advancement of many other countries. In the uniqueness of the Holocaust this central location is an essential element because only the Holocaust occurred almost in view of the centers of world civilization. While, as we have pointed out the magnitude of the *result* is only one out of at least five features that establish the absolute uniqueness of the Holocaust, the success achieved by the planners of the Final Solution constitutes certainly a very major distinguishing characteristic. Of the nine million Jews who lived on the European continent and could have been caught by the Germans, six million were slain, two out of every three. The world Jewish population was at that time 18 million— thus, one out of every three Jews living anywhere in the world was murdered. No genocidal persecution ever achieved such results.

At the time of the Crystal Night, November 9, 1938, six and one half years before the end of the national socialist era, there were hundreds of foreign correspondents in Germany. They reported details of the pogroms and, in addition to the newspaper reports, the numerous consuls (the major powers had a consulate in every larger city) reported confidentially even more details to their governments. The Germans had ordered the burning to the ground of all synagogues, destruction of all Jewish shops, mass arrests, and deportation of Jews to concentration camps. Every one of the 7,500 Jewish-owned shops that had escaped earlier destruction or "Aryanization"— expropriation— was now ransacked, and what could not be taken away was hacked to pieces. Close to 31, 000 Jews were herded on trains and deported to concentration camps. And all that not only in full, but in demonstrative view of the foreign press and the foreign diplomatic corps. Germany wanted to demonstrate— following the fiasco of the Evian Conference on Refugees— what was in store for the Jews if the countries continued to block the escape possibilities.

Did the world know in advance? Certainly it did. It knew during and after as well. The Governments had of course, reports from their diplomatic representatives, and also from their intelligence agents. The Vatican knew: hundreds of local clerics reported to their bishops and they, in turn, brought it to the attention of their superiors.

Most of all, as became known only much later, the Allies had broken the German code: Project ENIGMA (ULTRA) allowed eavesdropping Allies to know everything that went on in German-occupied lands and was transmitted in code. More than that: the SS had its own radio stations and the SS code, too, was broken by the Allies. From Charkov and Donets in the Ukraine, to Vitebsk and to Sinferopol in the Crimea, altogether eight stations, the *Einsatzgruppen* beamed their daily "progress reports" to Himmler's headquarters in Berlin and thereby also to the Allies.

But there were even more sources to inform the world of the progress of the Final Solution. Neutral Switzerland was teeming with spies who came and went and not infrequently, traded information. It was also the world's financial center. German business-men visited there, and at least one of them had been so horrified by what he knew was being done to the Jews that he risked his life and let Jewish sources have such detailed information that they rushed to have the tragic news forwarded to London, New York and Washington. We are now referring to the information obtained by the so called Riegner report. In addition, the Polish underground succeeded in smuggling a young Lieutenant out via Sweden. He, Jan Karski, a devout Catholic, now a Professor at Georgetown University, met with Jewish and government representatives in Britain and the United States to give them eyewitness data.

This author was as an American Intelligence Officer during World War II assigned for Liaison to the British MI 19 Intelligence outfit and saw, with his own eyes, reports of massacres and of the use of trucks carrying the Red Cross sign that were loaded with Jews. Shut tight, they went on a short trip during which carbon monoxide was released by a special attachment into the interior of the truck. As soon as the one load was dead, the truck returned for reloading.

Although the Germans tried to keep the mass murders a "secret," so many thousands of people were actively involved in carrying out the Final Solution that in Germany it was a well-repressed but definitely not unknown secret. The allies did, of course, follow newspapers of Germany and of its satellites, and occasionally a slip occurred and confirmed the accuracy of all other sources. Swedish newspapers occasionally printed information received from persons who had escaped from German-held territories and brought with them information full of gruesome details. Also, though to a lesser extent than Zurich, Stockholm was visited by German businessmen and professionals, traveling on their government-sponsored business. Thus in the Swedish *Socialdemokraten* a report was published on October 22, 1942 that was even able to name Eichmann as a prime mover in the "premeditated mass murder." Before that the Stockholm correspondent of London's evening Standard reported that in Vilna, alone, the capital of Lithuania, 60,000 Jews had been massacred.

On June 25, 1942, almost 3 years before the end of World War II, the highly prestigious *Daily Telegraph* reported "More than 700,000 Polish Jews have been slaughtered by the Germans in the greatest massacre in the world's history." The report names the use of poison gas and is accurate in other details of the horror, too.

The above report speaks of Polish Jews only. It was followed in the same paper on June 30 by another report "More than 1,000,000 Jews killed in Europe."

The *New York Times* repeated these items of the *Daily Telegraph* word for word in June 1942, but for the second article in July assigned it an inconspicuous place well inside the paper.

Did the world know? It certainly did, and the more archives are opened the clearer it becomes that not only the facts but the grisly details were known and confirmed to the Allied government. The public, too, had learned that persecution had long since turned into annihilation. Figures had even been published, but the news items, particularly in the United States, were not given any prominence when published; and, in the absence of a publicly sponsored uproar most people found it convenient to repress this uncomfortable knowledge.

Finally, the feature, which, more than any of the preceding, makes the Holocaust so gruesomely unique is that to which this book is devoted: that is the fact that this horror was committed not only with the knowledge of the so-called civilized world, but with its active participation.

* * *

As the documentation can leave no doubt that without this active participation in the German program only a fraction of those who perished would have been murdered, a weighty question arises: did Justice keep one eye closed when it put German leaders alone on trial before the International Military Tribunal in Nuremberg? Would not a parallel trial have been warranted of those leading figures in the Allied and neutral camps who, without formal agreement, knowingly and willingly cooperated in the German annihilation scheme?

Such a trial was, of course, impossible—for political reasons. But does this mitigate existing guilt?

[1] E. Gumpel Vier Jahre Politischer Mord. Berlin 1922

[2] Foremost among these are: I. Abella and H. Troper's *None Is Too Many*; L. Dawidowicz's *The War Against The Jews*; H. Druk's *Failure to Rescue*; H. Feingold's *The Politics of Rescue, The Roosevelt Administration And The Holocaust, 1938–1945*; M. Gilbert's *Auschwitz And The Allies*; R. Hilberg's *The Destruction of the European Jews*; Morse A.D. *While Six Million Died*; W. Laqueur's *The Terrible Secret*; M.N. Penkower's *The Jews Were Expendable*; Gerald Reitlinger's *The Final Solution*; B. Wasserstein's *Britain And The Jews Of Europe, 1939-45*; and D. Wyman's *Paper Walls* and *The Abandonment of the Jews*. All these constitute a must for serious students of the Holocaust.

[3] Akten Zur Auswaertigen, Deutschen Politik, 1918-1945, Series D, Vol. V, Document 642.

[4] Memorandum by Woerman, Chief PO Div. Auswaertiges Amt., August 10, 1938, Akten, Series D. Vol. V, Document 642.

[5] Akten, Series D, Vol. V, Document 643.

[6] Quoted in Reitlinger the Final Solution 21, 935. Also quoted in Nazi Conspiracy and Aggression VI87, 89 VI Jan. 31, 1939.

[7] Reichssicherheitshauptamt Abt. 4 NOE 247-009 Blitz

[8] "Admission of German Refugee Children", transcript of hearings held by subcommittees of Committee on Imigration of House and Senate, 76th Congress, 1st session, May 24, 25, 31, June 1, 1939 as quoted by Morse op. cit. p. 400.

[9] FDR Library, OF 3186 June 2, 1939. Watson to FDR, as cited by Feingold, op. cit.

[10] Moffat Diary, May 25, 1939 as cited by Feingold, op. cit. p. 331.

[11] National Archives, Morgenthau Diaries 668II 240-1, 692/25, 287–92, 693/82–91, 188–229, as cited by Wyman, *The Abandonment of the Jews*, p. 382. For details see chapter 3 of this work.

[12] Rom. 11:28.

[13] Rom. 11:1

[14] The dead little boy, Simon, was beatified, but in 1965 he was debeatified

[15] Martin Luther, Von Den Jueden und Ihren Luegen (Concerning the Jews and their lies) Wittenberg 1543.

[16] John Baker, Racism and the Bible, 1985.

[17] Wannsee Conference, January 20, 1942 in Wannsee, Berlin, the total annihilation of all Jews was formally decided.

Chapter 2
SETTING OF THE COURSE
The Fiasco Of The Evian Conference:
An American-British Conspiracy

On March 26, 1938 Jews in Austria and Germany were elated. Just two weeks ago, German troops had marched into Austria, and while every day since had been one of increased persecution, the end of the nightmare was now in sight. The marvelous news had come from those who had dared to listen clandestinely to foreign broadcasts, and it spread like wildfire. President Roosevelt had yesterday announced that he was calling an international conference to resolve the problems of the now homeless victims of German malevolence. The United States had always been viewed in Europe as champion of freedom and under her powerful influence and following her example, certainly many countries would provide the chance to get out of the German trap. The rescue, a new life seemed in reach.

Not only among the captive Jews, almost everywhere all kinds of rumors and hopes preceded the opening of the conference. Immigration to the U.S. was regulated by the Immigration Act of 1917, as amended in 1924, a completely outdated document. It was based on a system of national quotas assigned to the various nationalities.[1] The respective number assigned was in accordance with the needs and immigration figures of that time and did not take into consideration the drastically changed situation of the 30's. It permitted a yearly total of 152,744 immigrants and the lion's share went to Britain (65,000) which, together with Ireland had a quota of 83,574 allotted. Yet in no years since Hitler's ascent to power had the combined British-Irish figure exceeded 4,300 immigrants. Thus it was assumed that at least the unused British-Irish quota surplus, roughly 79,000 per year would be transferred to the German-Austrian quota, a total of 27,370 annually. Thus about 106,000 places

37

could go to refugees from Germany and Austria, without interfering with the total admissible figure.

In view of the fact that President Roosevelt had called the conference, some expectations were even more optimistic. Representative Samuel Dickstein of New York, Chairman of the House Immigration and Naturalization Committee, submitted a bill that from July 1, 1938, the beginning of the new fiscal year, *all* unused quota numbers from the year just passed should be allotted to refugees. Mr. Emanuel Celler, Representative from New York, promoted a bill to grant the President the power to increase the quota limits in accordance with the emergency.

Hearings for those bills were scheduled for April but never even started. The administration had won out with its position that the President should not be "restricted," it should be left to him to do the right thing at the approaching conference. The administration's argument was that debate of the bills in Congress would provide the numerous opponents with a chance to mobilize.

Among the 600,000 captive Jews of Germany and Austria, expectations rose to a feverish pitch as the conference date approached. It had become known that of the countries invited, only Italy, because of its friendship with Germany, had declined. Thirty-two nations, had risen to the challenge of humanity's need and would endeavor to resolve the immigration crisis.

Mainly middle and upper middle class, most Jewish families owned an atlas. At nightly meetings of groups of relatives and friends who wanted to start anew together, the maps of the world were studied to decide where to emigrate.

Switzerland was first suggested as seat of the conference, but she declined. She worried about anti-German remarks at the meeting and wanted to stay "neutral." France agreed to host the meeting, and it was called for Evian Les Bains, a luxurious spa on the French shore of Lake Geneva. The date was set as July 6 to 16.

On opening night, the Grand Ball Room of the Hotel Royal was crowded to the last standing place. Most of the thirty-two participating countries had sent delegations consisting of several members. There were journalists from all over the globe to observe and report how the world reacted to the brutal German crushing of the rights and lives of fellow human beings. There were also observers of nations not participating in the conference, including Germans, and there were representatives of Jewish organizations and of other charitable groups as well as just interested guests.

In hushed silence, the audience heard the opening address of the Chief U.S. delegate, Myron C. Taylor. Many already knew the essence of what he would say, but many were stunned by the content of the speech, almost all by the blatant bluntness of the statements, by the lack of even an attempt to veil in diplomatic phraseology the points Mr. Taylor made. The only trimmings were expressions of sympathy for "those unfortunate human beings," for "persons coming within the scope of this conference"—the word "Jews" was avoided by all kinds of verbal acrobatics. Besides expression of pity for those "political emigrants" this was the essence of the speech:

1. The U.S. will not make any changes in its immigration laws.
2. Neither will the U.S. change its "procedures," the ways in which those immigration laws are presently applied.
3. The U.S. does not expect other countries to change either their immigration laws or their procedures.
4. No country should have to carry a financial burden resulting from immigration. "Private organizations" would have to take care of that entirely.
5. Places of refuge must be found for those unfortunate "political emigrants."

Those in the audience who understood the full impact which that statement was bound to have on the other delegates were aghast. But before they could recover from their shock, Great Britain struck the second blow against the conference, the two thereby condemning hundreds of thousands to death.

Lord Winterton, the Chief British Delegate, had actually a key to the situation in his hand. The obvious haven, the Jewish National Home in Palestine, was not even mentioned by him. In the Balfour Declaration, Britain had pledged to "use their best endeavors" to "establish in Palestine a national home for the Jewish people." At the end of World War I, the League of Nations, the forerunner of the United Nations, had conferred upon Britain the administration of Palestine as a Mandate, the Mandate being to act on behalf of the League of Nations and to endeavor, as she had pledged, to establish in Palestine a Jewish national home. In fulfillment of that duty, Great Britain had to report regularly to the League of Nations Mandate's Commission about the progress in its administrative task.

In the Balfour Declaration, on November 2, 1917, the British had pledged

> His Majesty's Government view with
> favor the establishment in Palestine of
> a national home for the Jewish
> people... and will use their best en-
> deavors to facilitate the achievement
> of this object....

Less than two years later, Winston Churchill, then Minister of State for War and Air, reiterated this idea and spelled out its political intent and geographical extent: a Jewish State on both sides of the Jordan

> ... if, as may well happen, there
> should be created in our own lifetime
> by the banks of the Jordan, a Jewish
> State under the protection of the Brit-
> ish Crown... an event would have
> occurred in the history of the world
> which would, from every point of
> view, be beneficial, and would be
> especially in harmony with the truest
> interest of the British empire.[2]

The Mandate under which Britain administered Palestine went even farther than the Balfour Declaration, not only incorporating the Balfour Declaration into its preamble, but additionally stressing "the historical connection of the Jewish people with Palestine" and to the grounds for" reconstituting their national home in that country."

All Jewish attempts to bring the issue of Palestine before the conference were thwarted. No Jewish organization was permitted to address the meeting. Professor Chaim Weizmann, President of the Jewish Agency and as such recognized by the League of Nations as representing the Jewish people before the League as well as before the Mandatory power, Britain, not only was refused the opportunity to address the conference, he was even denied interviews with the British delegation prior to the conference. He also asked for an interview with the American delegate, before the opening, but was told he too had no time to meet with him. What was going on?

As to the other participating countries, most of them had come with little enthusiasm for receiving large numbers of mostly penniless refugees. Now after the United States had set the course for the conference and seeing the way Britain handled its Palestine obligation and altogether the near hostility with which Jewish organizations were treated, the others did not hesitate to come out with a loud and definite "not my country." The Latin American countries because they were under-populated and often controlled large land masses, had been centers of great hopes. One after another gave a negative reply. As some of them expressed later, they were weary of having the U.S. and Europe dump undesirables upon them. Some smaller European countries, the Netherlands, Belgium, Denmark pointed out that considering their size and density of population, they had already done more than their share. It was now on the others to come up with a comparable effort. France voiced similar sentiments, while Great Britain used a curious double argument: first, that the British Isles, themselves, were already overcrowded, and second, that nowhere in her vast, globe-spanning empire was there room for any large resettlement. As an afterthought, East Africa was vaguely mentioned as a future possibility.

The only country to come forward with a generous offer was the Dominican Republic which declared its readiness to accept immediately 100,000 refugees. This offer, however, was later on, as we will describe in detail in a subsequent chapter, whittled down to almost nothing in conversations with all too prudent Americans.

The conference was thus a complete fiasco. It had been scuttled even before the opening speech had been completed.

Even while the conference was still in session, the German newspaper *Der Reichswart Grenzbote*, saw it as a justification of the attitude the Germans employed towards Jews. It reported on July 13, 1938 "Jews are relatively cheap. Who wants them? Nobody!" And on July 15, one day before the closing ceremonies, the same conclusions were echoed by the *Danziger Vorposten* in an even more pointed way: "We see that one likes to pity the Jews as long as one can use this for a wicked agitation against Germany, but that no one is ready to fight the cultural shame of Europe by admitting a few thousand Jews. Thus the conference justifies Germany's policy against Jewry." *The London Daily Herald* summarized succinctly: "If this is coming to the help of the refugees, then what would the nations do if they meant to desert them?"

Thus the Evian Intergovernmental Conference was worse than just a total failure. It had exposed to the Germans the fact that they could go on with their persecution, the world did not care what Germany did to the Jews. It gave the Germans not only a green light, it served to justify their doings.

Unfortunately, it was also the first world-wide "attempt" to rescue, and the happenings at the conference set the trend for future rescue planning and action.

Even an abbreviated report on that meeting cannot omit a telling happening that occurred after the conference closed. The committee set up to continue the "work" worked in at least one instance. In an attempt to appease the Germans, apparently hoping that they might permit the refugees to take at least some of their possessions along, it sent a telegram to the Government in Berlin that actually contained a blank check for the treatment of Germany's Jews. That cable asserted that none of the 32 states had challenged the right of the German government to "legislate measures pertaining to certain of its citizens." The word "Jew" is again not used; whether not to offend the tender feelings of the Germans or those of the committee remains uncertain.

Among the Jews of Austria and Germany, distress assumed proportions even more engulfing than before the great hopes had been raised, the more so as hateful cruelties which seemed to have abated shortly preceding and during the conference climbed to new highs. But disappointment was everywhere outside Germany, too, among those who had been jubilant when Roosevelt made his announcement. Even those as close to him as New York Governor Herbert Lehman had no inkling of the true purpose of calling that conference. Lehman had sent a one word telegram to his friend: "splendid."

What had gone wrong, what had really happened? How genuine had been the U.S. desire to find immigration possibilities for the victims of that unbelievable barbarism?

The true motivation for the conference was later that year summarized by an official of the State Department and can be found in the National Archives. The report first describes the increase of persecution following the annexation of Austria. It refers to the pressure to liberalize its immigration policy and states that "Dorothy Thompson and certain congressman with metropolitan constituencies" were the principal sources of that pressure. To counteract that pressure, the Secretary of State Cordell Hull, the Undersecretary of State Sumner Wells and Assistant Secretary

George Messersmith determined that it will be best to

> "get out in front and attempt to guide
> their pressure, primarily with a view
> towards forestalling attempts to have the
> immigration laws liberalized."[3]

What cynicism! What brutal abuse of the agonized cries for help, to use these very pleas as an excuse to masquerade as a shining knight while actually planning to manipulate the force of these cries to scuttle any real attempt at rescue.

If this plot by the three ranking State Department officials does not constitute conspiracy, what does?

Unfortunately, this attitude of getting out in front (and divert) in order to forestall showed up in numerous actions of the U.S. State Department all during the Holocaust.

If there was any vague hope that other countries would fall for that scheme, it was naive. (By the way, several journalists pointing at that naivete, noticed that Evian spelled backward reads "naive.") Peru, referring to its negative reply stated almost teasingly that it was just following the example provided by the Americans' "caution and wisdom." One after the other, delegates rose to express pity for the victims, and to reiterate the theme "no—not my country. We cannot accept a substantial number."

The full disaster of Evian became evident in the weeks following the meeting. Many more Jews in Austria and Germany received from the *Gestapo* the dreaded notification that unless they emigrated within 14 days, they would be sent to a concentration camp.

Yet they knew that the world outside was aware of their anguish. Somehow a copy of the London *Times,* possession of which was, of course, a serious crime, had made its way to them. It was dated June 19, 1938. A report there stated "no specific charges are made, but men and women, young and old, are taken each day and each night from their homes and in the streets carried off, the more fortunate to Austrian prisons and the rest to Dachau and other concentration camps in Germany. These raids are not restricted to the rich, they include doctors, lawyers, merchants, employees, poor artisans and peasants. There can be no Jewish family in the country that has not one or more of its members under arrest."

Many Jews felt that the paper should have also mentioned the ruthless beatings and the torture one had to expect when arrested, but they saw that their plight was essentially known. Yet—why then was there no help?

Events after the conference demonstrated that not only had it not helped, it had increased the problem of obtaining a saving berth. Brazil had first been ready to accept the vice chairmanship of the committee that was to continue the efforts of the conference after it ended. But instead of becoming more involved in what they had seen and heard at Evian, the Brazilians informed the Intergovernmental Committee that they had decided to decline that offer and they did not even send a delegate to the committee's board meeting. In 1937, Brazil had admitted 2,003 Jewish immigrants, a "tear in the sea" only, especially considering that country's size and large empty spaces. The number dropped to 530 in the year of Evian.

Argentina, which for the same reasons as Brazil had been expected to accept a vastly larger number than up to the conference, had admitted 5,178 Jewish refugees in 1937 but reduced that figure in 1938 to 1,050. With one sole exception the figure kept shrinking sharply; for 1945 it is zero. Similar reductions of immigration figures could be observed all over the world.

When later on Roosevelt approached Mussolini with the suggestion to provide settlement territory for refugees in Ethiopia which was then part of Italy's colonial possessions, Mussolini declined and in his answer indicated that settlement in the interior of the United States should be considered.[4]

Four motivational conditions were mainly responsible for the decisions taken in the U.S. regarding the Holocaust. Together with some occasional other component they account for the trend and details of actions by the decision makers. The four are:

> The mood of the American population, the majority of which opposed liberalization of the immigration policy.
>
> The configuration of the American political system, specifically the composition of the Democratic party.
>
> A President who was determined not to risk a split in his party, nor even a weakening of whatever harmony there was in its ranks.
>
> Anti-Semitism which sometimes might have been unconscious and rationalized away, but which was

pervasive in some of the decision makers.

When Representatives Dickstein and Celler withdrew their bills which respectively called for adding all unused quota spaces to the refugees and authorizing the President to increase quotas, they knew why they did not go through with their plans. From all indications these bills would never have made it through Congress. Anti-immigration sentiment was strong and politicians were keenly aware of that. A public opinion poll conducted by the Opinion Research Corporation in March 1938, right after the Germans had marched into Austria and annexed, it showed 75% against admitting "a larger number of Jewish exiles from Germany." Less than one-fifth, 17% replied that they favored such a step and 8% had no opinion.

A *Fortune* magazine poll, in July, the month of Evian, resulted in 67.4% answering yes to: "with conditions what they are, we should keep them out." Note that two-thirds were against any admission of refugees. Even those who were for maintaining the present, restrictive quota system were in the minority. Only 18.25% were for maintaining the status as it was prior to Austria's annexation. And only one in 20, 4.9% were in favor of "should we encourage them to come even if we have to raise our immigration quota." The remaining 9.5% answered "No opinion."

A third poll was taken, again by another organization. A Roper poll conducted in December 1938, in the wake of the Crystal Night pogroms which had been widely reported in the media with many of their gruesome details showed an increase in the anti-admission sentiment. Now 83% opposed the idea of granting immigration to "a larger number of European refugees than now admitted under our immigration quota."

Anti-Semitism, so massive that we are discussing it separately below, was certainly a part of the anti-immigration mood of the country, but it was not the sole cause. This was 1938, the U.S. was still on the fringes of the 1929 depression, and fear that newcomers would take away jobs needed from those already in the country was genuine. The fact that newcomers mean also increased consumption, that many of them, as they actually did, created new jobs rather than occupy existing ones was not considered. Neither was the fact that even if the unused part of the British and Irish quota would have been added to the German one, this would have amounted to less than one tenth of one percent of the then population and could have had at the worst a minimal impact only. And, of course, the humanitarian element had no space at all in these kinds of considerations.

President Roosevelt was first of all a politician, and a shrewd and ruthless one at that. He was not going to imperil his fragile coalition for moral or humanitarian reasons. He had introduced many controversial issues and established a fragile balance in his coalition. He was not ready to put it to a test over an issue that, he knew, was loaded with emotion among supporters as well as opponents and which was in summary not popular at all. He was at that time preparing to run for an unprecedented third term of the presidency, and any rocking of the boat was out of the question. Those who worked closely with him, his Secretary of State Hull and Undersecretary Welles, all knew that they had to do everything to avoid the fallout from a decision out of favor with almost all of his adversaries as well as with many of his most loyal supporters. Yet, it was necessary to keep up the image of a great liberal and humanitarian.

To call a conference designated to ease the lot of Europe's refugees without changing immigration laws and procedures was just the right thing to do from this point of view. The conference, which according to Hull, Welles and Messersmith was to divert the pressure for a change in legislation, was to be played up big. He did so by appointing a man known for his pragmatism to lead the delegation. Roosevelt's friend, Myron C. Taylor was just the right man. Taylor being the former President of US Steel, Roosevelt would not be accused, as he often was, of being out on a fancy love-everybody dream trip. Taylor would carry weight also by the new title assigned to him for his assignment: Ambassador Plenipotentiary Extraordinary.

The fourth and certainly not the least component at the basis of American policy towards the Holocaust was anti-Semitism. Widely spread and shared by many decision makers, it was a potent factor shaping decisions on issues involving Jews.

In the nineteen twenties, a wave of vehement, rabid anti-Semitism had hit the U.S. We pointed out in chapter one how historical developments entrenched for almost two thousand years had prepared the ground for every new outgrowth of Jew-hatred. Such well-plowed ground must have been the basis of Henry Ford's reaction to reading "The Protocols of the Elders of Zion," the fraud that was starting to replace the blood libel as a cause for anti-Jewish attitudes and actions. True, Mr. Ford later admitted that he had erred and even offered his large real estate holdings in Brazil for settlement of Jewish refugees. (The Brazilian government refused to admit them). Yet before his change of attitude his newspaper, the *Dearborn Independent* , did much harm in activating more "prepared ground" and in encouraging overt anti-Semites.

The number of openly admitted anti-Semites never constituted a large percentage of the U.S. population. Anti-Semitism is not compatible with the image Americans have of their country. However, when it came to expression of attitude, it became evident that the heritage of almost two thousand years of race hatred, fanned more recently by Nazism and hate propaganda of people like William Dudley Polley and his Silver Shirts, the American-German Bund and most of all by Father Charles E. Coughlin had scored heavily. Coughlin's inciting speeches were broadcast every Sunday over 40 stations, and a Gallup poll conducted in December 1938 showed that as many as 15 million had listened to him once or more often. His regular listeners amounted to 3.5 million. Of the 15 million who did not listen regularly 51% agreed with his statements. Of those who listened regularly, 67% agreed with him. His publication *Social Justice* published (without naming the author) an article that was word for word a speech given in 1935 by the German Minister of Propaganda, Joseph Goebbels. Some papers, among them the one published by the Brooklyn Catholic diocese, which alone had a circulation of 100,000, published excerpts of Father Couglin's speeches, and thus his views gained wide circulation. Not to fall behind their Catholic fellow anti-Semites, Protestants conducted an anti-Semitic campaign on their own. The Reverend Gerald Winrod of Wichita, Kansas published his monthly *Defender Magazine* which too, had a circulation of 100,000. There were several more publications of the same type, bringing the hate message into hundreds of thousands of homes. Propaganda was quite clever using word-plays to stick to the memory—"refujew", "Jew Deal", etc.

The hostility against a wider opening of the gates to those who had to flee their land of birth gave cause to study more carefully the extent of anti-Semitic feelings, and starting early in 1938 up to 1941 a series of surveys was conducted that arrived at a conclusion frightening to anybody who consideres race hatred a phenomenon not only directed against the hated but also a short-coming of the hater.

These surveys showed a consistent pattern much more common than would have been expected. It was confirmed not only by the attitude towards rescue actions but also supported by similar surveys measuring straight anti-Semitism. The nine surveys recorded that 12 to 15% of those questioned were ready to support a general anti-Semitic campaign. Between 1939 and 1941 an additional 20% expressed sympathy for such a campaign, thus showing that one-third would have either supported actively campaigning anti-Semitism or would have been in favor of such action.

In fact in 1942, when the U.S. was already at war with Germany and Japan, Americans polled as to whom in the U.S. they considered most of a "menace" to their country answered "Jews" about 3 times as often as "Japanese" and four times more often than "Germans."[5]

Any move by the government that would have favored the refugees would have evoked new vitriolic attacks against Roosevelt, and he was eager to avoid that. Votes from the 4,700,000 Jews were safe for him. He was fully certain that whatever he did, the Jews would vote for him. There was, as one writer expressed it, "a torrent love affair" in existence between the Jews and Roosevelt. It was one-sided though.

By far exceeding those who wrote and read hate literature was the large proportion of the population in which latent anti-Semitism was present. It was a highly unpopular action to do *anything* that would benefit Jews.

The plot developed and put into action in the State Department, to use the Evian conference for the government's anti-refugee purposes, involved more than action by the United States. It became an international plot when Britain received an invitation to attend the meeting on refugee issues. For reasons quite different from the Americans', the British did not want such a conference. They were bound to see their country as the one that had the key to the solution because it was Britain which controlled immigration to what was internationally destined to become the Jewish national home.

For years the British had hedged on the fulfillment of their mandatory obligation. They had changed their mind regarding the Jews' position in Palestine and had acted in open violation of that assigned role.

Ruling Palestine was for the British of paramount importance because of the Suez Canal, Britain's lifeline to India and other Asian colonies. On one bank of the canal, they felt, they were securely anchored. They were manipulating the Arabs as they pleased and did not expect any problems with them. On the other side of the canal, they did now not wish to see a Jewish national home. They could not be certain at all that the Jews would fit into a colonial pattern. One of their first acts after obtaining the Mandate for Palestine was to divide the country in two. All the territory east of the Jordan river, which was 77% of the land covered by the pledge in the Balfour Declaration and the League of Nations Mandate, would become Arab Palestine. Only the remaining 23% would stay under the Mandate for the future Jewish national home. In the Arab part of Palestine, they established a puppet for whom they needed a throne, a member of the influential Hashemite family. They named the newly created Arab part of Palestine "Transjordan" and called its new leader Sheikh. After 1948, he elevated this territory to a kingdom and called it Jordan. With the exception of Great Britain herself and her close ally, Pakistan, no country recognized this division and the newly created Arab land. But Britain for the reasons described and for general appeasement of the Arabs also did not want a Jewish majority in the truncated part of "Jewish" Palestine, the land west of the Jordan river. It had therefore adopted a very restrictive immigration policy for Jews, while Arabs could and did come from all directions as Jewish settlers cleared out marshes, planted colonies and raised the living standards for all inhabitants.

Now, with the happenings on the continent, Britain experienced strong pressure to open the remaining part of the mandated territory to Jews fleeing Europe. The Evian conference could put Great Britain into a position which would cause much criticism and would be hard to defend. The best would therefore be no conference. Or even better, if one could turn things around and let them work for the British anti-immigration policy. One such possibility would be to let the conference take place, and exclude discussion of Palestine as a place for immigration. Such exclusion at a conference would serve as a trend setter and demonstration that Palestine should be excluded from future discussions, too.

But how could one achieve that? The answer was simple enough. The U.S. was eager for the conference to take place. President Roosevelt wanted to demonstrate to those who were pressuring for action as well as to the whole world that the U.S. did try to help. One had to get the help of the U.S. to insure that no discussion of Palestine would take place. The two countries acting together would dominate the meeting and be able to keep the Palestine issue out.

The first communication from the U.S. regarding plans for a conference on the newly created refugee crisis offered the British a handle for the tackling of the delicate Palestine question. On March 26, Joseph P. Kennedy, the U.S. Ambassador to Britain, had received a cable asking him to inquire whether "the British Government (on its own behalf or on behalf of the self-governing Dominions) would be willing to cooperate with the government of the United States in setting up a special committee... for the purpose of facilitating the emigration from Austria and presumably from Germany of political refugees..."

Britain would be ready to cooperate—but for a price.[6, 7]

The weak point of the United States, the one for which she would have to pay the price, was indicated right in the second paragraph of the letter to Mr. Kennedy. This second paragraph reads:"... it should be understood that no country would be expected or asked to receive a greater number of emigrants than is permitted by its existing legislation..." Certainly this rule would, to say the least, hamper the effectiveness of such a committee. It would have to deal with an extraordinary new situation by applying only old laws, created under different circumstances. There could be no doubt that the U.S. was aware of the restricting influence of that rule. It wanted most of all to protect itself from having to change its own immigration laws. Here was the point that could be used to assure exclusion of Palestine at the first, trend-setting meeting regarding the rapidly growing refugee problem. The British knew that President Roosevelt needed their participation. Britain was by far the leading power in Europe. Her Empire, including her dominions, covered a substantial portion of the globe, and in her colonies and dominions there was much space, particularly for people who were ready to start life anew. A conference dealing with refugee resettlement without Britain was hardly thinkable.

Yet it hesitated. The reason given was that their taking part would inject the issue of immigration to Palestine, and that in turn would stir up bitter passions and might lead to a disruption of the conference because Britain would definitely stick to her guns. The United States gave in to the threat but in turn assured Britain that the conference had been called with the understanding that there would be no change in the American immigration laws. "Procedures" had not been mentioned in the original letter to Mr. J. Kennedy, but were now added.

Not only had the United States and Britain, each on its own, conspired to use the conference for a purpose harmful to the refugees' cause; their efforts were mutually reinforcing. Britain would participate; and though it was directly interested in larger immigration to America (hundreds of refugees a week were being admitted for temporary stay in the British Isles and most of them wanted to continue to America), Britain would not press for increased American immigration quotas. If it were confident that the US would table the "Palestine Question", this action would make the Conference worthwhile for the United Kingdom.

Thus, the issue worked out to the mutual satisfaction of the U.S. and Great Britain, and thus it was a total disaster for the "persons coming within the scope of this conference."

[1] Nationality was determined by the immigrant's place of birth.
[2] Illustrated Sunday Herald (London) February 5, 1920, p.5
[3] National Archives 840.48, Division of European Affairs, Memo on Refugee Problems, attached to Division of American Republics, Memo of November 18, 1938.
[4] National Archives EDDF 840.48 Refugees 1319 1/2 December 10, 1938. Also Ciano Diaries 1939-45, p.5.
[5] Charles Herbert Stember, *Jews in the MInd of America*. A survey of public opinion polls.
[6] Confidential Memorandum NE: PHA Mac D 88 6-9.
[7] Foreign Relations of the United States. Diplomatic Papers 1938, Volume I General, p. 740.

Chapter 3
CONSPIRACY IN THE
AMERICAN HIERARCHY

The conspiracy aimed at thwarting efforts to rescue the hunted Jews of Europe from the clutches of the Germans was, in the American hierarchy, not restricted to specific cases. Not even to a large number of them, it was an *ongoing*, consistent policy concentrated in the State Department but also practiced by the War Department. Therefore when we report specific cases in this chapter, we must keep in mind that they do not constitute exceptional occurrences. They are part of a continuous, overall pattern as practiced by the authorities involved.

It was not a nameless group that practiced the anti-refugee policy in the State Department and not a nameless group either in the War Department. The Treasury's Chief Legal Counsel, Randolph Paul, names the group in the State Department as headed by the Assistant Secretary Breckinridge Long. They were Mr. R. Borden Reams, a major force in the anti-refugees activities, James Dunn and Wallace Murray, Departmental Advisors on Political Relations, Ray Atherton, Acting Chief of the Division of European Affairs, and Howard Travers, Chief of the Visa Division. Mr. Paul describes this group as *"an American underground to let the Jews be killed."*[1, 2]

In the War Department it was the Secretary of War, Mr. Henry Stimson who had to carry the responsibility for his Department's formally and actually counteracting Executive Order 9417 which stated "... it is the policy of the government to take all measures within its power to rescue the victims of enemy oppression who are in eminent danger of death and otherwise to afford such victims all possible relief and assistance consistent with the successful prosecution of the war...". The actual carrying out of the policy which counteracted that Executive Order was done by the Deputy Secretary of War John L. McCloy in cooperation with his staff, especially

Colonel Thomas Davis of the War Department's Operation Division. More about the role of the War Department in the later chapter on Auschwitz.

Excuses and explanations for the scuttling of rescue efforts range from the provocative to the absurd. Some excuses seem to be both, such as the refusal to rescue because it would relieve the Germans of the burden of supporting a part of the population for which they are legally responsible. (!)

A new possibility to save lives had been opened when the Germans became interested in exchanging Jews for German citizens who, as enemy aliens, had been interned in the United States and especially in Latin America where that number was quite high. One such deal had been effected between Germany and Britain. German civilians interned in South Africa, Egypt, and Palestine had been exchanged for Jews. By this procedure 463 Jews had been delivered by the Germans and another 4,000 had been earmarked for that plan by their German masters, but these exchanges had come to a stop because the British did not have any more exchangeable Germans. This principle would have permitted the saving of many thousands of lives if the State Department had pursued the matter: there were tens of thousands of exchangeable Germans in Latin America. The program also included the exchange of disabled German prisoners of war for Jews. Pressed into action by the War Refugee Board, a total of 800 German internees from the United Stated and from Latin America were exchanged. In turn, the Germans handed over citizens of the respective countries, and this group included 149 Jews who had been taken out of the hell of the Bergen Belsen concentration camp.[3]

As the Germans were eager to have their interned citizens from Latin America return home to Germany, and as the possession of a foreign passport offered some security anyhow, possession of a Latin American passport became potentially life saving.

Consuls of Latin American countries in Switzerland, Portugal, and even in the United States were offered, by relatives of Jews who were still in Europe, large sums of money for such passports and thousands of Latin American passports were obtained, mainly by bribery but from some of the consular officials for humanitarian reasons. The exact number of such passports remains unknown, estimates range from 5,000 to 10,000. The Germans respected such passports; they wanted, after all, the exchange program to succeed and the supply of Jews for "extermination" remained almost unlimited.

Jews holding such Latin American passports were put into special "exchange camps" in which life was incomparably easier—and certainly safer—than in camps which served as collecting places for deportations. The Germans now waited for the Allies to come through with their part of the deal. The State Department, faithful to its policy of using delay as one of the means to thwart rescue attempts, did not officially react to the situation, but secretly it protested the exchange plan. Such a procedure, it found, would mean favoring the Jews over non-Jewish citizens and should therefore be rejected.[4]

For those held in exchange camps, of which the one at Vittel, France, was the largest, the situation turned more precarious with every day that passed without the exchange that had been visualized by the Germans. In September 1943, Paraguay dismissed its consul in Switzerland and, within eight weeks, the Germans collected all Latin American passports, not only the Paraguayan ones. Pressured by the War Refugee Board's efficient and committed Chairman John Pehle and following an intervention by the Vatican (which, in these waning months of the Hitler regime, partially abandoned its hands-off-the-Holocaust stance) thirteen of the fourteen Latin American countries announced that up to the end of the war they would recognize these "special" passports as valid.

Pehle now drafted a telegram to be sent from the State Department to the U.S. Legation in Switzerland urging the legation to demand action in the matter of these passports. Switzerland represented most of the Latin American countries before the Germans and had omitted to protest the confiscation of all these Latin passports. The telegram demanded that the U.S. Legation prod the Swiss into an energetic protest.

This telegram was held up, for *seven fateful weeks* in the State Department.

Meanwhile, the Polish Jews in Vittel were separated from the rest apparently in preparation for deportation. The passports remained confiscated. Alarmed, the Union of Orthodox Rabbis in New York, in order to break the deadlock, sent a delegation to Washington. It found at the State Department only evasion but succeeded in meeting with Secretary Morgenthau. In his diary Morgenthau describes how the oldest of the rabbis "broke down... and wept and wept and wept." Morgenthau called the Secretary of State Hull and told him how that telegram had been blocked for seven precious weeks. The day after, the State Department sent the so delayed cable to Switzerland.

There, the official receiving it apparently knew what was expected in the home office and he (the First Secretary George Tait) cabled back:

> I do not like the matter at all in any of its aspects. *This group of persons* has obtained false papers to which they have no claim and has *endeavored to obtain special treatment* which they would otherwise not have received. We are being placed in the position of acting as nurse maid to persons who *have no claim to our protection.*[5][6]

Poor Mr. Tait who did not understand what had happened to his superiors. He did not know that, finally, this telegram was sent after intervention of the Secretary of State himself, and his objection was accordingly overruled.

The intervention by the Swiss Ministry of Foreign Affairs changed the situation entirely. The holders of these passports were now not only recognized as using them legally, but a neutral country of importance to Germany protected the bearers of these passports and had even staged a demarche on behalf of them. The issue was now not any more just the exchange but the fact that the holders of these passports were under Swiss protection. This was in April, 1944, and in May the German Foreign Office formally announced that no one at that time in an exchange camp would be deported.

But for 238, most of them orthodox rabbis, the German reversal came ten days too late. They had been in Auschwitz previously, and in the last moment Latin American passports had arrived. These passports had been obtained as a result of a tremendous effort of Jewish groups. The 238 were to be exchange for disabled German prisoners of war in a POW camp in Texas. Via a collecting camp they had been sent to the Vittel exchange camp. It all seemed to be a dream, but it turned out to be a most cruel nightmare. When the Germans, due to the endless delays, thought that the United States was reneging on the deal, they picked as the first ones to be deported those who had been in Auschwitz before. After waiting for month after month in the paradise of Vittel, the dream ended abruptly for the 238. They were shipped back to Auschwitz—this time "for good."

Josiah Du Bois, the former Chief Legal Counsel of the Treasury Department, refers to the case of the 238 as "murder by delay." For week after week, the State Department had delayed action on behalf of those for whom every day, every hour, could bring disaster. The main guilt for these 238 lives rests certainly with the Germans. But they share it with the conspirators in the State Department.

Another case in the chain of consistent actions intended to obstruct rescue attempt involves at least 2,000 persons. For that number, the scene could have changed from horror to the subtropical paradise of the Caribbean islands.

By Executive Order issued in April 1938, the Virgin Islands had been given the right to admit in emergency cases alien visitors without a visa. In August 1940, the Legislature of the Virgin Islands decided to admit 2,000 refugees in accordance with that Executive Order, and the Governor of the Islands, Mr. Lawrence L. Cramer signed on November 12 of that year a decree for admission of 2,000 persons. Near panic ruled in the State Department when it learned of that rescue possibility.[7] As soon as he learned of that invitation, Breckinridge Long started to lobby against it.[8] He went to see President Roosevelt who sent him to Secretary of the Interior Harold Ickes, under whose jurisdiction the Virgin Islands were. Ickes refused to counteract the islanders' decision. Long then went to the Justice Department where he found a more sympathetic ear. Again he went to Roosevelt who found Long "extremely agitated." In the meantime, Ickes had made his support of the islanders' decision public. The main argument of Long's was that the refugees would use the islands to seep into the United States. He wanted the entire undertaking scuttled, not even allowing the admittance to the Virgin Islands of those who held quota numbers for immigration to the United States and who had waiting times lasting from a few weeks to several years.

Long tried to convince everybody that with those 2,000, German spies might enter the hemisphere. He used that spy argument frequently, although during the entire war not a single spy was ever found among refugees. To place a spy among refugees would have been anyhow impossible for Germans to do. If a Jew would stoop to such a role, the risk that he would turn into a double spy and do more harm than good to Germany was obvious. Besides, there was no environment in which a spy would have been faster detected than in a group of Jewish refugees. They knew what a real refugee was and were themselves looking with suspicion at everybody who spoke German and did not seem to be Jewish. In any case, Long peddled the spy argument. He now had a great idea. He went to see Admiral Alan Kirk, Chief of Naval Intelligence. He told the Admiral "if the Navy could declare it a restricted area for strictly naval reasons" that would "prevent the raising of the political questions involved in this refugee and undesirable traffic which is going on", and in this case "we would have no more trouble."[9]

Long finally succeeded in spite of Ickes' holding firm. Roosevelt was won over by the State Department's position and the President's last words in the matter were, "I have sympathy; I can not however do anything which would conceivably hurt the future of present American citizens."[10]

One has to wonder what the admission of several thousand persons, most of them middle class, hard working, and quite successful in their previous activities, would have done to those Caribbean islands. There is a good possibility that the Virgin Islands, which today subsist on a minor portion of Caribbean tourist traffic and which have a regrettably high percentage of its native population on welfare, would have become, a Taiwan of the West, a center of industrial and commercial activity in the region with tourism developed to satisfy even the most demanding expectations. Here is one of the occasions at which politics quite possibly prevented an economic upswing of an area. It can hardly be seen in which way "the future of present American citizens" could have been jeopardized by upholding the invitation which the islanders themselves had extended.

After having looked at the murder of 238 Jews who were deported from Vittel to Auschwitz and after having reported the "successful" scuttling of the Virgin Islanders' rescue action for 2,000, let us now look at the grave accusations raised by ranking lawyers in the Treasury Department and the "Report to the Secretary of the Treasury on the Acquiescence of this Government in the Murder of Jews" as reported in Chapter I. This document charges the government with more than mere acquiescence in the murder. It charges, as we do: conspiracy. That report accuses the State Department, actually certain officials of the State Department, of using "this govern-ment machinery to *prevent*[11] the rescue" and of doing that by employ-ing "concealment and misrepresentation" and the "issuance of false and misleading statements." This document deals with two phases of activities that willfully obstructed rescue efforts.

From several German sources, each independent of the other, Dr. Gerhard Riegner, the representative in Switzerland of the American Jewish Congress, had learned of the fateful German deci-sion taken in January 1942 at Wannsee, to murder all the Jews of Europe. He had also established that the process of mass murder was proceeding with German thoroughness and that many thousands were being slaughtered daily. After having this confirmed from various sources, he sent early in 1943 a telegram through the U.S. Legation in Switzerland to his superiors in the United States. The informants had each risked their lives to get this information out of Germany and into neutral Switzerland, and now it was on the way to the States. What else could one do? But was it on the way?

The telegram communicating the horror in detail was answered by the infamous telegram #354 of Feb. 10, 1943, this time without delay. The telegram in fact ordered the Legation in Switzerland *not to forward in the future information of that kind* .The State Department did not want to know and, even less the public, of the decision to enact the Final Solution and that this decision was already in full swing of enactment. Such knowledge would, of course, create pressure for rescue actions and therefore had, in the view of the plotters in the State Department, to be suppressed. Riegner, did not, however, trust the State Department and managed to get the news to Rabbi Wise, the chairman of the American Jewish Congress. There was of course a delay, and every day thousands of Jews were being killed. Wise saw the Deputy Secretary of State Sumner Wells who unaware of the "stop information order" telegraphed to the Minister in Switzerland requesting the latest information from Riegner. The Minister, Mr. Leland Harrison complied and asked that future information regarding the Final Solution "should not, repeat not, be subjected to the restrictions imposed by your 354 and that I be permitted to transmit messages from R. (Riegner) more particularly in view of the helpful information which they frequently contain." This reference to "354" brought to light that "certain persons" in the State Department had tried to keep the Department as well as the public unaware of the Final Solution and its progress.

The plotters in the State Department soon had the chance to do more work that would profit the German plan. And this time it did not involve death to 238 and the rejection of rescue for at least 2,000. This time they had to gather all their strength: it involved very concrete rescue possibilities of more than 100,00 humans.

By the beginning of 1943, after Germany's defeat at Stalingrad and its loss there of its entire 6th Army, after the Germans were in retreat over most of the Eastern Front, and the United States, at full strength, had not yet started the invasion in the West, the defeat of Germany was only a question of time.

Then, most of the Jews in the Balkan countries—though in frightful circumstances—were still alive. The satellites were ready to distance themselves from Germany, especially from the Final Solution, as they feared retribution. This was a chance to negotiate with them the saving of their Jews. It was a chance which was not utilized for an incredible reason. The Allies did not want to save the Jews of the Balkans; they did not want to save any larger group of Jews. Intervention with the Hitler—appointed dictators of Rumania, Hungary, Bulgaria, and Greece would have saved close to one million Jews. This is confirmed by the fact that after more than 400,000 Jews had been deported from Hungary to Auschwitz, an appeal to the Hungarian strongman Admiral Miklos Horthy, resulted in his ordering the deportation stopped. The order ended the deportation of Jews from Hungary during Horthy's rule. The Germans alone could not do it. They needed the local authorities who knew who was Jewish for the rounding up of those destined for the crematoria.

As no such demarche was forthcoming, in February 1944, Rumania on its own offered to save its Jews. Its dictator, Ion Antonescu had deported 185,000 Jews into the Transnistria, the barren area between the rivers Bug and Dnjestr. There they lived, or more exactly died, under the most inhuman conditions. There were hardly any living quarters, no food, no clothing to protect them from the icy winds that swept the plains. Daily many dozens died of starvation and others from the cold and exposure. On February 13, 1943, *The New York Times* carried a headline, *Rumania Proposes Transfer of Jews*. In a report written by C.L. Sulzberger one of the owners of *The New York Times*, it stated that, in fact, Rumania offered to transfer for the amount of 20,000 Lei per person (about $2.40) 70,000 Jews from Transnistria "to any refuge selected by the Allies."

The proposal was quite specific as to details. The released 70,000 would first be transferred to Bucharest where they would be accommodated in specially selected buildings, and they would then be brought by Rumanian ships flying either the Red Cross or, as arranged with the Catholic Archbishop of Bucharest, the Vatican flag, to any destination chosen by the Allies. Palestine, the proposal said, would be the most convenient location to bring them to, but other possibilities would be considered.

It was assumed that these 70,000 were just the initial group, and that the others still alive in Transnistria would soon follow. What a chance—from the storm swept plains of Transnistria into freedom!

The State Department must have known by February 13 of this opportunity, but it did not follow it up. On April 20, a message arrived in the State Department in which Riegner asked for permission to issue a license to pay to Rumania, in Rumanian currency, the amount of $175,000 for the freeing of these 70,000, a ridiculously small amount. He also suggested the freeing of a fund for supporting Jewish children who were in hiding in France and whose parents had in most cases already been deported, and also a license for funds to finance the escape of young Jewish persons via the Pyrenees into Spain. The issuance of a license to spend that money was in the jurisdiction of the Treasury and that office should —considering the urgency—have been informed by telephone. The whole matter, as Treasury officials later assured, could have been settled by phone in five minutes and the cable to the American Legation in Switzerland to issue the license could have been in Switzerland the same day.

For two more months, from April 20 to late June, the State Department did nothing, but withheld information of that request for a license from the Treasury. The latter finally found out by a leak that such a request was held back by the State Department. Though the Treasury urged fast positive action, it took 3 more weeks before a meeting between the Treasury Department and the State Department could be arranged. At this meeting, Mr. R. Borden Reams opposed granting that license because the matter would not work out anyhow. This , of course, was not a valid reason for not having the license ready in case it did work out. In fact showing such a license would prove to the Rumanians that the United States meant business. (This, however was exactly what was apparently to be prevented.) The request had been made and immediate action was required as one could not meaningfully negotiate without the license. There were no expenses involved for the United States as Jewish organizations would carry the expense. And it was made certain that no foreign funds would fall into Rumanian hands; all payments were to be made in Rumanian leis.[12]

Rabbi Wise discussed the Riegner plans with President Roosevelt, and the President approved of these plans. In spite of the presidential approval, Breckinridge Long *delayed* the issuance of the license *for another 45 days*, claiming that it would bring dollars into the enemy's hands, although it had been made certain that payment would be made in foreign currency and although both the Treasury and the White House had approved the plan. *Five months had elapsed* since the April 20 report and request by Riegner, before on September 28, the State Department sent a telegram to the Legation in Bern informing it that the Treasury had granted the license. But the Minister there had learned what the attitude of his superiors was. He did not issue the license and telegraphed instead that the British opposed the whole deal for reasons of economic warfare.[13]

Still another delay. And in Transnistria people were dying like flies, and deportation to Auschwitz seemed the only possible alternative. Harrison's telegram regarding the British opposition to something that did not require British consent was, for the obstructionist conspirators in the State Department, a God-given chance for new delay. They did not inform the Treasury of this new complication, but the news of Harrison's telegram was leaked to Treasury by an unnamed source. Unfortunately communication with the Legation had to go via "State", so the Treasury composed another telegram and gave it to the State Department for sending it to Harrison. It ordered Harrison to issue the license; Britain had no right to object and all measures to protect economic warfare interests had been effectively taken. Reams argued with the Treasury officials against ordering Harrison to issue the license, and his argument is, again, both provocative and absurd. He was against the entire action because it gave preference to a "special group of enemy aliens" who alone were by that action being helped.[14] Long however recognized that Reams' argument would not halt the action and—finally—on October 26 gave orders to Harrison in Bern to issue the license.[15] This was *more than six months* after the Treasury had been requested to issue that license, a procedure that could have been taken care of simply by telephone.

But this is not yet the end of the so tragic story. As the economic warfare argument did not work because it was so demonstratively inapplicable, the British let the cat out of the bag, and the British Foreign Secretary, Eden, who in the course of the Holocaust came out several times with overtly anti-Semitic statements, cabled now the true reason for the British objection. Harrison still did not issue the license, allegedly because there was a change in the situation, as the British, who so far had expressed displeasure only, had now lodged a formal protest. Of this and of his still not issuing the license, Harrison informed his superiors in Washington only 17 days after receipt of the President-approved order.

Eden, in, for a diplomat, unbelievably blunt manner, stated in fact that they did not want these Jews to be saved, and with this note he admitted the true reason for Britain's objection to the issuing of a license. The claim it would interfere with economic warfare aims had been only an excuse. This is the essence of the British message:

> The Foreign Office are concerned with the difficulties of *disposing*[16] of any considerable number of Jews should they be rescued from enemy occupied territory... difficulties of transportation, particularly shipping and of finding accommodations in the countries of the Near East for any but a *very small number*[16] of Jewish refugees. They (the Foreign Office) foresee that it is likely to be almost if not entirely impossible to deal with anything like the number of 70,000 refugees whose rescue is envisaged by the Riegner plan. *For this reason*[16] they are reluctant to agree to any approval being expressed even of the preliminary financial arrangements.[17]

In speaking of difficulties of finding shipping, the British Foreign Office note overlooks the fact that the Rumanians offered to supply the shipping.

In any event, the reason of "not enough shipping available" that was given by the Allies for not saving the Rumanian and/or Bulgarian Jews was not just a poor excuse. It was an outright lie. The United States sent huge supplies to Europe. A "bridge of ships" had been established across the ocean and one freighter after the other, heavily loaded, came from the United States, unloaded and returned either entirely or almost empty. Sometimes, it was difficult to find ballast. There was no shortage of shipping to prevent the Allies from moving 100,000 non-Jewish Yugoslav, Polish, and Greek civilians to temporary havens in East Africa, Egypt, and even to Mexico.

As the Germans retreated from Greece, they left behind a country robbed of every bit of food. Food and medical supplies in large quantities were moved to Greece in the period in which there was no transportation for the Jews in Transnistria for whom the choice was to die from starvation and exposure or to survive—for deportation to Auschwitz.

Neither was there transportation for the 4,000 Yugoslav Jews whom Yugoslav partisans had smuggled to the Adriatic island of Rab, near the Yugoslav coast. As there was danger that the Germans might retake the island, transfer was sought to the already liberated part of Italy. Yugoslavs were at that time evacuated with the help of Allied shipping from Yugoslavia to Italy. But the Jews had to remain on the little island close to the Yugoslav mainland. Yugoslav partisans were in control of part of their country and had opened a corridor to the sea. Thus the refugees from Rumania and Bulgaria could have been evacuated to Italy by crossing the narrow Adriatic, if that chance had been seized. Besides all that, there was really no problem with shipping to the United States. Three Portugese liners with a total capacity of 2,000 passengers were on a regular schedule, sailing from Lisbon to the United States. Every week, there were two sailings by these ships, and there were also smaller ships available in Portugal and Spain. The British attitude of not wanting to save them was fully shared by Britain's co-conspirators in the State Department. The use of the formulation "dispose of them" in the British note is telling. The Germans had decided to dispose of the Jews by "extermination." The British and the American co-conspirators did their best to dispose of them by pushing them into Eichmann's hands.

And during all these delays, the Germans were pressing to make Rumania *judenrein*. One deadline set by Eichmann, May 1, 1943, had already passed. Anyhow, the number of Jews left in Transnistria reduced itself steadily.

At a staff meeting at the Treasury, Randolph Paul, the Chief Legal Counsel said: "I do not know how we can blame the Germans for killing them when we are doing this. The law calls (it) para delicto—of equal guilt." Morgenthau said: "When you are through with it, the attitude is not different from Hitler's."Herbert Gason, a staff member replied: "You are unfair. We do not shoot them. We let other people shoot them and starve them."[18] [19]

For the 30,000 Jews remaining in Bulgaria, after deportation of all Jews from the Bulgarian occupied part of Greece, the issue of possible rescue was similar to that in Rumania, except that they had not been herded into a "death by exposure and starvation" area.

From the State Department's receiving Rumania's offer to transfer 70,000 of its Jews, it had taken *ten months* to the issuance of even a preliminary license. After the license was issued, negotiations went on and on. Britain remained adamant in its refusal to let the Rumanians—just as the Bulgarian Jews—be saved by providing a haven in Palestine. Turkey was approached. She was, after some negotiations, ready to let the refugees enter but only if, continuing the voyage, entry into Palestine was guaranteed. This would have provided the possibility of traveling all the way by land and circumvented the —in any case, trumped up—issue of shortage of shipping space. But Britain refused to provide such a promise.

Rumanian and Bulgarian Jews could also have been brought to North Africa, by then already under Allied control. But this plan was opposed by Robert Murphy, President Roosevelt's special envoy for North Africa and by the French General Henry Giraud.[20] The rescued persons could have been kept in camps organized like prisoner of war camps which would have been paradise for them, yet would have provided the Allies with full control over their movement. The French had a hand in decisions because the African territory had been largely French prior to German occupation.

Other propositions included having already liberated Jews brought to the United States under P.O.W. rules and have them interned there. This too was allegedly impossible for reasons of "shortage of shipping."

As a sham, after long delays, three camps were opened which did not save any lives. One was the Fedala camp in North Africa near Casablanca. Refugees from Spain used it, 630 altogether. This was 1944 and Spain was quite safe by then. Germany was heavily on the losing side of the war, and an invasion of its "non-belligerent ally" was not only unlikely, it was impossible. And deportation from Spain to one of the German camps was extremely unlikely. Contrary to expectation, Spain behaved relatively well towards Jewish refugees. In spite of the non-belligerent alliance with Germany, there were no deportations. To prevent their murder, Franco had Spanish passports issued for 300 Sephardic Jews because Spain recognized them as descendants of Jews who had been expelled from Spain in 1492. They came to Spain straight from Bergen Belsen.[21, 22]Most refugees in Spain did not want to go into the uncertainty of a new situation when they did not have to. The same applied to another camp in North Africa, Phillipsville in Algeria. It was a former Allied military camp; and one could proudly announce that still another camp for refugees holding up to 7,000 had been made available, but there were few takers. The Allied authorities had in mind that refugees from the liberated parts of Italy would wish to be sent there, but there was little such desire. Finally, a camp was opened even in the United States. It was located in Oswego in the state of New York, close to the Canadian border, and it held one thousand persons. The opportunity was fully used but again by refugees who had already been liberated, mainly coming from Italy. They were held there as though they were in a prisoner of war camp. No Jews from Transnistria, none from Bulgaria, for any of those camps that served mainly decorative purpose.[23]

Just as during all these months nothing was done regarding the Rumanian part of the Riegner plan, so was also the part of the plan sabotaged that dealt with the need to provide funds for hiding of children in France and for the smuggling of young, strong persons over the Pyrenees mountains into Spain. It took money to follow up either of these two suggestions. If one wanted to persuade Frenchmen to hide Jewish children one had at least to pay for their upkeep, and often had to give a bribe to prod them into action at all. Nothing was forthcoming from the United States to promote such action.

The story of the hidden children began on July 16, 1942. This was the day the Gestapo, with the cooperation of the Paris police, raided the houses in which Jews lived, particularly apartment houses in Paris's Jewish quarter that housed most of the more impecunious Jews. To their horror the Jewish families were herded into buses without even the chance to take anything with them and driven to the assembly area, the Velodrome d' Hiver. Even from hospitals were the Jews rounded up. A man who had undergone a cancer operation only the day before was among those crammed into the buses. It was clear that the next stop would be deportation; and, as difficult as the decision was, some parents had left their children behind, hoping somebody would take care of them. Many children were actually picked up by various Frenchmen but others perished—particularly small ones. Some mothers who had taken their babies along saw them die in the Velodrome where there was almost complete lack of food, little water, and no milk. There were no facilities to lie down, not even straw. Nearly four thousand children, aged two to fourteen, who had been found by the police wandering the streets or crying in the abandoned apartments were crammed in the infamous box cars and shipped to Auschwitz. Fortunately for them, many did not survive the voyage in the windowless freight cars where they remained without water and food and without toilet facilities during the entire time of transportation. For many French people who had taken in "abandoned" Jewish children, this proved to be more of a burden than they had expected. Food was scarce and rationed, and one could not apply for ration coupons for a hidden child. The fact that there was suddenly a child around could be reported by some neighbor, and that meant danger of Gestapo interrogation and arrest. To help such adopting families carry the additional burden and to motivate them not to abandon the Jewish child or children they had taken in, funds were required and—because foreign funds transactions were controlled—the licensing of exchange money was needed. Besides, the raid of July 16 had been just a beginning; more such raids took place. First they had been restricted to the occupied part of France, but soon the formally unoccupied zone of France, the part called "Vichy France" started deporting too.

Just as the endeavors on behalf of the first part of Riegner's plan were thwarted, so was the second part, the attempt to help the hidden children and to smuggle some younger persons into Spain. What a difference between the actions of the United States and the intent expressed in Executive Order No. 9417.

When Pinkney Tuck, Charge d' affaires at the U.S. Embassy in Vichy France, protested to Laval, Hitler's strong man in unoccupied France, and called the treatment of Jews "inhuman" and "revolting," a member of Breckinridge Long's staff complained to Deputy Secretary Sumner Wells that Tuck had exceeded his instructions.[24] The pressure by the U.S. Embassy in France to admit at least some of the tens of thousands of endangered children, energetically supported by Eleanor Roosevelt as well as by the American Friends Service, was too powerful for the Breckinridge Long clique to overcome. The Pressure succeeded and entrance permits were obtained first for 1,000 children, and later this figure was raised to 5,000.[25]

Under pressure, it appeared to be at least one generous life-saving act on the part of the State Department; however, it was neither generous nor life-saving.

As to generosity, let us have a look at the figures of entries into the United States and compare them with the number of admissions permitted under the restrictive immigration laws. The following figures tell the story better than words could. Between Pearl Harbor and the German surrender, thus between December 7, 1941, and May 9, 1945, the quota assigned to countries that were under German control was about 208,000. During that time, only approximately 21,000 refugees entered. Thus only about one out of ten available spots was used, and this did not include the use of any surplus figures like the huge one from the British-Irish quota.[26] The unused quota numbers from German-controlled countries amounted during that time of daily massacres to 190,000. Not so generous was the readiness to admit 5,000 refugee children without their parents.

And not in time either. For leaving France, an exit permit from the Vichy Government was required. One could not apply for the exit permit prior to having entry to the United States assured because many of the children were in hiding, and it was unsafe to direct the attention of the puppet government to any Jewish child. When exit permits could finally be applied for, the Vichy dictator, Pierre Laval was hesitant. Laval argued that it would mean rewarding lawlessness if one would now let children leave who had been in hiding. Besides, it would be cruel to separate the children from their parents. Finally, exit permits for 500 children were promised. While their documents were being readied and checked and the technical preparations to put the 500 on the train to Lisbon were being hurriedly made, the Allies, on November 8 landed in French North Africa. On that day the first group of children, 100, had arrived in Marseilles and all that was now needed in terms of documents was the U.S. visa, which should be issued without problems. But the American consulate was closed with the beginning of the invasion of French territory. American interests were represented by Switzerland. All Swiss attempts to obtain exit permits were in vain. The old exit permits were declared invalid as Vichy France and the United States were now at war. The children did not get out any more.

As reported at the beginning of this chapter, each one of the cases recorded here was just a part of a continuous chain of actions aimed at throttling immigration and thereby of pushing the desperate ones into the wheels of the Final Solution machinery. Besides specific actions, there were general measures to make immigration impossible or close to that. One of the most effective measures contrived by the conspirators in the State Department was the need for each of the two American sponsors—or the organization sponsoring that person—to fill out a most discouraging form. It was four feet long on each side, thus altogether eight feet of form in six copies. The entire form had to be sworn to, and it stated that false statements constituted perjury. Certainly only very few people would take the time to work on such a monster of a form in order to help others. Anyone handed such a form must have correctly guessed that an authority that concocted such a form was most unlikely anyhow to grant a visa, so why should the American sponsor submit to the drudgery of filling out an 8 foot form and to undergo, by doing so, a degrading inquiry into one's personal affairs including to reveal under oath all details of one's financial status. With these new forms developed by Breckinridge's staff, the plotters had found a powerful tool to reduce the number of those who could apply for entrance into the United States.

But this was by far not the end of the inventiveness displayed by the Breckinridge Long clique. One June 5, 1941, it sent instructions to the various consulates which amounted to an almost complete obstruction to the visa granting process as far as Jewish refugees were concerned. That communication instructed the consular offices not to issue visas to anyone who had close relatives in territory controlled by the Germans or in the Soviet Union. In practical terms that meant almost total exclusion of Jewish refugees as nearly everyone had a parent, brother, sister, son, or daughter left in the German's power, more rarely in the U.S.S.R. It prevented the brother who had succeeded in escaping from trying to save his sister or other brothers or his parents.[27] Only the few who had escaped with their entire family could hope to get somebody else out—and if it was not that, catch 22 applied. A devilish device. First, the news of that rule was not announced publicly so those who did not know could not even keep the fact of a remaining family member a secret. But the news leaked out on June 21, 1941, when *The New York Times* reported this exclusionary measure. As reason for this measure, Long used the old canard of refugees being recruited by the Germans to spy for them. If you have a close relative in German-held lands, the Germans can blackmail you to work for them as a spy, the reasoning went.

Although a search of documents fully available in the years after the war's end shows that not one refugee was proven to have acted as a spy, Long claimed to have proof of actual cases for his exclusionary rule. The result of the State Department's claim was catastrophic as other offices assumed that the State Department must have knowledge, and this was particularly true as far as the consuls were concerned. They were the ones who issued the visas, and the claim of espionage practices by refugees made them approach the issue of granting a visa with a most negative expectation.

The close relatives rule did not prevail for long in its absolute form because in cases of relatives still in Europe, special security investigations became possible. However, such investigations, which included the right to appeal, lasted many months, usually about nine months. And every day counted. Nine months after the beginning of such an investigation, the applicant had usually already for several months been reduced to ashes.

Even devising a form for the sponsors which looked and was prohibitive, even the enactment of the close family exclusion rule, and even the sowing in the minds of the consuls abroad the suspicion of widely spread espionage among Jewish refugees, did not suffice to call these steps the final ones in the endeavor to keep the refugees locked in Europe. There was still the danger that other countries might admit too many of "these people" as Long often refers to the Jews in his diary. The Caribbean countries were warned of the danger of refugee-spies to cut off that possible escape route, too. Certainly the smaller countries in Central America, in fact in all the Americas, were bound to assume that the U.S. State Department had knowledge not available to them. Therefore, information from Washington that stressed the spy risk, influenced other countries to keep those "undesirables" out.

The degree to which the United States immigration policy succeeded in blocking the escape route becomes impressively evident when one compares the number of persons who could have been admitted in full accordance with existing laws, with the number of those who actually entered. The total number of admissions permissible according to the immigration laws was 152,700 annually, 0.12 percent of the then population.[28] In the actual years since Hitler came to power, January 1933 to the end of 1944, therefore, 1,832,000 new admissions were permissible. To admit that many would not have required raising the total number, just to have all quotas filled. The number of actually entering newcomers in these 12 years was close to 240,000.

If one looks only at the years most critical to the refugees, the war years 1941-44 (all U.S. data use the fiscal year system) and restricts those admissible to the quotas of countries under control of the Germans, the following figures show how even the so restrictive immigration laws were abused for blocking rescue.

In 1941, of all the spaces available to those who fell under the "German occupied quotas" 28,929 persons entered the United States, almost exactly one half of those who could have come. One out of two who fulfilled the quota requirements remained excluded.

In fiscal 1942, it was worse. Only one out of five of the legally permitted spaces was utilized. To be exact: the 11,702 newcomers constituted 19.2% of the legally admissible ones.

As there was no powerful opposition or protest, the screws were tightened even further in the following year, 1943. Nine out of ten available life-saving spaces remained unused. To be exact 5,944 newcomers entered the United States, 9.8% of the possible number.

And in 1944, the new arrival figure was even smaller. As 4,793 were newly admitted, the percentage of used quota numbers for countries under German control had slipped to 7.9%. Eleven out of twelve available numbers were wasted, eleven who could have started life anew were pushed back into the hands of their assassins.

When one studies Breckinridge Long's diaries and his private written communications, one cannot be surprised at all by the machinations he employed to seal off the American escape route as well as (to the best of his ability) escape to Caribbean countries. Long fantasied that not only were refugees spies for Germany, but, after everything that Germany did to them, he sees them as German sympathizers who left the Fatherland only out of cowardice. They wanted to be away from a place of combat. He writes

> Some are certainly German spies and others are sympathizers, the last coming here because it is away from the scene of combat and looks like a safe place.[29]

One of the means Long used to obstruct rescue actions was to suppress information about the Holocaust and about how very little the United States did to help. In November 1944, the House Committee on Foreign Affairs held hearings because of public pressure to learn what was being done in terms of rescue activities. On November 26, Long testified before that committee, and his testimony was *false*.[30] He testified that since 1933, 580,000 newcomers had entered the United States. This was more than twice the actual figure.[31] Fortunately the press knew better; and when he was confronted with the fact that he had supplied false data, he admitted to have given "erroneously" the so exaggerated figure. Unfortunately he had used the same false figures before when "informing" the President. The newspapers, he complains, which had reported this "erroneous" acting of his were "the radical press and the Jewish press" and they were making life for him "somewhat uncomfortable."

When Josiah Du Bois had called the methods employed by the State Department "murder by delay" he did not know how sharply he had formulated a principle that Long recorded in a communication to friends of his.

> We can delay and effectively stop for a *temporary period* of *indefinite length* the number of immigrants into the United States by simply advising our consuls to put every obstacle in the way and to require additional evidence and to resort to various administrative advices which would *postpone* and *postpone* and *postpone* the granting of the visas. However this could be done temporarily only.[32]

Yes, temporarily only, but for an "indefinite length."

Those who see Long as a dull bureaucrat would be surprised to note how enthusiastic he could be if he succeeded in his plotting. After he had sent out cables to the consuls advising them how to handle visa applications, he entered into his diary triumphantly:

> The cables practically stopping immigration went![33]

The cases and actions described in this chapter are just some of the most blatant—and to their victims most deadly—incidents of conspiracy in the American hierachy. The one with the most catastrophic result will be reported in Chapter 6 "How the Allies Kept Auschwitz Operating." There the conspirators' headquarters shifts from the State to the War Department, but the conspiracy in the State Department continued.

[1] Morgenthau Diaries 688II 138 694/67-68; U.S. House of Representatives Problems of World War I and its Aftermath, Part II the Palestine Question p.181; Fred Israel The War Diary of Breckinridge Long 308-309, as cited by Wyman Abandonment p. 191, 383.

[2] Emphasis added.

[3] Foreign Relation of the United States 1944 v. 1-1076, Morgenthau Diaries 758/71 Ira Hirschmann's Second Report, 16 Exhibit K, War Refugee Board History 286, as cited by Wyman, Abandonment, p. 277, 403.

[4] Memo to Bermuda Conference (n.d.) War Refugee Board 3 Bermuda Conference as cited by Wyman, Abandonment, p. 276.

[5] Foreign Relations of the U.S. 1944 v. 1, 1023-24, Tait to Huddle 4/19/44.

[6] Emphasis added.

[7] National Archives, State Department File 811.111 Refugees 282 as cited by Wyman, *Paper Walls*, 112, 113, 256.

[8] Long Diary, Nov. 13, 1940 as cited by Feingold, op. cit. 115, 155, 332.

[9] Long diary, 4/22/41 as quoted by Feingold op. cit. 157.

[10] FDR Library/OF 3186, Dec. 18, 1940, FDR to Ickes.

[11] Emphasis added.

[12] Harrison to State Dept. 4/20/43; Hull to Bern 5/25/43 State Dept. 862 4016/2269; Wise to Wells 5/3/43 State Dept. R. 3821; Harrison to Secretary of State 6/14/43; 7/3/43; m 7/10/43; State Dept. 862 4016/2274, 2276, 2278; Meltzer, Conversation w. Goldmann 5/12/43 State Dept. R 3827; Riegner Jarvik interview 10/4/78 as quoted by Wyman, Abandonment 179-80, 381.

[13] Morgenthau Diaries 681 85, 88-89, 68II 66-75.

[14] Reams to Long and Mathews 10/25/43 State Dept. 862 4016/2292; as quoted by Wyman, Abandonment 181, 382.

[15] Long memo 10/26/43 State Dept. 862 4016/2292. Morgenthau Diaries 688II 70-72 as quoted by Wyman, Abandonment 181, 382.

[16] Emphasis added.

[17] Morgenthau Diaries 688 I/166, 688 II/47A 48-49 as quoted by Wyman, Abandonment 182, 382. Also Wasserstein 246-249.

[18] Morgenthau Diaries 693/200-1 as quoted by Wyman, Abandonment 183, 382.

[19] There is rich literature available on this entire subject of obstruction of rescue of Rumanian Jews; also of 30,000 Bulgarian Jews. Morgenthau wrote two detailed reports in Colliers, 1947; Joseph Tennenbaum in Congress Weekly, Feb. 2, 1953, 527 and Josiah Du Bois in his *The Devils Chemists*, Beacon Press, 183-88.

[20] Foreign Relations of the U.S. I 70-71, Dec. 17, 1943, Aide Memoir from British Embassy, as cited by Feingold, op. cit. 185, 335.

[21] Hays Memo to Baraibar 3/18/43 Carlton Hayes papers, Box 3 Jordana; excerpts and Summary of reports on Spain from Conard 11/20/43 American Friends Committee Country Spain RS 6, as quoted by Wyman, Abandonment 280, 404.

[22] Two hundred more Sephardic Jews were saved the same way by receiving Spanish passports.

[23] Even this measure was objected to by the Secretary of War, Henry Stimson, who protested to Roosevelt that the issue "concerns a very deeply held feeling of our people." National Archives /SDDF, 840.48 Refugees/5499, March 31, 1944, Stimson to Pehle as quoted by Feingold, op. cit. 261-262.

[24] Atherton to Welles 9/3/42 State Department R/3080; also The New York Times 9/5/42, 3 and Foreign Relations of the U.S., 1942, v. 2, 710-12 and Contemporary Jewish Record 12/42, 648-9 as cited by Wyman, op. cit. 36, 361.

[25] Ibid.

[26] Annual report of the Immigration and Naturalization Service 1946 as quoted by Wyman, Abandonment 136, 374.

[27] Foreign Relations of the United States, 1941 I 619-620, Department of State Bulletin IV 6-2; 41, 748, The New York Times June 18, 1941, 1.

[28] From 1933 to 1944 243, 862 immigrants, not all Jews, arrived in the U.S. R.M. Davis *Refugees in America*, 1947.

[29] Emphasis added.

[30] Emphasis added

[31] U.S. Census of 1940

[32] Breckinridge Long to Adolf Berle and James Dunn, June 26, 1940. Breckinridge Long papers, Box 211 as quoted by Wyman, *Paper Walls*, 173.

[33] Long Diary 1940, p. 140 as quoted by Wyman, *Paper Walls*, 174.

Chapter 4
CONSPIRACY IN THE
BRITISH HIERARCHY

No country was as consistent and as callous in its actions aimed at sealing escape routes to those who tried to flee for their lives as was Great Britain. And no country had as many individuals in decision-making positions and as many government offices involved in that undertaking. Next to the Germans, who as the designers of the Final Solution and as its executioners are in a category of their own, the British carry the heaviest guilt for that abomination, that total collapse of human morality, the Holocaust.

For at least three fateful years, one and a half years before and approximately the same period after the outbreak of World War II, the actions of Germany and Britain left an odd mark on the pages of history. The Germans, in order to fulfill their plan to make Europe "judenrein"—clear of Jews, were trying hard to make the Jews emigrate. The Germans used mass murder and torture as well as offers of German ships for emigrants even—modestly—contributing rare foreign currency to the expense of the voyage. The British, to the contrary, mobilized their diplomatic services as well as naval units, army, and police detachments in addition to their intelligence services to seal the only open major escape route.[1]

As we will point out and document in this chapter, some of these actions aimed openly at *preventing Jews from leaving* and countering the Jewish endeavor to flee by stopping it "at the source."[2] There was also the specific undertaking of barring, except for token numbers, the vast expanse of the British Empire to anything approaching substantial Jewish immigration. The British Empire spanned the world. With its colonies and dominions it constituted the largest commonwealth in human history. Most of these lands were thinly populated and craved more European immigrants. There was enough space to rescue hundreds of thousands and, at the same time, to provide these mostly underdeveloped economies with the energy of a people who were eager to build a new life for themselves. Yet, a British official expressed the prevailing attitude bluntly by stating that the empire had "an absorbing capacity (of) nil!"[3]   A Canadian senior official expressed the same position when asked how many Jewish immigrants he thought should be admitted after the war, he answered "None is too many."[4]

Let us first glance at some of the British dominions. Australia, New Zealand, and South Africa, plus the huge Crown Colony of India, together admitted fewer refugees than the Japanese—then in control of Shanghai—permitted to enter that city. Australia had been calling for more immigrants. Yet between 1938—when after annexation of Austria, persecution reached new highs—and the end of World War II in 1945, Australia admitted a total of 6,479[5] Jewish immigrants, averaging to about 800 annually. South Africa, which was quite eager to attract white immigrants, accepted an even smaller number and the figure dwindled to a trickle as the persecution and thereby the urgency increased. In 1938, the vast territory of South Africa admitted 566 escapees from the Holocaust. In 1939, the figure was reduced to 300 and in the six years during 1940-45 a total of 216 were admitted.

In the African colonies the chances for rescue were even lower than in the South African Dominion. There was talk about allowing immigration to Kenya and also to Tanganyika, but the following figures show that these colonies were, for all practical purposes, excluded from becoming havens for the hunted of Europe. The thinking was in terms of dozens to be admitted, not of many thousands as the situation demanded and would have permitted. In November 1938, Prime Minister Neville Chamberlain announced to the House of Commons that *thirty* German and Austrian refugees had been sent to *Kenya*. The British Governor of Kenya declared that this colony was ready to admit "carefully screened Jews of the right type, i.e. Nordic, from Germany or Austria."[6] The actual number admitted into that large region did not exceed twenty five families per year.[7] In the little country of Luxembourg the Jewish population had been entirely upper middle and upper class, professionals and experienced businessmen, accustomed to designing and implementing major economic projects in both developed and underdeveloped areas. In 1941, the Foreign Minister of the Luxembourg government in exile asked the British Foreign Office to find havens in the British Empire for his Jewish citizens, who were threatened with deportation to the East. Tanganyika was mentioned, but he was told that it was "not possible in existing circumstances for the United Kingdom to admit refugees whether of allies or other nationality on compassionate grounds alone"[8] and that visas for Tanganyika were not available.

It was easier to obtain entrance into the British Isles, where many of the refugees had relatives, than into British colonies or dominions. Faced with the relatively large numbers of refugees admitted to such small countries as the Netherlands, Belgium and even tiny Luxembourg, the United Kingdom and Northern Ireland with a population of approximately 46 million, admitted in the course of the twelve years of Nazi rule, a total of approximately 0.15% of their own population figure. Many of the 71,000 Jewish refugees admitted during that period were in the British Isles in transit only. More than a third of them had obtained an American quota number and waited for that number to come up.

The breakdown of civilized thinking that occurred during the Holocaust is not only evident from the closing of the rescuing gates; it seems to us that the *reasons* given to justify those brutal actions were at least as immoral as blocking the escape itself. The various countries used the standard excuse that the applicant's occupation was not needed in the country to which admission was sought. It aparently did not occur to the officials of those countries that this was no excuse for letting fellow humans be murdered. Yet such an excuse is comparable to the one of the ship's captain who passes by drowning persons and refuses to take them aboard because there is no profit, no advantage in it for either him or the shipping company. The British answer to the Luxembourg request—no admission on compassionate grounds—is comparable to such a ship captain's action.

To mention just a few other British colonial areas that refused to rescue the drowning, *Southern* as well as *Northern Rhodesia,* both craving for white immigrants, refused entrance to Jews, except a few dozen, mainly people who already had relatives living there. In the Western Hemisphere the same rule was applied for British colonies. When at the Bermuda Conference on Refugees, in April 1943, U.S. Senator Lukas mentioned the possibility of admissions to British Honduras, the British answered that there were already twenty refugees there, and that there was no room for additional ones because it was difficult for Europeans to adjust and to be productive in that climate. It was not mentioned why it would be harder to adjust for 200 or 2,000 who would find strength living with more persons of a similar past than it was for 20, isolated from everything their life had been before.

Another British colony in the Western Hemisphere, Trinidad, came into the limelight in October 1941. A ship had docked there that carried approximately 85 Jewish refugees. They had left Marseilles nine months earlier equipped with Brazilian visas issued by the Brazilian consul in Marseilles. The Brazilian Government had refused to honor these visas, and their attempts to find a country that would admit them had been a cruel nightmare. The ship had called at many ports, but nowhere had the refugees been admitted. Port calls included Dakar in West Africa where the Vichy French had detained the ship for four months. From Dakar, they had sailed to Casablanca. There, they were not only denied admission, but were put into a detention camp. In October they had arrived in Buenos Aires on a Spanish ship. Admittance refused. And now they asked for asylum in Trinidad. The decision of the colonial government was not to admit a single one of them[9] and this decision was backed up by the Colonial Office.[10] That there was space for a haven in the Caribbean was confirmed by Britain's shipping 3,000 persons to Jamaica. These 3,000 were mentioned by the British when they reported at the Bermuda Conference on how they had done everything possible to admit refugees to the empire. Not mentioned was the fact that these 3,000 proved both that there was shipping as well as a haven—if it was not for the purpose of saving Jews. The 3,000 shipped to Jamaica were all British—evacuated from Gibraltar.

There was one area in the Western Hemisphere that the British dangled before various refugee organizations. Britain's South American colony of Guiana was an almost uninhabitable territory that had been offered in the 1920's to Syrians who were seeking settlement, an attempt that ended in total failure. Britain now offered to sell land there at a modest price for the settlement of Jewish refugees. The colony had an equatorial climate, being only five degrees from the equator, and the territory considered for resettlement of the refugees was 250 miles fron the nearest port, with which it was connected by a path only. At best, a few hundred unusually hardened young pioneers experienced in agricultural work might, with outside assistance, have been able to really settle there. Dr. Isaiah Bowman, President of John Hopkins University and a top expert in resettlement issues, compared the Guiana suggestion to a plan to build a city on the South Pole. This would be possible but it would be prohibitive.[11] The British offer was clearly meant for diversion and decoration. As the Jewish organizations hesitated to act on it, it was withdrawn in the course of the 1943 Bermuda Conference. Among themselves those shaping the refugee policies were quite united and their machinations were well coordinated. Ranking officers of the Foreign Office, worked hand in hand with high officials of the Colonial Office in the development of these plans as well as in their enforcement.

Contrary to their counterparts in the U.S. Department of State and War Department, there was hardly any attempt in the British hierarchy to conceal the anti-refugee character of its policy which was actually an anti-Jewish one. Those who may be inclined to feel that it is too grave a charge that anti-Semitism was involved in the British reaction to the disaster which engulfed European Jewry should be aware that Winston Churchill pointed his finger on more than one occasion at what he bluntly called anti-Semitism in the civilian bureaucracy as well as in the armed forces. As quoted by the Churchill biographer Martin Gilbert, Churchill stated in a letter to the Colonial Secretary Lord Cranborne.

> It may be necessary to make an ex-
> ample of these anti-Semitic officers
> and others in high places. If three or
> four of them were recalled and dis-
> missed and the reasons given, it
> would have a salutary effect.[12]

Unfortunately one of the "others in high places" who were anti-Semites and whose biases were reflected in their actions was the man who was, next to the Prime Minister, the most influential person in the British Government, Sir Anthony Eden. After twelve years of being a leading member of the House of Commons, Sir Anthony was, in 1935, appointed Secretary of State for Foreign Affairs, and held that position until 1938. From 1939-40, Eden was Secretary for the Dominions. For half a year in 1940, he was also Secretary of War, and for the rest of the war period—1940-45—Secretary of State for Foreign Affairs. He had thus held ministerial positions in three departments: Foreign Affairs, Dominions, and War, and thereby had the chance to build up a following in all three departments. Each department was a major factor in dealing with the issue of rescue action.

And Sir Anthony Eden was a Jew-hater.[13]

He is described as hating Jews in unequivocal terms by his private secretary, Lord Harvy of Tasburgh. When a conflict arose between Arab and Jewish interests, he could not be objective; he favored the Arabs.[14] When the chance arose to save 70,000 Rumanian Jews, he *feared* that Rumania would release those Jews who were destined to die and declared that it would be too much of a problem to "dispose" of them.[15]

When George Becker, President of the American ORT, first heard of the excuse of lacking transportation and space to place rescued Jews, he replied "If 100,000 Germans would offer to surrender we would find some way to get them out."[16]

And when the deportations from Hungary were keeping Auschwitz gas chambers and crematoria working full blast to "dispose of them"—12,000 Jews almost every day from sunrise to sunrise, Dr. Weizmann, who represented the largest Jewish organization, and his right-hand man, Shertok, asked to see Eden. Sir Anthony asked his Private Secretary:

> What do you say, must I? Which of my
> colleagues looks after this? Minister
> of State or Mr. Hall? At least one of
> them responsible should be there to
> see these two Jews. Weizmann does
> not usually take much time.[17]

Mr. Eden did not meet with Weizmann and Shertok on this vitally important matter but made Mr. Hall see "these two Jews." The Colonial Office was fully cooperating with—and often outdoing—the Foreign Office in anti-Jewish actions. This was not surprising considering the persons who held decision-making positions there. The head of the Colonial Office's Mideast Department was Harold Frederick Downie, who expressed his attitudes towards Jews, after reading an article by a Jewish author as follows:

> "This sort of thing makes one regret
> that the Jews are not on the other side
> in this war."[18]

He could have hardly expressed more clearly his hostility against Jews. He saw them as enemies, just as the Germans. No wonder that this head of the Mideast Department was one of the main promoters of the canard that Jews were spying for their assassins. Downie viewed them as being "on the other side in this war"; to spy for the Germans was, from this perverted view, therefore only natural.

Downie's attitudes were not at all isolated. They were basically those which one could find throughout the Colonial Department. The Deputy Undersecretary of the Colonial Office, Sir John Shuckburgh, wrote in 1940 regarding the Jews of Palestine "... they hate us and have always hated us, they hate all gentiles."[19] Could it be that this gentleman simply applied the psychological process of projection and projected his Jew hatred onto the Jews in making them hate all gentiles as he hated all Jews? "They have always hated us" since time immemorial or since Sir John has "always" hated Jews?

One of the Jewish traits about which Shuckburgh complained was that "the Jews have no sense of humor..."[20] He does not elaborate what specifically was so humorous in the Jewish situation.

We mention here still one more comment by a ranking official of the Colonial Office expressing the general attitude prevailing among those in the British hierarchy assigned to deal with Holocaust issues. Mr. J.S. Bennett was a former First Secretary to the British Legation in Cairo and was a Middle East expert assigned to the Colonial Office. His expertise qualified him so well that he referred to the lot of European Jewry as *"Zionist sob stuff."*[21]

With individuals of the above-described anti-Semitic attitudes concerned full-time with issues related to the Holocaust, one cannot be surprised by the positions so often favoring the effectiveness of the Final Solution. British hostility against rescue actions was the more regrettable, as it was Britain which held the key to the solution of the problem, or at the very least, the capacity to make a very major contribution to solving the problem. Britain controlled immigration to what was then Palestine, and Palestine was a natural answer to the issue of the homeless Jews. Not only had it been destined by Britain as well as by the international community to be the Jews' homeland; it was most favorably located to receive the masses of Jews from central as well as from Eastern Europe. The Danube, navigable all the way from Germany, through Austria, Czechoslovakia, Hungary, Yugoslavia, Bulgaria, and Rumania, presented an inexpensive way of transportation without the need to land—even for a moment—in any place to which visas might not be obtainable. In addition, in Palestine the newcomers would find a large, well—organized Jewish community, keen on helping their brothers and sisters and eager to rescue as many as possible. And as to absorption power, the Jews there were firm believers in a principle that had proved correct before and did so again after the war, when Israel within three years, 1948-1951, doubled its population! It was the principle that each newcomer stands on the shoulders of the one who immigrates after him.

But Britain, concerned with its colonial empire, wanted an uninterrupted area of unconditionally controlled territory on both sides of the Suez Canal. With hardly any air transportation in existence at that time, "the canal" constituted the lifeline to Britain's colonies in the East, among them India, Burma, Singapore, and Hong Kong. According to the Mandate for Palestine, British rule was to end when the Mandate's purpose, a Jewish national home that could rule itself, had been established. This was not at all what Britain really wanted. To express it in the simplest yet correctly descriptive way, Britain intended to "pocket" Palestine for good.

As the world was apparently moving towards another war, strategic interests could be used prominently as the alleged reason for taking Palestine away from the Jews. The goodwill of the Arabs, whose British-dominated countries lined the lifeline to the East, made a convincing argument. Actually Britain knew that there was no goodwill to be expected on the part of the Arabs, who were either docile or, when nationally conscious, adamantly set against the British. Typically, future Arab leaders like Nasser and Sadat were admirers of Hitler. When war came, they worked for a German victory, thereby showing the weakness of the appeasement policy. The Jews offered a Jewish army, consisting of volunteers from Palestine and from all over the world, and such an army would have been an asset in the war against Germany. But the British adamantly refused to agree to the idea although the proposal for such an army was favored by Churchill. Solidifying the British presence in Palestine and incorporating it into the British Empire was for the then-ruling Chamberlain government a much more desirable aim.

The great step towards breaking the pledge of the Balfour Declaration and towards reneging on the obligation assumed by the Mandate, was being prepared by the Foreign Office. Eden's return to the leadership of the Foreign Office during 1939-45 bespeaks the influence he retained in that ministry. His influence in the government was a steady, uninterrupted factor. And he was a steadfast promoter of the plot to formally terminate all planning for a Jewish homeland.

On May 17, 1939, the British White Paper was published. In blunt language it abrogated the pledge of the Balfour Declaration and the duties assumed under the Mandate. It left no doubt about its meaning. "His majesty's Government now declares that it is not part of their policy that Palestine should become a Jewish state." It then named the measures by which that goal was to be achieved. During the next five years, immigration of Jews will be limited to a total of 75,000. After that, Jews would be admitted only if the Arabs agree. The High Commissioner would be given the right to prohibit and regulate sales of real estate to Jews, and five months later he promulgated these restrictions: In circumscribed regions amounting to 64% of the land, Jews could not buy land that previously belonged to Arabs save for exceptional cases. In another 31% of the land, Jews could acquire such lands only in specified cases. Only 5% of the anyhow truncated Promised Land was open for purchases by Jews without special restrictions. The timing for the White Paper's publication was well chosen to keep criticism to a minimum. Following the Crystal Night pogroms, persecution of the Jews in German-held lands had reached new highs. Also at that time, the United States had removed herself from the list of possible critics by refusing admission to children of the persecuted by letting the Wagner-Rogers initiative die in Congressional committees. In the same month, the St. Louis sailed with Jewish refugees from Hamburg for Cuba and, as Cuba cancelled the visas the refugees had obtained, it was obvious that a scandal was brewing. This would help divert attention from the British proclamation and would exclude the United States even more clearly from those entitled to criticize the British White Paper.

Yet, powerful voices arose in the House of Commons. Leopold Amery, who had been Secretary for the Colonies but was out of power at that time, spoke vehemently against the repudiation of obligation assumed.

> I could never hold my head up again to either Jew or Arab if I voted tomorrow for what in good faith I repeatedly told both, Jews and Arabs, was inconceivable, namely that any British government would ever go back upon the pledge given not only to Jews but the whole civilized world when it assumed the Mandate.[22]

The following day a man whose name will live when the names of
those who plotted the White Paper and conspired to get it approved,
will long be forgotten, addressed the House of Commons on the
same subject. Winston Churchhill—like Amery, out of power under
the Chamberlain government—said

> As one intimately and personally and
> responsibly concerned in the earlier
> stages of our Palestine policy, I could
> not stand by and see solemn engage-
> ments into which Britain has entered
> before the world to set aside for rea-
> sons of administrative convenience
> or—and it will be a vain hope—for the
> sake of a quiet life. Like my Right
> Honorable Friend I should feel per-
> sonally embarrassed in the most acute
> manner if I lent myself by silence or
> inaction to what I must regard as an
> act of repudiation.[22]

A poll conducted two months before the publication of the White
Paper showed that the public continued to favor continuation of
Jewish immigration to Palestine.[23] The major daily newspapers
however, with the exception of the Manchester Guardian, supported the White Paper.

Churchill's and Amery's statements did not swing the House of
Commons. The White Paper was accepted, and those who had been
plotting the theft of Palestine carried the day. A theft it was because
the Mandate provided the only legality of a British presence there.
With the Mandate repudiated, they had no right to it.

But whatever their legal situation, the conspiracy that had earlier
abused the Evian Conference to prevent Palestine from even being
considered as part of the solution to the refugee problem had won
out again. The theft of Palestine, which should and could have
provided a new home for the victims of German persecution, was
"legalized"—by the thief himself.

While the American conspirators acted largely on the admitted
principle of "postpone and postpone and postpone" (until rescue is
not possible any more), their British counterparts used delay as just
one of their several tools. They did not hesitate to take open action

even when the excuse of acting in the interest of their country was obviously not applicable. Typical examples of this were the refusal to save thousands of children from the eminent danger of murder. In 1943, when the Germans wanted to exchange German civilians who had been interned by the British at the start of the war for 5,000 Jewish children in German controlled lands, the British refused that offer on the grounds that those children were not citizens of the British Empire.[24] A year later, in 1944, the Joint Distribution Committee[25] persuaded the Swiss to accept 5,000 Jewish children from France against guarantees that these children would leave Switzerland at the end of the war. However, the British accomplices to the Holocaust refused to promise to grant those children entrance certificates to Palestine valid *after the war's end* even though, according to the White Paper, 75,000 were admissible.[26]

In the case of the children, the British could not even apply their standard argument that admission would involve security risks for the country because the Germans used such opportunities to smuggle spies in with the refugees. This argument, which made those still insisting on rescue action appear unpatriotic, was entirely fraudulent. We have pointed out before that for a German spy, there was hardly a place more likely to lead to discovery than in a group of Jewish refugees. Jews knew each other's ways and experiences, their customs and ways of reacting. They had mutual friends or acquaintances and were, as people in danger always are, suspicious themselves. Besides, in every country there were numerous natives who admired Hitler and who could provide much more information and were, for the Germans, incomparably more reliable than any Jew might have been. We are calling that security argument fraudulent because the Downies and Breckinridge Longs and others who regularly invoked it in order to scuttle rescue measures *knew* that it was false. There was a point at which even the Foreign Office complained that the security argument was regularly resorted to by the Colonial Office as well as by the High Commissioner for Palestine, yet when they were requested to name a case in which German agents had been brought to the Middle East posing as illegal Jewish immigrants, not one such case could be produced.

It was one thing by Britain to declare the gates of Palestine barred (except for the pittance of certificates which it was ready to issue while making certain that Palestine could not become a Jewish state), and it was quite another matter to keep the doors really so tightly blocked. People who see their relatives and friends perish and know that it is only a question of time before they will be next, do not ask whether it is "illegal" to save one's life. This is true in any case but the more so if the one who proclaimed the law is viewed as an illegal occupier, a power that tries to steal the land which not only meant saving one's individual life, but also rescue for the persecuted, hunted, and massacred group to which one belongs.

Fighting that "illegal" escape to Palestine brought the plotters in the Colonial Office together with those in the Foreign Office, and they called for the armed forces to implement their cruel policy. In a House of Commons debate on July 20, 1939, Mr. Malcolm MacDonald, the Colonial Secretary, had to admit that a "Division of Destroyers" supported by five smaller launches was being employed to ascertain that those who had escaped Hitler did not escape the British capture as they approached Palestine.[27] Those who had fled the German destroyer and his cohorts were now hunted down by four destroyers of His Majesty's Royal Navy: HMS *Hero* (flagship), HMS *Havock*, HMS *Henward*, and HMS *Hotspur*. These were among Britain's newest and fastest fighting ships—all four commissioned just two years earlier. At least one other destroyer, the *Ivanhoe* was also used in that lopsided warfare. Those conspiring in London to block the saving gate of Palestine really meant business. The ships had been authorized to open fire "at or into any ship that was suspected of having illegal immigrants on board and that did not obey the warning to stand by."[28]

They had been authorized to shoot, and shoot they did. Thus it happened that on the very first day of World Way II, on September 1, 1939, while German dive bombers rained death on Warsaw and a dozen other Polish cities, His Majesty's ship *Lorna* opened fire on a rickety overcrowded refugee ship, *Tiger Hill*, as she approached the Palestine coast to unload her cargo of misery, 1417 survivors of man's inhumanity against man. She did not, could not, heed the order to turn back toward Germany. The encounter between HMS *Lorna* and the *Tiger Hill* ended with a victory for the Royal Navy. Killed in the encounter were Dr. Robert Schneider, a young man who had been a physician in Czechoslovakia before he had been deprived of human dignity and all possessions; and Zwi Binder, a young pioneer from Poland whose hopes to till the land peacefully in a Kibbutz died within sight of the land he had been longing for years to reach.

The first two persons killed by British bullets during World War II *were not Germans but Jewish escapees* from the German hell.

Aggressively pursued diplomatic efforts also were applied in full cooperation between the Jew haters in the Colonial and the Foreign Offices to keep the escape routes blocked.[29] In the effort to keep prospective immigrants out of Palestine, a veritable diplomatic net was thrown out over all the countries through which they might pass. A special effort was directed by the accesories to the Holocaust who worked out of the Foreign Office to those states whose ships might carry escapees who were able to reach a seaport. In line with Mr. Downie's spirit that Jews were just as dangerous enemies as the Germans, the now-available files of the respective ministries show that the planners of a war against the Jews spoke in the spirit of warfare of the various "fronts" on which they battled the escapees. So does, for example, Foreign Office file 371/252411 speak of the "Bulgarian front" when it refers to the diplomatic pressure on Bulgaria to aid Britain in her desire to stop the refugees "at the source." Viscount Edward Frederick Lindsay Woods, Earl of Halifax, Secretary of State for Foreign Affairs 1938-40, demonstrated the importance of the diplomatic offensive by a five-page directive dated July 21, 1939 in which he demanded that the ambassadors of the following countries "be summoned" to the Foreign Office and "be spoken to on the subject": Brazil, Iran, Liberia, Mexico, Panama, and the Dominican Republic.[30] At the same time, it was considered imperative to stop these potential escapees from the Holocaust right in the countries from which they sought escape. Mr. Alec Randall, who in matters of refugees was functioning as the Secretary for Foreign Affairs' right-hand man, clarifies: "countries... which may be regarded as countries of origin... are Poland, Hungary, Yugoslavia, Rumania and Bulgaria. One or more of these countries must be crossed in transit before embarking for Palestine. I am to enclose drafts of dispatches to His Majesty's representatives at Bucharest, Budapest, and Warsaw. Instructions have already been sent to His Majesty's Ministers in Belgrade and Sofia in telegrams of which copies are enclosed for convenience of reference."[31]

By tradition, the King does not involve himself in political issues, but this continent-wide chase of Jews was entered into even by the King; and it was done by his demanding the harshest of measures: preventing the victims from leaving the places of increasingly brutal persecution. In February 1939, three months after the Crystal Night had revealed to the whole world details of the Nazi horror, King George VI's Private Secretary advised the Secretary for Foreign Affairs that the King hoped that the Jewish refugees, to whom the message also refers as "these people", be prevented from *leaving*[32] their country of origin.

> "The King had heard... that a number of Jewish refugees from diferent countries were surreptitiously getting into Palestine and he is glad to think that steps have been taken to prevent these people leaving their country of origin."[33]

But notwithstanding the Crown's endorsement of even such a brutal measure as preventing the escape of "these people" from "their country of origin," there were Britishers who stood up against their government's policy and did so firmly in the House of Commons. There, on July 20, 1939, a major debate on the Palestine policy took place. The discussion, unusually impassioned and long, lasted until 11 p.m. The official record of that day's debate fills 122 pages (pp. 762-884). The Secretary of State for the Colonies defended the policies by claiming that they were in the British interest, and he thus implicitly took for granted the principle that the aim justifies even the most cruel means. He was assisted by the more conservative members of the House of Commons who, by their support, joined those who by action—not by inaction—made themselves co-responsible for the effectiveness of the German's undertaking and by sealing the escape routes became accomplices of the so-often and so-openly announced German Final Solution. Ironically, those supporting the government's policy included the representative in the House of Commons of a learned institution of worldwide renown, Mr. Pickthorn, the member of Cambridge University. Most members associated with the military also backed the government's policy, but Captain Victor Cazalet stated,

> "If there is anyone who under those conditions would turn back those people he would deserve neither the title of British nor of Christian."

Mr. Duff Cooper, who later serving in Churchill's government was to become Minister of State for Information, said in defense of large-scale immigration into Palestine and in support of meeting the obligations of the Mandate:

"We should decide that it is our policy first and foremost to make a real home for the Jews in Palestine... Before these islands began their history, a thousand years before the Prophet Mohammed was born, the Jew, already exiled, sitting by the waters of Babylon was singing: 'If I forget thee O Jerusalem, let my right hand forget her cunning.'"

And Sir J. Haslam in defense of an "open the gates policy" stated

"The Jews regard Palestine as their native land whether they were actually born there or not. Millions of them who have never been to Palestine at all, regard that country as their home, just as millions of people of the British race who have never set foot in this country regard this country as their home... As long as I can remember Palestine has been known as the Promised Land. Promised to whom? It was promised to the Jews by Lord God Almighty. Almost every book of the Old Testament and many of the New Testament repeats that promise."

Again, the government used the powerful argument of security, claiming that, with the refugees, enemy agents would enter the country... and the government won out again.

In the meanwhile conditions on the continent had deteriorated further. Pogroms were set in motion even in countries which were not yet formally under the German heel but where, stimulated and encouraged by the German example, persecution of Jews quickened its pace and sharpened its methods.

As we want to report next on the British conspiracy that resulted in the deaths of the refugees crammed into the SS *Struma*, we have first to outline the conditions which made it possible that so many persons could be crowded into such a small rotting and unseaworthy boat.

In the last days of January 1941, Rumanian Jews fell victim to a pogrom staged by the Rumanian Nazi party. It was reported in many details in the Western press, including in *The New York Times*, and major British papers in their issues from January 29 to February 2, 1941. This is an excerpt of the lengthy report:

"Sofia January 29. This I believe is the first eyewitness account to reach the outside world of the Iron Guard horror in Rumania... Jewish leaders believed that dead throughout the whole country would exceed 2,000... Dozens of Jews—women and children as well as men—were literally burned alive. I am not speaking of those who were burned to death in hundreds of buildings to which guardists set fire after shooting and beating the inhabitants and looting the contents of their homes. I am speaking only of Jews who were beaten senseless on the streets, robbed, then doused with gasoline and set afire.

In the Bucharest morgue yesterday, a military surgeon showed me the charred bodies of nine persons burned beyond recognition. All of them, he assured me, had been picked up in the streets of the Jewish quarter following the most frenzied stage of the pogrom last Wednesday.

Trusted friends have told me and officials have confirmed numerous cases of Jewish women whose breasts were cut off, not to mention sadistic mutilations like gouged-out eyes, brandings and bone breakings.

Perhaps the most horrifying single episode of the pogrom was the "Ko-

sher butchering" last Wednesday
night of more than 200 Jews in the
municipal slaughterhouse.

The Jews who had been rounded up
after several hours of Iron Guard
raids were put into several trucks and
carried off to the slaughterhouse.
There the Green-shirts forced them to
undress and led them to the chopping
blocks where they cut their throats in
a horrible parody of the traditional
Jewish methods of slaughtering fowls
and livestock.

Tiring of this sport after a few score
had been thus dispatched, forty to
fifty armed legionnaires mad with
hate beheaded the rest with axes and
knives. Some mangled bodies were
disposed of by pouring them down
manholes to the sewers usually used
to carry off animal remains.

What this report does not mention or what was omitted by the media
as too much of the ghastliness, is that many of the bodies so
slaughtered were hung up in the slaughterhouse on meat hooks and
signs reading "Kosher Meat" were put on these headless torsos.

The American ambassador to Bucharest, Franklin Guenther
Scott informed Washington of a detail which the papers apparently
felt to be too gruesome to print. His telegram informs the State
Department that the torsos, altogether 50, had been skinned like
carcasses of slaughtered animals before they were hung up on the
meathooks.

Only when one tries to realize the panic with which Rumanian
Jews lived after that pogrom, can one understand that they boarded
a ship as clearly rotting and unseaworthy as the *Struma*. Frantically,
they had been looking around for a ship to get them away from
Rumania and to bring them to the only place where they knew
friendly arms were reaching out for them and where they could find
a new home. But it seemed impossible to find a ship. Agriculturally

rich Rumania had been obliged to deliver to Germany large quantities of cattle and wheat. For this purpose the Germans had taken over practically all ships to bring foods up the Danube. Yet the Germans had not requisitioned a small, old cattle boat, which, rickety and ramshackle, was rotting on a Danube dock. Its name was *Macedonia* and the Germans did not want it—too risky to entrust it with cattle for the trip up the Danube.

The Jews in their understandable panic got hold of the *Macedonia* and succeeded in getting her registered under the flag of Panama. She was renamed *Struma*. Officially she was fifty-six feet long, according to an editorial in *The New York Times* on March 13, 1942, only 50 feet. It sounds unbelievable, but 767 human beings were packed into this small boat built ages ago to transport cattle on the Danube and now set to help in the humans' escape by sailing the high seas. It is unbelievable that the *Struma* carried that many. Even more incredible was the fact that she succeeded in limping into Istanbul on December 16, 1941 after four days at sea. But this was all she could do.

The Turks did not permit the vessel to disembark. On the other hand, it was obvious that this wreck of a ship could not go anywhere. Turkish engineers who examined the broken engine declared it to be beyond repair. The Jewish Agency offered to provide transportation if admittance to any location not under German control could be granted.

The British refused admittance to Palestine although through their own intelligence report, the British legation in Ankara was fully aware of the "appalling" conditions on board where there was hardly enough standing room, one toilet only and one tiny kitchen. The stench from urine and feces was literally suffocating.[34] This was especially so in the hold in which, taking turns for reasons of space, one half of those on board had to be at any time.[35] All intervention with the government in London as well as with the British embassy to Turkey was in vain. Eleven days after the ship's arrival, the British informed the Turkish Foreign Ministry of their final decision:

> "His Majesty's government saw no reason why the Turkish government should not send the Struma back into the Black Sea if they wished."

The new year, 1942, started, and all during January the Jewish Agency tried to move the government in London to change its position. It was in particular Lord Moyne, Secretary of State for the Colonies and Leader of the House of Lords, who insisted on not changing the official decision and on pressuring the Turks to send the vessel back into the sea. During all that time the wretched 767 on the *Struma* were not permitted to leave the boat even for seconds. They remained prisoners on the boat. The Turkish authorities interdicted any contact with land except the bringing in of a minimal quantity of food by the Istanbul Jewish community.[36] Diseases, especially dysentery, spread, and at least two on the boat had become mental casualties. The humans on that vessel had to suffer conditions to which the cattle for whom the boat had been used previously never had to submit.

On February 9, after the *Struma* and its load of human misery had been in Istanbul for six weeks, the Turkish Government informed the British embassy that unless a solution of the problem would be reached by February 16, the boat would be sent in the direction from which it had come. As the engine remained unusable, this meant that the boat would be towed into the open sea.

We are claiming in this volume that by concerted action most governments conspired to seal the escape routes and that they made themselves accomplices to the German annihilation plans. It is interesting to note that Mr. A. Walker of the Foreign Office's Refugee Department recorded the following in a Foreign Office file:

> "The Black Sea is rough at this time of
> the year and the *Struma* might well
> founder. I do not like at all the idea
> that we may be acting as accomplices
> in bringing about the death of these
> miserable people."[37]

This minute is dated February 24. A second minute, dated February 25 reads:

> "The ship is today reported sunk with all on board."

The Turks had been made aware that, even according to the limitations of the White Paper, thousands of entry certificates into Palestine remained unused, and they had postponed the departure date of February 16 for another week. But with no change in the British attitude forthcoming, the *Struma*'s captain received on February 23 the final order to leave immediately. The refugees tried to prevent the crew from casting off. Then 80 Turkish policemen clubbed their way on board. The refugees fought them with their bare hands. Literally crawling over the shoulders and heads of the solid mass on deck, the policemen reached the docking lines, cast off, and a tugboat towed the vessel with all its men, women and children aboard, through the Bosporus and five miles into the Black Sea. There the *Struma* was left helpless. Next morning an explosion occurred which tore that floating coffin into pieces. Of all the humans on board, only one, an expert swimmer, survived. Within less than half an hour the icy waters had swallowed the last one of the others. Seven hundred and sixty-five humans had been murdered, victims of not only the Germans but also of the British Foreign Office by its cooperation in the matter with the Colonial Office and the High Commissioner for Palestine, who had repeatedly insisted in messages to his superiors in London that they should remain adamant.

There was a debate in the House of Lords following this disaster. The accomplices to the mass murder defended their actions largely by invoking the need for "security" of the British Empire. Lord Josiah C. Wedgwood answered in specific terms.

> "The Jews have certainly more cause to hate Hitler than anybody in the world. In Palestine you have the additional argument that Hitler can get Arab agents more easily and cheaply than anybody else. That allegation regarding the Jews is a barefaced excuse which supplies fresh evidence of anti-Semitism on the part of people who admit quite openly that they do not like Jews."[38]

The catastrophe of the *Struma* had roused many comments and condemnations. It was, however, not the first one, and not the last one either in which escapees from terror and victims of the White Paper and of even more stringent immigration policies for Palestine perished en masse in an attempt to save their lives. Shortly before the *Struma* catastrophe, on December 12, the 100 ton *Salvador* loaded with refugees who were trying to flee from German-controlled Bulgaria to Palestine sunk in the nearby Sea of Marmara. Two hundred and four humans drowned. The *Salvador* had been a rotting sailboat that had a small auxiliary motor. The Bulgarians refused to let it sail under the Bulgarian flag; but with a bribe it received permission to sail under the registry of Uruguay, and the Bulgarians washed their hands of it. She had no bunks, of course no cabins. For a short trip along the coast, she could have taken up to 30 or 40 passengers. Instead 327 were stuffed into her. Most were Rumanian citizens. Under German pressure Rumania had ceded part of her territory, the Dobruja, to Bulgaria, and the Jews there had suddenly become unwanted "foreigners." Bulgaria was at that time under full German control and expelled her Jews into Rumania where the Iron Guard and its followers would take care of the "Jewish problem." The British had intervened with both Bulgaria and Rumania to prevent escape, and fast clandestine action was necessary if one wanted to flee. When the boat was already so full that there was mainly standing room only, the Bulgarian authorities eager to get rid of the foreign Jews stuffed even more human cargo into the hold. One of those who tried to save his life "illegally", as many thousands had done by that time, was a journalist who described what happened…

> "The Bulgarian authorities insisted on our departure and refused to allow us time to prepare for the voyage… Cramped one against the other we were driven aboard, towed out into the Black Sea by a tug and abandoned to our fate."

He then describes how a passing motor boat towed them part of the way towards Istanbul, but there they were not permitted to stay and the boat tried to make it into the Sea of Marmara.

> "Suddenly a violent shock aroused us. We had been hurled into a reef. The ensuing scenes were terrible. Prayers and shrieks mingled with the howling of the gale and in the pitch darkness the white crested waves broke over us and water poured through thousands of fissures as the ancient craft began to break up. There were hardly any life belts (sic "life preservers") on board and they disappeared instantly. There was one small rowing boat aboard and we were 300. Suddenly the vessel broke its back

and precipitated everyone into the
raging sea."[39]

Two hundred and four humans who thought they had saved their
lives and were on the way to the Promised Land drowned. This
number included 66 children.

And what was the reaction to it in the offices in London that had
by their policy forced those who wanted to escape murder to try it
with ships which were expendable? Mr. T.H. Snow, the then Chief
of the Foreign Office's Refugee Section, put it into writing:

> "*There could have been no more convenient disaster* from
> the point of view of stopping this traffic."[40]

As convenient as that disaster was for Mr. Snow, it did not stop that
traffic because it simply could not. The *Struma* disaster followed and
so did the sinking of more ships crowded with refugees, because to
save his life the human will reach for a straw—or for a boat like the
Salvador or the Struma or—somewhat later—the Mefkurie with her
350 on board, or nameless even smaller vessels that turned out to
have been just floating coffins.

* * *

Those in the Foreign Office in London, just as those in the State
Department in Washington who, as the handling of the Rumanian
offer to release 70,000 Jews in Transnistria showed, did their best to
prevent the rescue of "too many Jews," were hit with a bombshell in
May 1944 by a German offer. Since their defeat at Stalingrad and the
surrender there of the crack 6th Army, those involved in war crimes
grew increasingly worried. One who had the best of reasons to be
concerned was Heinrich Himmler. He was, next to Hitler, the most
powerful man in Germany, being not only the Supreme Leader of
the S.S. and thereby of the Gestapo, but also held the position of
Minister of the Interior and was as such head of all police forces.
Eichmann was far down the bureaucratic ladder, but he was the one
who handled the Final Solution. In May 1944 through Eichmann, an
offer was made to the Allies which was nothing short of sensational.
Hungarian Jews were already concentrated at collection points as
deportations were just about to start. Eichmann on April 25, 1944,
announced to Joel Brand, a leading figure in Hungarian Jewry and

a member of the Relief and Rescue Committee, that the Germans were ready to release one million Jews against delivery of certain goods. The demand was for 2 million bars of soap, eight hundred tons of coffee, two hundred tons of tea and an item which was bound to be the by far most difficult to agree to, 10,000 trucks. To make the offer more acceptable to the United States and Britian, these trucks would be used on the Eastern front only.[41] Brand was told to get ready to bring that offer to the attention of the Allies.

On May 19, Brand, accompanied by a certain "Bandy" Grosz, a shadowy figure who had done some dirty work for the Germans, was put into a small German aircraft and flown to Istanbul. There Brand immediately established contact with emissaries of the Zionist organization, and within hours the message went out to London and to Washington.

The first reaction in the State Department, as well as in the Foreign Office, was to doubt the legitimacy of the offer. How seriously could Brand be taken, and if what he said was true, was it the outcome of a whim of some lower level Germans or did it come from the top German echelon? These doubts were soon dispelled as not valid. Brand in his interviews expressed the opinion that the demand for 10,000 trucks might be negotiable. Other goods were mentioned too. Mr. Laurence A. Steinhardt, the American ambassador to Turkey named cocoa in addition to the goods initially mentioned.

In any case those in the Foreign Office and also those in the State Department, who had so far successfully blocked the rescue of large numbers of Jews, were determined not to let this offer succeed. The routine excuses of lacking shipping and, even the more decisive claim that they could not come up with locations where even temporary havens could be established were brought up again. Lord Moyne, when hearing of that offer, called out, "Save one million Jews? What shall we do with them? Where shall we put them?"[42]

There were however other reasons, too, which spoke against acceptance of the offer by the Allies. To deliver trucks to an enemy with whom one is at war was a decision which truly demanded thorough deliberation. The condition that they would be used on Germany's Eastern front only was clearly intended to create a split between the western Allies and the Soviets.

It was also correctly suspected that the offer was made to start talking to the western Allies with the hope that they might agree to a separate peace.

But all this should not have excluded the opportunity to use the German desire for goods and possibly for peace talks to a least slow down the annihilation process that was just then reaching its height in Hungary -from where 12,000 Jews were being deported every day to Auschwitz. Ambassador Steinhardt, recommended keeping negotiations going.[43]

The principle which Breckinridge Long used to thwart rescue efforts, "postpone and postpone and postpone" could now delay the murder of 12,000 daily and, with the end of the war approaching, this might have meant survival for most of those who would otherwise have been deported.

But the British did everything they could to make it clear right away to the Germans that there was no chance of any agreement regarding the goods-for-blood offer.

First, they lured Brand from neutral Turkey to territory which was British controlled, to Aleppo in Syria. There Brand was arrested. From Aleppo, he was brought to Cairo, Lord Moynes' headquarters and center of anti-Semitic scheming. In Cairo, he remained under arrest. Jewish organizations pleaded with the British to release Brand and to send him back with, or if this was not possible, without, a delaying message, as his continuing arrest was an almost provocative signal to the Germans that the Allies did not want to have anything to do with that matter and were rejecting any kind of negotiations. The British, however, apparently wanted just that. Brand implored them to let him return; this rude way of reacting to the German offer would be at the expense of the Jews still left— including Slovakia's Jews of whom many had not yet been deported.

The American War Refugee Board urged Britain to send Brand back and not signal to the Germans that there was no chance of negotiation. President Roosevelt's agreement with that policy was obtained by Secretary Morgenthau and by John Pehle of the War Refugee Board.[44]

This whole suggested deal was too important to be left to Breckinridge Long and his staff to handle. The new Assistant Secretary of State, Edward R. Stettinus took the matter of the German offer into his own hands and said that "the Germans must be made to think that we take them seriously."[45]

But all these suggestions assumed that the British desired to save Jews, while they actually did all in their power to prevent such release. The attitude that prevailed in ruling British circles toward the rescue of Jews is characterized by the reaction of Sir Robert Bruce Lockhart, Director of the Political Warfare Executive, to the suggestion in 1944 to use leaflets to warn European populations not to aid in the murders and therefore not in the deportations. Among the excuses he gave for the rejection of that proposition was that the supply of paper was limited and that "our other commitments are heavy."[46] As the top echelons in the United States, including President Roosevelt, favored negotiations regarding the German offer in order to stall and thus to save as many as possible, the British made a gesture toward the United States. They finally informed the United States that they would consider the German offer if those released could be brought to Spain and/or Portugal. Certain that these countries would—if at all—agree to receive more refugees only if the United States and Britain guaranteed that at the end of the war those admitted under such a program would leave Spain and/or Portugal and as Britain knew that such a guarantee had been declined before, this British-qualified offer amounted to a rejection.

Actually the German offer to release Jews for goods including trucks was highly negotiable as events soon proved. Germany, with the approaching collapse of its Nazi regime, was keen on changing its policy regarding the Jews but an excuse to do so was needed. The demand for goods as sent through Brand was apparently such a very negotiable excuse. As the Brand offer was rejected in the most demonstrative manner—Brand was held under arrest until October 7, when chances for progress in that matter had vanished—other attempts to show a change in their policy were made by the Germans via Switzerland. There a group for the American Board of Orthodox Rabbis, Isaac and Recha Sternbusch, joined forces with Dr. Reuben Hecht, an imaginative Swiss citizen. Hecht had shown his ability to get things done before in being instrumental saving 2,200 Jews by getting them with the S.S. *Sakarya* "illegally" into Palestine. The Sternbusch-Hecht group recruited the services of just the right man for negotiating mass releases by the Germans.

J. Maria Musey, a former president of the Swiss Confederation, had exhibited sympathies for the German cause and could therefore more easily establish German connections. Himmler agreed to show his good will. Upon receipt of 12 Swiss-produced tractors he released and brought right to the Swiss border on August 21, 1944, 318 Hungarian Jews from Bergen-Belsen concentration camp. This release to Switzerland was followed by 1,368. All these had originally come from Hungary. Almost all of them were Orthodox, many rabbis among them. Sally Meyer, Chairman of the Swiss Union of Jewish Congregations representing the JOINT, negotiated with the Germans. These endeavors brought another 1,200 from the Theresienstadt detention camp to the Swiss border. All this shows how concrete the possibility was to get hundreds of thousands of Jews out of Rumania or have at least deportations stopped by negotiating, a procedure which was firmly rejected by the British and in which the Americans followed suit: The reason—no negotiations with the Germans for anything. This small group achieved such results from Himmler that he counteracted Hitler's order to have all Jews still assembled for deportation, or already in concentration camps, liquidated.

The German offer regarding a million Jews was made in May 1944; the war ended in May 1945, and during that time Himmler's willingness to release Jews and to establish for himself a kind of alibi could have been used for saving very large numbers without delivering a single truck. But the evidence shows that the British did not want to save them—that they were rather afraid of the prospect of a major rescue action. A British cabinet meeting on May 31, 1944 decided to torpedo the German rescue offer. It constituted a "danger" and may "lead to an offer to unload an even greater number of Jews on our hands."[47] This meeting of the cabinet committee on refugees was attended by Eden.

From the very beginning, from the sabotage of the Evian Conference to the arrest of Brand and the scuttling of rescue opportunity created by the developing German collapse, the British had effectively conspired, in the words of His Majesty, "to prevent these people leaving their country of origin."

[1] For details of these British actions, see the works cited in Chapter 1 note 2 especially Wasserstein and also William Perl, Operation Action, 1983.

[2] British Public Records Office, F.O. W10846/1369/48268

[3] Christopher Sykes, *Cross Roads to Israel*, 1965, 47

[4] Abella and Troper, op. cit.

[5] Abella and Troper, op. cit. Immigration Table V. All figures apply to fiscal year.

[6] Quoted by Sherman, *Island Refuge*, 106.

[7] Ibid.

[8] PRO F.O. 371/2 25254/496 W 12667/48

[9] Government of Trinidad to Colonial Office, October 9, 1941 PRO FO 371/29220 W 12001/570/48

[10] Colonial Office to Foreign Office October 11, 1941 same file as above. n. 1 and 2 as quoted by Wasserstein, op. cit. 142.

[11] FDR Library PSF Hull folder, November 21, 1939, Bowman to FDR as quoted by Feingold, op. cit. 109

[12] Premier papers 4/51/9 as quoted by Gilbert, op. cit. 49

[13] Diaries and papers of Oliver Harvey (Lord Harvey of Tasburgh) entry of April 25, 1943 as quoted by Wasserstein op. cit. 34.

[14] Eden to Harvey September 7, 1941 BL 56402 as quoted by Wasserstein, op. cit. 34.

[15] Morgenthau Diaries 23; Joseph Tenenbaum *They Might Have Been Rescued* Congress Weekly, February 2, 1953, 5-7 as quoted by Feingold op. cit. 183, 355.

[16] Long, Stephen S. Wise Papers, Minutes of the Meeting of the American Delegation to the Bermuda Conference, April 28, 1943 as quoted by Feingold, op. cit. 205.

[17] Foreign Office Papers 371/42807 WR 49 folio 70 as quoted by Gilbert, op. cit. 255.

[18] Minute by Downie, March 15, 1941 PRO CO 733/445 Part II - 76021-308 as quoted by Waserstein op. cit. 50.

[19] Minute by Shuckburgh, April 27, 1940 PRO C0733/426/75872/16 as quoted by Wasserstein op. cit. 50.

[20] Minute by Shuckburgh, December 5, 1940 PRO CO 733/430/76021/35/3.

[21] Minute by J.S. Bennett, April 18, 1941 PRO CO 733/444/75872 as quoted by Wasserstein, op. cit. 50.

[22] House of Commons cols. 1937-54, 2015-16 and 2168 May 22-23, as quoted by Wasserstein, op. cit. 22, 23 and 2168 May 22-23, 1939 as quoted by Wasserstein op. cit. 21-22.

[22] Ibid.

[23] A public opinion poll in March 1939 showed that 60% favored continued Jewish immigration to Palestine with only 14% against it and 26% expressing no opinion as quoted by Wasserstein, op. cit. 23

[24] Hilberg, op. cit. 721

[25] A major Jewish welfare organization concerned with resettlement.

[26] Long-Campbell talk January 11, 1944, 840.48, Refugees 5017 ASD

[27] PRO House of Commons Debates, July 20, 1939.

[28] Palestine Gazette, Extraordinary Issue, April 27, 1939.

[29] Joint memorandum of Colonial and Foreign Office, January 17, 1940 PRO FO 371/25238/274ff W 766/38/48.

[30] PRO FO 371/24092/2829

[31] Ibid.

[32] Emphasis added.

[33] PRO FO 371/24085/ W 4190/451/48 April 6, 1939. Also FO 371/24085 W 3567/551/48 February 28, 1939.

[34] S.O. (I) to Admiralty, February 5, 1942 PRO FO 371/32661 I/28 W 2093/652/48 as quoted by Wasserstein op. cit. 144

[35] British Legation in Ankara to Foreign Office December 29, 1941 PRO PREM 4/51/1/40 as quoted by Wasserstein, op. cit., p. 146. Emphasis added.

[36] One woman about to give birth was brought to an Istanbul hospital where a stillborn baby was deliverd. When the Struma, with her family on board left, she was still hospitalized.

[37] A. Walker minutes February 24, 25, 1942 PRO FO 371.32661/75 (W 2810/652/48) as quoted by Wasserstein 152 op. cit.

[38] PRO House of Lords debate March 10, 1942.

[39] The New York Times, December 16, 1940, 4.4

[40] Minute by Snow, December 17, 1940 PRO FO 371/25241/389 (W 12451/38/48) Emphasis added.

[41] Yehuda Bauer, The Holocaust in Historical Perspective, pp. 109-13, Seattle 1978; Kastner affidavit Jan.4.1946, copy in 266 World Jewish Congress Archives, N.G. 2994 Nuremberg Documents, Columbia University Law Library as quoted by Penkower, 349, op. cit.

[42] Hilberg, The Destruction of the European Jews, op. cit. 728.

[43] Steinhardt to State Department 6/5/44, 6/21/4, J. Brand, H 4, as quoted by Wyman, Abandonment, 244, 394.

[44] Morgenthau Diaries 741/48; Foreign Relations of the United States, 1944 as quoted by Wyman, Abandonment, 244, 394.

[45] Hausner, Jerusalem Eichmann trial, quoting from a memorandum of conversation between Stettinus and Nahum Goldmann, June 7, 1944 as quoted by Feingold, op. cit. 273, 347.

[46] Minute dated December 1, 1944 PRO FO 371/42897/25 (WR 1732/1554/48) as quoted by Wasserstein 299.

[47] Minutes of Meeting, May 31, 1944 PRO CAB 95/15/32

Chapter 5
SOVIET POLICIES THAT SUPPORTED
THE FINAL SOLUTION

In assessing the part that Soviet policies played in the German Final Solution, we have first of all to recall the often forgotten fact that during the first two years of World War II, the Soviet Union and Germany were allies. Together they planned the attack on Poland which triggered the war. They decided on a mutually agreed undertaking that once the German forces invading from the West had reached a certain line, the U.S.S.R. would invade from the East. Germany and the Soviet Union agreed on how to share the spoils of their aggression—that is, they agreed to divide up their conquered neighbor.

The pact between the U.S.S.R. and Germany was formally signed on August 23, 1938, by Molotov, the Soviet Union's Foreign Minister and by von Ribbentrop, the German Foreign Minister (the latter was hanged for crimes against humanity after conviction by the Nuremberg war crimes tribunal). For the festive ceremony of the signing, the hall in the Kremlin was decorated with the swastika banner flying next to that of the U.S.S.R. Stalin delivered a toast in which he said he was drinking to the health of the Fuehrer, so beloved by the German people. If this was not encouragement, what would be? Toasting that monster, drinking to his health just a few days before German planes and tanks would start bringing death to thousands of Poles, and the SS Einsatzgruppen would advance into Poland ready to begin their task of slaughtering hundreds of thousands of people.

Clearly, much more was made certain by that pact than the invasion of Poland. France and Britain had left no doubt about it: if Poland were attacked, they would live up to their treaty obligations and enter the war. The limit had been more than reached; it had been exceeded as Britain and France stood passively by when Germany committed four major acts of aggression and international lawlessness: the military occupation of the Ruhr territory; the march into and annexation of Austria; the occupation and annexation of the Sudeten; and, finally, occupation of the rest of Czechoslovakia. Thus Hitler and Stalin knew what they were starting by guaranteeing Hitler the security that he need not worry about his major neighbor to the East when fighting against the French and the British. The green light had been given to Hitler; his generals no longer had to be concerned about the Soviet Union while fighting the West. Most likely Hitler would have started the war anyway, but now, with the Soviet alliance, war had become an absolute certainty. Only nine days after the U.S.S.R.-German treaty was signed, on September 1st at dawn, German planes started raining death on the population of Warsaw and other Polish cities, and German tanks broke through the border defenses. And with the advancing German military machine came the SS Einsatzgruppen. The Soviets knew well that by giving Hitler a free hand to start his war, they also provided him with the possibility to enact his plans to annihilate the Jews. Besides all the other proof, there was the formal circular of January 31, 1939 sent to all German diplomatic stations which followed Hitler's statement before the Reichstag on January 30, 1939, in which he asserted his intent to annihilate the Jews of Europe.

To fully understand the support which the Final Solution received from the Soviet Union, we have to keep in mind the engulfing influence which the Soviet information and propaganda system exercises upon the thinking and, thereby, upon the actions of the Soviet population. The Government exercises an absolute monopoly over the distribution of news. Public television did not exist in the early 1940's, but radio, newspapers, and public speeches and announcements were not only tightly controlled; they were used to the fullest extent to form opinions, to keep the thinking "correct," and to initiate desired action and forestall undesired ones. Because of the importance which news items in war time exercise upon the life of the community as well as of the individual, news reports are eagerly listened to and read. This was particularly true in the days of the rapid developments of the earlier phases of the German-Soviet war, and that is where the other major Soviet contribution to the German Final Solution program lay: the functioning of the Soviet news and propaganda system during the time of war with Germany.

After two years, the Soviet policy of alignment with Germany backfired. Its basis had been the hope that Germany, on the one hand, and France and Britain on the other, would tear each other to pieces and that all three parties would then be at the mercy of the Soviets. The rapid German victories in the West had, however, strengthened Germany so much that it thought itself now ready to attack its erstwhile partner. Not to lag behind Germany's expansionism, the Soviet Union, too, had begun to swallow its neighbors. In addition to invading the Eastern part of Poland, the Soviets invaded three small Baltic neighbors, Latvia, Lithuania, and Estonia, and incorporated them into the Soviet Union as an "integral part." The U.S.S.R. had also invaded sections of Rumania. The Northern Bukovina and Bessarabia, too, were occupied and annexed. All these remain today part of the Soviet Union.

During the two years of the German-Soviet alliance, the U.S.S.R. suppressed information that was unfavorable to Germany. The German atrocities committed against the Jews in Poland and elsewhere were taboo for the Soviet information machine. The news media in the West underplayed these happenings, but the Soviet information system either entirely quashed this news or reported it in a way and place which minimized the issue to almost nothing.

Due to consistently applied policy, the vast majority of Soviet citizens were either not, or at best, only vaguely, aware of the mass murders which the approaching German occupation would bring to them.

Detailed instructions on how to act and of what to do in case of falling within the German advance were issued incessantly and brought up to date almost hourly by the Soviet radio stations. These instructions were closely observed by the population which, without government instructions, would not know how to act under the hectic and completely unfamiliar circumstances. Accustomed to being ordered around, the Soviet people were particularly liable to do as advised by the media.

The Germans, of course, tried to bring their viewpoint to the populations of the invaded areas, broadcasting on a wave length likely to be heard when one tuned in to local stations. In this way, German propaganda also reached the Soviet population, and it contained massive anti-Semitic material. While the inhabitants of these soon-to-be-occupied areas were exposed to that barrage of hateful anti-Semitic propaganda, there was not one word over their own stations to combat it, not one hint to counteract the often specific German charges, cleverly adapted to issues of the locale and holding the Jews responsible for the war as well as for special local problems.

With so much of the German focus directed against alleged misconduct of the Jews and with their own stations silent on these issues, the Soviet population was bound to assume that this part of the enemy's contentions was true. At the very least, people had to assume that, from the Soviet point of view, what happened to the Jews was of little interest. Although the Germans were constantly talking and writing about them, the issue was not worth mentioning by the Soviet media. Although the Soviet information and propaganda system vehemently attacked German lies and tried to disprove them, not even the repeated German claim that General "Yankel" Kreiser, a Soviet General whose real name was Jacob Kreiser, a Jew, used Russians willfully as cannon fodder and that his order should be disobeyed was countered by the Soviet media.

Yet, the issue of Jews was not a minor one in the Soviet Union. At the start of the war against the Germans, there were about 5,000,000 Jews in the territories under Soviet control. The Soviet census of January 1939 counted 3,020,171 Jews. The natural increase between that date and June 1941 is estimated by population experts to have amounted to at least 100,000. To these roughly 3,100,000 have to be added the 1,900,000 Jews who lived in the newly "acquired" territories—Eastern Poland, Lithuania, Latvia, Estonia, and those in Northern Bukovina and Bessarabia. The inhabitants had all been given Soviet citizenship with the annexation of their lands. In the Soviet territory as it then existed, there were thus roughly 5,000,000 Jewish Soviet citizens alive in 1941. This figure does not include approximately 250,000 Jews from western Poland who had fled into Poland's eastern part to escape the advancing German forces. Of the latter—and fortunately for them—a substantial but uncertain number had been deported by the Soviets as "undesirable" to the Central Asian area of the U.S.S.R. or to the northern sections of the Russian Soviet Socialist Republic.

Most of the Soviet Union's 5,000,000 Jewish citizens lived in the country's western areas, most exposed to the threat of German occupation. At one time or the other, Jews in the following areas and numbers fell under German control:

White Russia	375,000
Ukraine	1,533,000
Occupied areas of the Russian Soviet Socialist Republic	250,000
Annexed areas	1,900,000
	4,058,000

This is a minimal figure.

The number of 4,100,000 would be a realistic, but low estimate. Of them, approximately two million, one half of all, were killed.

There can be no doubt that these more than 4,000,000 of her citizens were under very special risks if they fell into German hands. What special measures were taken by the Soviet Government to protect that highest risk group of its citizens? The answer is: none. No special measures whatsoever. To the contrary, there was silence regarding the murderously anti-Semitic German propaganda while other claims were vigorously denounced. This made it appear that the anti-Semitic aspects of the announcements were not disagreed with. The consequences of this policy were manifested by large sections of the Soviet populations cooperating with the German annihilation. This collaboration was responsible for the loss of huge numbers of Jewish lives.

To counter the German "kill the Jews" propaganda would have been the more imperative as the old Russian anti-Semitism was still very much alive in spite of more than 20 years of Soviet Rule. And anti-Semitism never had a rest in the newly annexed territories, particularly in the Baltic Republics and in Poland. In the Soviet Ukraine, Jew-hatred was just as strong as in the newly acquired Baltic countries and, all in all, the Germans could reasonable expect a favorable reception for their anti-Jewish broadcasts and leaflets. It is exactly for that reason that the Soviets avoided countering the anti-Jewish aspects of German propaganda and that, in deference to the prevailing anti-Semitic feelings, they decided to keep entirely away from the issue of the Jews. This policy was quite likely supported by the anti-Semitic attitudes of the Soviet decision makers, but if one neglects entirely the moral and humane issue, there was some realism in that reasoning. Building on the endemic anti-Semitism especially in the Polish and Ukrainian population, the Germans claimed that the Soviets were fighting to protect the Jews. For the Soviets, to have stood up in any way for the Jews would not have been popular; it would have tended to support the German claim that communism was a Jewish invention and served Jewish interests. It would have likely weakened the desire to fight the German invaders who promised to free the country from the "communist Jewish yoke."

The Soviet policy of keeping entirely away from this issue proved catastrophic for the Jews, as the news media censored the mentioning of Jews as specific targets for murder when they accused the "fascist monster" of atrocities.

Jews in the Baltic countries had, up to a year prior to the German invasion, lived under a rule that permitted access to foreign news. They did not know specifics of what had happened in Poland. Yet they were frightened enough when the invasion of their homelands started to try to flee in masses toward the eastern parts of the Soviet Union. Although they had been Soviet citizens since the annexation and although it had since then all been one country, they were stopped by Soviet "border" guards when they reached the line which had once divided their Baltic states from the U.S.S.R. They pleaded with the guards to let them pass, explaining to them that they were Soviet citizens with the same rights and duties as any other citizens. This was to no avail. No imploring helped. The guards were under strict orders. Many of those who had reached these border lines returned to their homes where they were killed by the Germans.

There is a vivid description by Yankev Rasen, a Jewish scientist who survived.

> We are not permitted to go farther...
> Regardless of how much we implore
> the Soviet border guards, we get one
> answer only: "Nobody is allowed to
> cross. These are orders. Move back,
> twenty steps. We will shoot if you do
> not. Get moving! One, two—fire."
>
> For twelve horrible days and nights
> we have stayed near the border. During that time crowds of thousands of
> more refugees have arrived here.
> Most of them are Jews with an occasional non-Jew among them. They lie
> in ditches nearby and in the fields and

woods. They implore the guards to let
them go on so that they can save their
lives. Properly documented members
of the communist party are allowed to
pass... others have no right to be
saved.
Suddenly the frontier guards disappeared. The Germans had come
within 10 to 15 km of the dividing
line... But how far can one flee when
the dreadful enemy is so near?[1]

Mr. Rasen could have added: "especially when the enemy is motor-
ized." He and those who had waited it out to the last could finally
cross, but they were all too soon overtaken by the Germans. By
ingenuity and luck Rasen survived.

Those who had returned to the cities and those who had stayed
there were the worst off. Particularly in the Baltic countries a very
active Jewish life had existed. There were numerous Jewish organizations, whose lists were obtained by the advancing Germans. Also,
in cities that had been part of the Soviet Union prior to 1939, the
Germans succeeded in lining up almost all the Jews. In Byalistok, a
city in White Russia, of a Jewish population of 50,000, only 900 Jews
survived, as reported by the chairman of the postwar Jewish
Committee for the Province of Byalistok. From the capital of White
Russia, Minsk, government agencies and government personnel
with families were evacuated in haste, but there, as well as in other
cities, no special evacuation of the by far most endangered section of
the population took place. Of the 90,000 Jews who lived in Minsk
before the war, at least 85,000, more likely as many as 88,000, were
murdered. Of course, towns where the Einsatzgruppen had a major
installation were the worst off. Vitebsk housed a headquarters unit
of the Einsatzgruppen. An SS radio station was located there that
reported its daily achievements to the Reichssicherheitsamt in Berlin. Of Vitebsk's 50,000 Jews, only 500, one out of a hundred, survived.

The name of a ravine on the outskirts of Kiev, Babi Yar, stands
next only to Auschwitz as a symbol of German inhumanity during
the Nazi era, as well as for Jewish martyrdom. It also symbolizes the
support which Soviet policy supplied to the effectiveness of the Final
Solution. Reports on the Babi Yar carnage are both detailed and well

documented. They consist of German documents and other evidence produced in two major war crimes trials, the international one at Nuremberg and a trial conducted in the later postwar period before a German court in Darmstadt.

On September 29 and 30, 1941, in a 36-hour period—the Germans were very exact in their record keeping—33,771 Jews were machine gunned and those who were still not dead were buried alive. Not even the assembly line death factory at Auschwitz when working at full capacity killed that many in such a short period. How was Babi Yar possible? How could the Germans assemble and kill that many Jews without known resistance? It is here that Soviet policy and actions have to carry a heavy burden of guilt.

On September 19—the dates are important—The German Army Group South had breached the faltering defenses of Kiev, the capital of the Ukrainian Soviet Socialist Republic, a city of about 1,500,000. Attached to Army Group South was the slaughtering Einsatsgruppen unit Commanded by SS Colonel Blobel. He expected considerable "difficulties from such a large scale action" as his task—killing Kiev's Jews—demanded. One of the problems was that Jews lived not just in certain districts but were distributed all over the city. Yet, this Kiev mission was to be "carried out exclusively against Jews with their entire families." Immediately he started rumors that Jews would soon be evacuated for "resettlement." On September 28, the rumors seemed to be proven true. Overnight 2,000 announcements had been posted throughout the city declaring that the next morning, September 29, all Jews had to assemble at a certain road crossing located near a railroad station at Kiev's outskirts. The Jews were to take warm clothing along and also their "documents, money, valuables..." Jews found not to have shown up would be shot. The SS expected at the most 6,000 Jews to fall for the trick. After what they had done in the more than three months since the invasion of the Soviet Union and after previous German actions in Poland, the Germans did not think that so many would be fooled to show themselves to be Jews and walk into the trap. Next morning to the surprise of the SS, the streets leading to that road crossing were fast teeming with large masses of Jews, estimated by the Germans at that time to amount to 30,000—later proven by the official headcount of victims to have been 33,771.

Much of the way toward the assigned gathering point led along Lvovskaya Street, one of the major streets of the city. Along it moved on that fateful September 29 an odd mass of desperate people. Most of them were elderly or women. Almost all of the younger men had, to their good luck, been drafted into the army. And there were children of all ages, approximately 6,000 of them, including the babies. The renowned Soviet writer Ilja Ehrenburg, who interviewed eyewitnesses of that death march writes: "A procession of the doomed marched along endless Lvovskaya, the mothers carrying their babies, the paralyzed pulled along on carts."

While, in the early afternoon, latecomers, mainly invalids and very old people were still arriving, the first hundred were already led toward the ravine. When they were out of sight they had to pass a line-up. Forming a narrow corridor on each side were SS and Ukrainian voluntary police equipped with rubber truncheons, brass knuckles and wooden clubs who beat them severely and shouted "run." Once through that passage, deadly frightened of more beatings and their spirits broken, the Jews were ordered to undress completely and, then, naked as they were, to proceed to the edge of a deep, wide ditch. There they were machin- gunned; the bodies fell or were kicked into the ditch, covered with a thin layer of dirt—and the next hundred were brought in for the same procedure. Small children were thrown alive into the ditch and perished as it became slowly filled with more bodies and dirt. Later groups had to dig their own ditches.

Full evidence for that unbelievable massacre was produced in the two war crimes trials. The Nuremberg International found Colonel Blobel guilty as charged and had him hanged. By 1967, 11 of the main participants had been apprehended and were charged before a German war crimes court. The trial lasted 4 months, 175 witnesses were heard, and a large number of documents was introduced, all of which corroborated the unbelievable facts. One of the defendants died in prison; the other ten were found guilty as charged and received prison sentences of varying lengths. Never charged were those responsible for the Soviet policy that multiplied the number of the ones whom the Germans would have caught anyhow. The Babi Yar carnage was committed more than three months after the Germans had entered Soviet territory. There was abundant time to warn Soviet Jews and to exhort the population to try to aid their fellow citizens, to save them by hiding them from the expected killing. Moreover, contrary to the newly acquired lands— and the west—there was no active Jewish life in the U.S.S.R.; there were no lists of Jewish organizations, no Jewish community that could have been tricked to be halfway helpful in a plan for "resettlement." It was relatively easy for citizens of the old Soviet Union to disappear among their comrades.

Whatever the Germans did, the Soviets stuck to their policy of denying existence of the special danger to Jews. After the war, they resisted the idea of a special memorial at Babi Yar. A sports stadium was planned for that location. But opposition among non-Jews was too strong to be wisely neglected. A memorial was finally erected there. But it commemorates the murder of Soviet citizens only. The word Jew does not appear on the memorial, as if this action had not been conducted according to the German document "exclusively against Jews and their entire families."

A procedure often followed by the Germans was to have prisoners of war lined up and then order those who were Jews to step ahead. Knowing that worse treatment awaited them than their fellow prisoners, not all Jews followed the order, but some usually did. The Germans then addressed the rest of the prisoners, exhorting them to point out those whom they knew to be Jews. Following up the line of German propaganda steadily beamed at them they were told: "Think of all the misery of the war. The Jews are responsible for the war. Your government knows and cannot and does not deny it." The exhortation was as a rule followed by one or the other of the prisoners pointing out Jews among those standing in line, if there were any and if they were known to him as such. The Jews were then taken away and, sometimes still in the sight of the others, but always still in hearing distance, shot.

There were, of course, cases of heartwarming loyalty to each other among prisoners, but pointing out Jews to the Germans when exhorted to do so was not at all an unusual incident. Anti-Semitism was particularly rampant in units that contained large percentages of military drawn from the recently acquired areas of the Baltic republics, and from eastern Poland, or the Ukraine. Units with a relatively larger percentage from these areas were likely also to contain a larger percentage of Jewish draftees. With the annexation, many young people from the new areas had been drafted into the Red Army, and these areas, as most of the western part of the U.S.S.R., were the main locations of Jews in the Soviet Union.

Anti-Semitism, brought to a pitch by the steady bombardment by German propaganda, was so unchecked that it heavily afflicted even the partisan movement. In some partisan units, comradery included Jews with no or hardly any discrimination. But there were other units. A Jew who wanted to join the partisans often found himself received with suspicion. He was taunted and often had to be afraid of his own comrades. Some Jewish partisans were even executed, framed with the absurd charge that they were spying for the Germans. It even happened that partisans chased Jews out of the forests which the Jews had entered to join the partisan forces. According to survivors of attempts to join, partisan leaders shied away from giving the impression of truth to the German propaganda—not rebuked by Soviet announcements—that the whole partisan movement was inspired by the Jews and that its main purpose was to aid the Jews. Acting that way, partisan leaders only followed the policy of the government to do everything possible not to appear friendly toward the Jews, as this might cause loss of public support. While the commanders might have been aware of such political considerations, the individual translated it into an occasional bullet into the back of one of those "suspect Jewish infiltrators." It speaks for the basic goodness of human nature that in spite of such policies there were numerous acts of individual heroism, non-Jews risking their lives to save a Jewish comrade. Yet the overall mood was prevailing anti-Semitism.[2]

Viewing happenings in the partisan units, we must be aware that while conditions initially allowed much authority to individual commanders, the partisan forces soon became part of the Red Army and were under its control. Unlike most armies, the Red Army is most concerned with the political attitudes in its military, even in fine nuances and trends, and had a political commissar just for the control of "correct" thinking assigned to the units. The partisans were doubtlessly under the political control of these Red Army commissars, as control over partisan forces was centrally exercised.

The Soviets were quite aware of their failing to evacuate those who were so much more than anybody else at risk to fall victim to the enemy's lust for murder. To counter such accusations and to create good will toward the U.S.S.R. in the West and thus increase pressure for an early opening of a second front, the Soviets founded a special committee. They named it the Jewish Antifascist Committee, and loyal communists who filled the bill of being qualified to promote propaganda effort abroad were appointed to it. Two men were sent abroad. One was Itsik Feffer, a Yiddish writer of considerable talent, the other one was Solomon Mikhoels, a well known Yiddish actor. Feffer had shown his reliability by ridiculing the Jewish religion and tradition and by writing about Stalin's "wondrous heart." Mikhoels, too, throughout his career had proven himself well versed and anchored in communist ideology.

Early in 1943, they were sent to New York. There, meetings were called, and each time the number of those attending grew. Most Jews were captivated by the personalities of the speakers and happy to see, for the first time after many years of isolation, Jews from the Soviet Union, the more so as their message indicated a turn in the attitude of the U.S.S.R. toward Jews and Judaism. They heard of course of the massacres, but they also were told about the hundreds of thousands whom the Soviets had allegedly saved by evacuating them to safety before the advancing German troops could capture them. Feffer and Mikhoels visited not only the United States but also Canada, Mexico, and England. In 46 cities, they spread the tale of how the Soviets had snatched hundreds of thousands of Jews right from the advancing Germans, and how many more would be saved if only some relief would come to the heroic Red Army by early establishment of a second front.

As is often the case with a good lie, the Soviet fable of mass evacuation of Jews was built upon an element—entirely twisted though—of a true happening. When in the time of the German-Soviet alliance, the Soviets annexed the Baltic countries and marched into other territories and occupied them (Bukovina, etc.), they found that most Jews belonged to one or the other Jewish organization, almost all of them "dangerous" and "undesirable" from the Soviet point of view. One policy the U.S.S.R. took over from the Czars was: "If you do not like someone's political ideas, to Siberia he goes." In following this principle, Jews by the tens of thousands— especially Zionists and also members of the social democratic anti-Zionist *Bund*— were deported *prior to the war*— to Central Asia and to the cold northeastern regions of the Russian Soviet Socialist Republic. They did then not know how lucky they were to be classified as undesirable or even dangerous. These newly acquired areas being heavily populated with Jews, it is estimated that 250,000 undesirables, maybe even more, were thus deported during that period in which the Soviet Union attempted to digest her new acquisitions.

The fable of mass evacuations in the face of the advancing Germans was not only spread by the messengers of the Jewish

Antifascist Committee. It was, almost at the end of the war, continued by an American, who, with the convenient name of Goldberg, had been invited to visit the U.S.S.R. He names one person only as the source of his post factum report, a "Rabbi Shekhter." Mr. Goldberg's claims were broadly publicized by the American communist press. Not mentioned of course was that the evacuations he reported had taken place before the war and that no document—not even a hint of a post invasion evacuation—is to be found in any Soviet publication, including *Izvestya* or *Pravda*. Yet some 3.8 million people are reported to have been evacuated from the Ukraine alone, to escape capture by the invading German armies.

By the way, both Feffer and Mikhoels were later shot by their masters. They were suspected—not without reason—to have been affected on their trip abroad by feelings of Jewish identification and were liquidated in the purge which Stalin conducted in 1952 against Jewish intellectuals.

Of the four million Jews in Soviet-held lands who at one time or the other were in an area controlled by the Germans, two million were killed. Even if warnings would have gone out by the Soviets and instructions on how to try to evade capture; even if the population had been exhorted not to cooperate with the Germans but to the contrary to try to aid Jews in escape or hiding attempts; even if the flood of German anti-Semitic propaganda had been countered by the so active and so listened to Soviet propaganda machinery, the great majority of these two million Jews would have perished anyhow. But if one takes a very conservative estimate, at least one out of ten could have been saved.

This leaves us still with a figure of 200,000 humans who could have been saved if the Soviets had not followed the policies described above. And this includes some 33,000 children. This figure does not take into consideration that the Soviets, whose front was much nearer to Auschwitz than the Allies and whose medium-distance bombers were for at least four months close enough to destroy the death factory, never attacked that murder complex. Yet, such an act would have saved the lives of many tens maybe even of hundreds of thousands.

Figures are impersonal; statistics are experienced with relatively little emotion. If we just think of the 33,000 children as playing in the street, near or in their homes while inhuman men in faraway Berlin decided their death, we may be capable of assessing better what Soviet policies did in support of the Final Solution.

[1] Yankev Rasen, Mir Viln Lebn, New York, 1949, pp. 22-25.
[2] Moshe Kahanovich, *The Fighting of the Jewish Partisans in Eastern Europe*, (Hebrew) Tel Aviv, 1954.

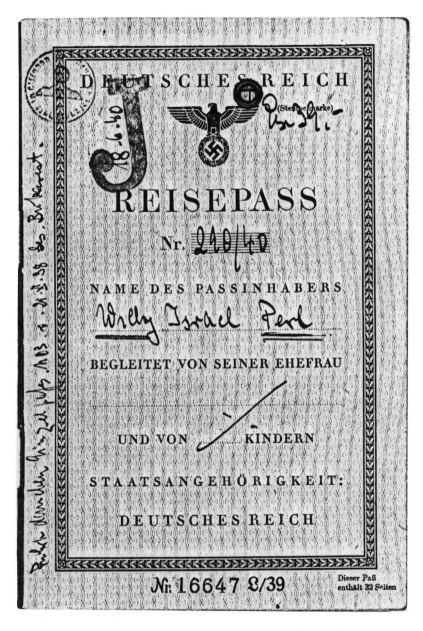

A Jew-Passport (the author's). The idea originated with the Swiss. They suggested the marking of all passports belonging to Jews so that Switzerland could prevent its "Judaization" by keeping Jews out. The Germans accepted the idea and marked all passports held by Jews with a large red "J" and added to each Jewish male's name "Israel", to each Jewish female's name "Sara".

Dr. Heinrich Rothmund, Chief of the Swiss Federal Police, the spiritual father of the Jew-Passport. He suggested the idea to the Germans and obtained their agreement. This policy became a death sentence to tens of thousands because it made the crossing of any border next to impossible. Rothmund forced thousands who had nevertheless secretly made it into Switzerland to be returned to their assassins in Germany.
(From the author's collection)

January 13, 1944

REPORT TO THE SECRETARY ON THE ACQUIESCENCE
OF THIS GOVERNMENT IN THE MURDER OF THE JEWS.

One of the greatest crimes in history, the slaughter
of the Jewish people in Europe, is continuing unabated.

This Government has for a long time maintained that
its policy is to work out programs to save those Jews of
Europe who could be saved.

I am convinced on the basis of the information which
is available to me that certain officials in our State Department, which is charged with carrying out this policy,
have been guilty not only of gross procrastination and wilful
failure to act, but even of wilful attempts to prevent action
from being taken to rescue Jews from Hitler.

I fully recognize the graveness of this statement and
I make it only after having most carefully weighed the shock-
ing facts which have come to my attention during the last
several months.

Unless remedial steps of a drastic nature are taken, and
taken immediately, I am certain that no effective action will
be taken by this Government to prevent the complete extermination of the Jews in German controlled Europe, and that this
Government will have to share for all time responsibility for
this extermination.

The tragic history of this Government's handling of this
matter reveals that certain State Department officials are
guilty of the following:

(1) They have not only failed to use the Governmental
machinery at their disposal to rescue Jews from Hitler, but
have even gone so far as to use this Government machinery to
prevent the rescue of these Jews.

(2) They have not only failed to cooperate with private
organizations in the efforts of these organizations to work
out individual programs of their own, but have taken steps designed to prevent these programs from being put into effect.

Government report in which the U.S. State Department is charged with ''Acquiescence in
the Murder of the Jews'' and with conspiracy to prevent rescue. Shown here page 1 of the
18 page document (The Morgenthau Papers).

121

~~CONFIDENTIAL~~   November 15, 1938.

Mr. Duggan:

Mr. Drew:

Mr. Achilles' memorandum regarding the refugee
program is so complete that I have little to add to
it. He has written very frankly and the memorandum,
I believe, should only be read before representatives
of this Department and Foreign Service Officers.

Fri, Dec 2, a.m.

REFUGEE PROGRAM

Germany was concerned primarily with the documentation
of such refugees. These facts were not, however, widely
known. Dorothy Thompson and certain Congressmen with metropolitan constituencies were the principal sources of this
pressure.

After the absorption of Austria by Germany on March 12,
with the resultant immediate and ruthless application of the
Nuhremberg laws to Austria, pressure on the Department to
"do something" immediately increased. It was obvious that
this pressure was going to be both exceedingly strong and
prolonged. The Secretary, Mr. Welles, Mr. Messersmith and
Mr. Moffat decided that it would be inadvisable for the Department to attempt merely to resist the pressure, and that
it would be far preferable to get out in front and attempt
to guide the pressure, primarily with a view toward forestall-
ing attempts to have the immigration laws liberalized. The
idea of the Evian intergovernmental meeting was suggested by
Mr. Welles and approved by the President on March 22

The Evian conference was not a failure; it was a fraud. This document, "written very
frankly," gives the true reason for calling that conference. It was not to help the refugees,
but to prevent liberalization of immigration laws. Shown here upper part of page 1 and
lower part of page 2. (Refugee Program, National Archives).

SUMNER WELLES

Assistant Secretary of State Sumner Welles, according to the document above, was the originator of the Evian intrigue. (Library of Congress)

BRECKINRIDGE LONG

Breckinridge Long: The U.S. Immigration Czar. (Library of Congress)

Frederick Charles Blair, Long's Canadian counterpart, was even more successful than
Breckinridge Long in thwarting the rescue.
(From *None Is Too Many*, by I. Abella and J.H. Troper)

Mackenzie King, Canadian Prime Minister, fully supported the anti-Semitic policy of Blair. Mackenzie King was an admirer of Hitler (Hitler: "a very decent man," "sweet," "He might come to be thought of as one of the saviors of mankind.") King plotted with Blair and others to block, almost completely, the Canadian escape route.
(From the author's collection)

This is what the American military saw after entering Nordhausen concentration camp. (US Army Signal Corps)

BUCKINGHAM PALACE

28th. February, 1939.

My dear Lord Halifax,

The King is very much obliged to you for your
letter to me of yesterday, in which you give such a clear
explanation of the question of the Dantzig Jews.   His
Majesty now understands the position, which is certainly
rather a complicated one.

The King had heard from Gort on his return from
Palestine that a number of Jewish refugees from different
countries were surreptitiously getting into Palestine, and
he is glad to think that steps have been taken to prevent
these people leaving their country of origin.   His Majesty
quite appreciates that the Government is doing all that
it can to find a solution to this most difficult problem.

INDEXED

The Right Honble.
    The Secretary of State for
        Foreign Affairs.

The British tradition that keeps the king out of politics did not prevent King George VI from joining those who conspired to seal the emergency exits from the Holocaust. In this letter the King informs his Foreign Minister that he is "glad to think that steps have been taken to prevent these people leaving their country of origin."
(British Public Records Office)

Sir Antony Eden, British Foreign Minister; One of the main conspirators.

The prosecution Staff (author is the fourth from right) at the War Crimes trial in Dachau. Being a prosecutor there provided the author a close view of the annihilation program's effectiveness due to support from collaborators inside the Allied camp. (From the author's collection.)

His Majesty's Forces in action. Clubbing, on an intercepted refugee ship, those who tried to save their lives "illegally." (From the author's collection)

100/3/08.

SECRET

4th May 1939.

Port & Marine,
C.I.D. Haifa.
C.I.D. Jaffa.

Subject: Co-operation with H.M. Ships.

Further to secret circular No: 100/3/C/8 dated
April 3rd. 1939.

2.   A destroyer flotilla composed of H.M. Ships
"Hero" (flag-ship) "Havock", "Hereward" and "Hotspur"
arrived at Haifa on April 29th. to assist the Palestine
Government preventive service in patrolling the coast,
and preventing the landing of illegal immigrants and
contraband.

3.   The Commander of H.M. Ships has decided that one
destroyer will be on patrol continuously.   The
destroyer on patrol will communicate by W/T to H.M.
Ships in port who will transmit reports to Duty Officer,
Haifa C.I.D. (telephone No: 532 Haifa) who, in turn,
will dispose of such reports as may be necessary.

4.   Reference para. 1 of the instructions to Police
contained in my previous circular; Port and Marine will
notify H.M. Ships when aircraft are leaving on seaward
patrols.

5.   Aircraft on patrol will communicate by W/T direct
with Haifa Civil Airport who have been directed to relay
messages to H.M. Ships and Duty Officer, Haifa C.I.D.

DEPUTY INSPECTOR-GENERAL.
C.I.D.

Copy to :- R.A.F.
          Nablus District.
          Gaza District.
          Signals.

Secret document showing that an entire flotilla was dispatched to thwart the rescue of
survivors. It coordinated its actions with the Royal Air Force that was engaged in the same
undertaking. (From the author's collection)

The refugee ship SS Parita broke through the British blockade and went right up the center of a Tel Aviv beach. (From the author's collection)

The beached ship being unloaded. (From the author's collection)

Jews from Greece being loaded for "extermination."
(Yad Vashem Archives, Jerusalem)

Some were pressed into open freight cars. (Yad Vashem Archives, Jerusalem)

Admiral Miklos Horthy, Hungary's ruler. He sent 400,000 of his citizens to their deaths. (From the author's collection)

Wien, am 18. März 1938.[1]

Der Erzbischof von Wien

Sehr geehrter Herr Gauleiter,

    Beigeschlossene Erklärung der Bischöfe übersende ich hiemit. Sie ersehen daraus, daß wir Bischöfe freiwillig und ohne Zwang unsere nationale Pflicht erfüllt haben. Ich weiß, daß dieser Erklärung eine gute Zusammenarbeit folgen wird.

    Mit dem Ausdruck ausgezeichneter Hochachtung

und Heil Hitler!

+Dr. Theod. Innitzer

Theodor Innitzer, Cardinal and Archbishop of Vienna welcomed the Nazi takeover of Austria and stressed his support for the Nazi regime by adding to the letter, written in his handwriting, the salute by which Nazis greeted each other: "Heil Hitler."
(From the author's collection)

Some evaded deportation, but, if found in hiding, they were shot.
(Yad Vashem Archives, Jerusalem)

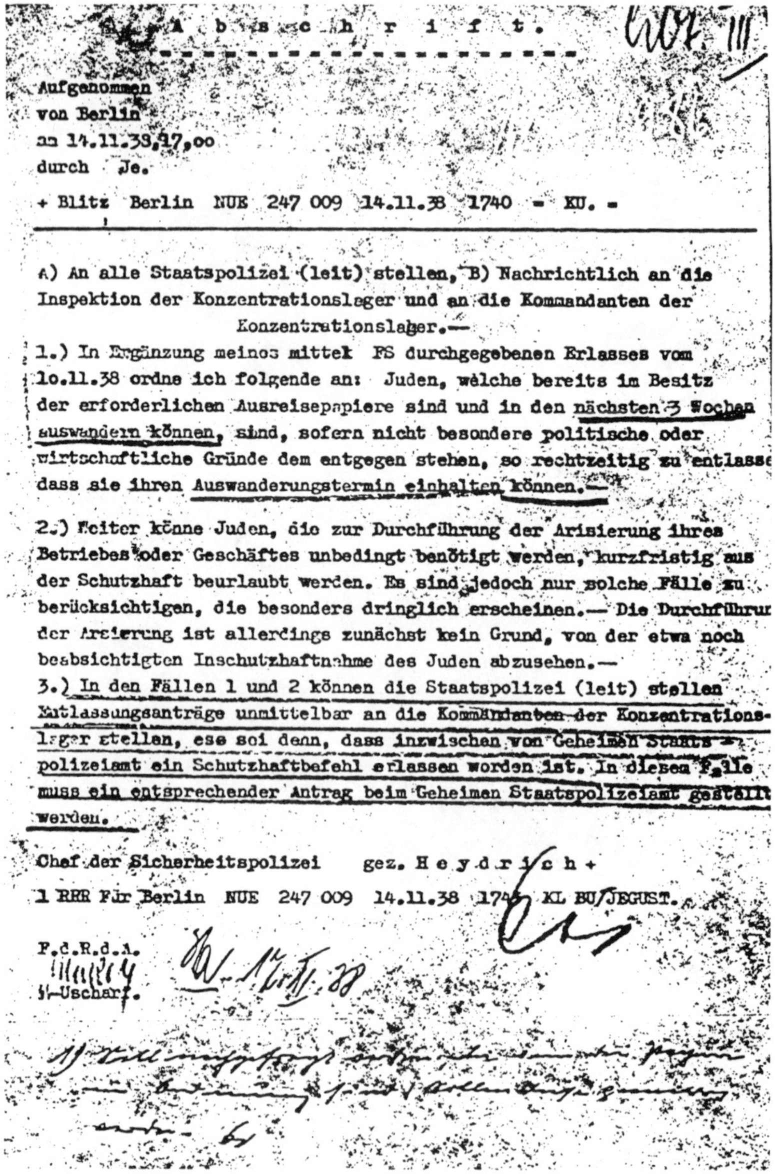

A b s c h r i f t.

Aufgenommen
von Berlin
am 14.11.38,17,00
durch Je.

+ Blitz Berlin NUE 247 009 14.11.38 1740 - KU. -

A) An alle Staatspolizei (leit) stellen, B) Nachrichtlich an die Inspektion der Konzentrationslager und an die Kommandanten der Konzentrationslager.—

1.) In Ergänzung meines mittel FS durchgegebenen Erlasses vom 10.11.38 ordne ich folgende an: Juden, welche bereits im Besitz der erforderlichen Ausreisepapiere sind und in den nächsten 3 Wochen auswandern können, sind, sofern nicht besondere politische oder wirtschaftliche Gründe dem entgegen stehen, so rechtzeitig zu entlasse dass sie ihren Auswanderungstermin einhalten können.—

2.) Weiter können Juden, die zur Durchführung der Arisierung ihres Betriebes oder Geschäftes unbedingt benötigt werden, kurzfristig aus der Schutzhaft beurlaubt werden. Es sind jedoch nur solche Fälle zu berücksichtigen, die besonders dringlich erscheinen.— Die Durchführur der Arisierung ist allerdings zunächst kein Grund, von der etwa noch beabsichtigten Inschutzhaftnahme des Juden abzusehen.—

3.) In den Fällen 1 und 2 können die Staatspolizei (leit) stellen Entlassungsanträge unmittelbar an die Kommandanten der Konzentrationslager stellen, es sei denn, dass inzwischen vom Geheimen Staatspolizeiamt ein Schutzhaftbefehl erlassen worden ist. In diesem Falle muss ein entsprechender Antrag beim Geheimen Staatspolizeiamt gestellt werden.

Chef der Sicherheitspolizei gez. H e y d r i c h +

1 RRR Für Berlin NUE 247 009 14.11.38 1740 KL BU/JEGUST.

F.d.R.d.A.
SS-Uscharf.

Blitz telegram by Reinhold Heydrich, National Commander of the SS, to all commanders of concentration camps ordering them to release those Jews who can emigrate within three weeks. Tens of thousands could have been saved right then. But in response, the Holocaust conspirators blocked the emergency exits even more effectively by tightening their exclusionary measures. (From the author's collection)

Haji Amin el-Husseini, Muslim leader and Grand Mufti of Jerusalem. A Holocaust
conspirator of major influence. He lobbied in Berlin for a total halt to Jewish emigration
and had a conference with Hitler shortly before the Wannsee conference, at which time it
was determined to proceed with the ''complete'' biological Final Solution and steps for
implementation of that program were determined.
(Jabotinsky Institute Archives, Tel-Aviv)

The Grand Mufti and Hitler meeting shortly before the Wannsee Conference which decided on the total biological annihilation of all Jews. (Jabotinsky Institute Archives, Tel-Aviv)

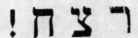

ר צ ח !
סיר הארולד מק מייכל,
הידוע כנציב העליון לפלשתינה (א"י),

מבוקש עבור רצח

800 פליטים יהודים במימי הים השחור באניה "סטרומ"

MURDER!

SIR HAROLD MAC MICHAEL

Known as High Commissioner for Palestine

WANTED for MURDER

OF 800 REFUGEES DROWNED IN THE
BLACK SEA ON THE BOAT STRUMA

Sir Harold Mac Michael, High Commissioner of Palestine. By his reports to London he urged even firmer blockading of the Palestine coast. He was largely responsible for the STRUMA disaster. Shown here on a "Wanted" poster of the Jewish underground. (From the author's collection)

Heinrich Himmler, next to Hitler, most powerful in the Third Reich. When Germany's defeat had become unavoidable in the spring of 1944, he offered to free one million Jews in exchange for goods needed by the Reich. The Allied reply was to arrest his messenger. Thus, an opportunity was missed to start negotiations with the condition that mass killings be suspended while negotiating. At least tens of thousands could have been saved by such a maneuver, but Sir Anthony Eden did not want those Jews to be freed. He saw no way to "dispose" of them if they were released. Himmler disposed of them.
(Deutscher Bilderdienst)

Cover illustration for Salem in the Army, a reading and writing primer for the Syrian army.

"Annihilate the Jews." A primer for Syrian soldiers. (From the author's collection)

Chapter 6
HOW THE ALLIES KEPT AUSCHWITZ OPERATING

Five hundred thousand human beings were slain after the Auschwitz murder complex came within bombing range of the Allied forces.

In November 1942, the airfields at Foggia, in southern Italy, had been seized from the enemy, and the U.S. 15th Air Force immediately established itself there. First, only short-and medium-range missions were flown but in April 1943 full combat strength had been reached and with it, the capacity to fly missions deep into Eastern Europe, including Poland. Destruction of the murder factory at Auschwitz, that burning shame of mankind's history, was definitely within the capacity of the U.S. Air Force.

Even before that, however, it was reachable by Soviet aircraft. Medium-range bombers, because they fly lower and are better able to target, could have been used by the Soviets. From British bases, Auschwitz would have been in range, too, had the Soviets agreed to a "shuttle run" in which the planes would have flown on, after bombing, to Soviet airfields, refueled, and then returned. But the figure of approximately 500,000 slain at Auschwitz does not even take into consideration earlier bombing possibilities from England or the U.S.S.R. It is the one that starts in April 1943, figuring only raids from Italy.

Basic to the issue is, of course, the question of whether Auschwitz was known to be a death factory. Another question is whether the Allies intended to interfere with the daily slaughter.

The answer to the first question is: Yes, it was known.

The answer to the second question is: No, the Allies decided not to stage bombing raids, or even a single raid, on the death camp.

That decision involved more than one person. It was taken and, in the face of numerous pleas for bombing, executed by groups of people. A conspiracy of bad will and of deceit is responsible for the

147

full functioning of Auschwitz up to the date the Germans themselves, decided that, with the war approaching its end, it was time to dismantle that testimonial to their bestial deeds.

Even if the crematoria and the gas chambers had been totally destroyed in an early raid from Italy, not all of the half million slain after that would have survived. The Germans did not, at that time, possess the manpower or the material to rebuild the facility. But certainly, the daily trains from Hungary bringing in 12,000 victims almost every 24-hour period would have had to stop, as would those trains unloading the condemned from the West. Yet a part of the half million would have met death anyhow although the German capacity to "exterminate" in an assembly line fashion would have been eliminated. It has been estimated that almost 450,000 persons could have survived if Auschwitz had been destroyed in April 1943.

We feel that this figure is probably too high, but even if we assume that one out of two would have, in any case, been killed, this leaves us with 250,000 who would not have had to perish had it not been for the conspiracy in Washington, London, and Moscow. A quarter million lives.

Now as to what was known, how much and when. The first experimental gassings in Auschwitz occurred in September 1941, one and a half years before the 15th Air Force had gained the capacity to intervene. At that "trial run" for the future benefit of Jews, 700 Soviet prisoners of war and 300 Christian Poles were locked into a sealed basement. Poison gas was then pumped in. The cries for help lasted all night. In the morning all thousand human guinea pigs were dead. That gas was, however, rejected. It worked much too slowly for mass production. It took half a year before the news of the killing of these 1,000 prisoners penetrated to the West. But news *did* leak out. The first gassing in Auschwitz by a "much improved" industrialized procedure occurred on May 4, 1942, about one year before the U.S. planes from Italy could have interfered; and, by that date, 1,759,000 had already been murdered in the gas chambers there.

The *Polish Fortnightly Review*, an official publication of the Polish Government in Exile, published in its issue of July 1, 1942, the first news item reaching the outside world and mentioning the use of poison gas in Oswiecin (the Polish name for Auschwitz). That mass murders were being committed in German concentration camps in

Poland had by then been reported on several occasions, in the press as well as by the British Broadcasting Company. That Auschwitz was a camp at which particular brutal procedures prevailed had become known, but the first knowledge of some details came from an emissary of the Polish underground. This emissary was Jan Karski, a young Christian Lieutenant in the Polish army. He was smuggled into Sweden with first-hand knowledge about conditions in Poland, and, in January 1943, he reported that the arrivals to Auschwitz were undressed and then put into chambers in which they were suffocated.

On June 1, 1943, the London *Times* carried a report that the Jews of Cracow, a large city in western Poland, had, with the exception of 1,000 who had been killed right in the streets, been deported to Auschwitz. This followed a report on March 26 in the *Times* that the 6,000 Jews of Salonica, Greece had been pressed into cattle cars and deported to Poland. There was standing room only for the trip of several days, and each car had just one slit to let air in.

On January 19, 1943, Gerhart Riegner, the representative of the World Jewish Congress in Switzerland, cabled the home office in New York that recent deportations to Auschwitz had increased in number, and that between July 15th and July 30th, 6,500 Czech Jews, among others, had been deported to Birkenau.[1]

All this happened before the U.S. Air Force had established its base in Foggia.

The real break in learning about details of the procedures as well as the exact layout of Auschwitz came with the escape on April 10, 1944 of two young Jewish prisoners who managed to get their report to Geneva Switzerland, London, and New York in unbelievably fast time. Rudolf Vrba, and Alfred Wetzler, both natives of Czechoslovakia, had been in Auschwitz for two years and knew it very well. They had managed to survive so long because, to utilize their considerable physical strength, the Germans had assigned them to work details which were hard to handle. Very bright, they managed to avoid capture after their escape, too, and to make it to Zilina, a town in Slovakia whose Jews had not yet been deported. There they wrote a 30-page report about Auschwitz, detailing locations of various German installations, maps, routine activities of the Germans, and exact information about the ways the slaughter occurred, from the moment of arrival to the moment of death. They described the height of the crematorium towers and the exact location of each of them. There was a distance of 1,000 feet between the slaughter place at the Birkenau section of Auschwitz, where the four gas chambers and crematoria were located, and the barracks in which prisoners were kept. Only the tail end of the long barracks complex came within that distance of the actual killing places. The gassing is described as taking place usually immediately after the arrival and after "selecting" those to go to the showers, first. Those who seemed physically strong were sent to the barracks—for slave labor. On average, about ten percent were thus temporarily saved. Those to be gassed were marched into the assembly halls. There they each were given towels and soap; then the door to the adjoining gas chamber was opened. There were four such chambers. The largest had space for 2,000. SS men went up to the roof of the building and poured the gas in. Once the right temperature, in what was to look like showers, was reached, the gas became effective. After a procedure which, altogether, lasted half an hour, everyone was dead. The bodies were then removed to be examined for gold teeth, which were broken out and collected. An SS report shows that from May 15 to May 31, 1944, 40 kilos (88 lbs.) of gold were thus obtained for the German treasury. After examination, the bodies were carted out by prisoners' details to the adjacent crematoria.

The Vrba-Wetzler report was most efficiently handled by the Jews of Zilina and those of Bratislava, the capital of Slovakia to which it was smuggled.

The Hungarian copy arrived in Budapest in the first days of May, 1944, but most Jews never learned of it. A few days before, on April 25, Hungarian Jewish leaders received from Eichmann a stunning offer: the Germans were ready to trade, as Eichmann expressed it "goods for blood." One hundred Jews for each truck, one million Jews for 10,000 trucks, the vehicles not to be used on the western front. Later on, coffee, tea, and soap, besides trucks, were named as trading possibilities. The offer was rejected by the Allies, but the Budapest Jewish leadership did not want to rock the boat by publicizing the escapees' report that showed the Germans in—to say the least—an unfavorable light. They kept the content of the Vrba-Wetzler report from their brethren.

Then in May 1944, just as the report warned, the Hungarian Jews were herded into the trains. Up to four trains a day left Budapest, each carrying about 3,000 Jews. They were pressed closely in these cattle cars, one against the other, with hardly room to stand. There were no toilet facilities. Many died during the journey, and the bodies were still in standing position on arrival. The stench from excrement, urine, and the sickening smell of bodies and vomit cannot be imagined.

On May 22, 1944, one copy of the escapees' report, was given to Monsignor Guiseppe Burzio, the Vatican's Charge d'Affairs in Bratislava. For reasons unknown to this author and to other researchers, it was annotated in the Vatican five months later on October 26, 1944. The copy smuggled into Switzerland arrived there in the middle of May. Copies were made to be sent to Britain, the United States, and also for the press. The one for the United States was handed to Mr. Roswell McClellan, the representative in Switzerland of the U.S. War Refugee Board. He composed an eight-page summary which he cabled to his home office on July 6.[2] Again there was delay at a time during which every lost day meant that thousands of lives had been extinguished.

Western journalists had confirming evidence at hand, previous fractional descriptions that fitted in and also corroboration from two more sources. In 1944 a Christian Polish Major, as well as two more Jews, had escaped. Their reports, though not as detailed as Vrba-Wetzler, corroborated the more complete one. The media people sent their consolidated reports to their papers, and *The New York Times* carried the news—in an all too short article on June 29.[3] *The Manchester Guardian* printed two reports which too, revealed the horrors of Auschwitz, one report on June 27, the other on June 28.[4] In the meantime, the Czechoslovakia Government in Exile, located in London, acted officially. The Czech Foreign Minister Hubert Ripka sent a copy of the report to Mr. Anthony Eden, the British Foreign Minister. During the same period, concise details were broadcast by the BBC.

We could adduce more information about news reaching the West, but we want to avoid being repetitive. We repeat: the answer to whether one knew in the West about the murder factory at Auschwitz is an unequivocal YES.

There were three ways in which the Allies could handle the issue of the Auschwitz death factory, and the three were not exclusive of each other. They could, in fact, have been employed simultaneously. In giving thought to possible action, we must be aware that by then, spring of 1944, it was clear that German armed forces had suffered in the long-drawn, exhaustive battle for Stalingrad; their army was in retreat all along the eastern front, a retreat which contained some elements of Napoleon's abandoning of Russia. In Africa the famous Africa Corps had been beaten. In addition, Sicily had been conquered by the Allies, who had already taken part of Italy. And most important: the Luftwaffe had been practically chased out of the skies. The puppets in Hungary, Rumania, Bulgaria and Slovakia, knowing that they had joined the wrong side, were frightened. To gain, in this last moment, the good will of the Allies seemed the straw to which they had to hold on. The horrible German war crimes might be charged to them, too, and the Bulgarian Minister to Ankara, Nicholas Balabanoff showed this concern clearly. In June 1944, he complained about the Allied barbarism perpetrated by the bombing of cities, and he hastened to add that the situation of Bulgaria's Jews would be absolutely normal if the bombing stopped.

The same situation prevailed in Hungary: terror at the thought of having Budapest destroyed at the time when the war was coming to an end! On July 8, 1944, Hungary's strong man, Admiral Horthy ordered further deportations stopped. That order proved effective, but it had been issued only after Horthy had close to 400,000 of his citizens sent to their deaths.

It is important to analyze what caused this stop order because we can learn from it what might have caused such a command to have been issued much earlier. Doubtlessly, appeals by the Pope and the King of Sweden played a part in issuing this stop order, but there is every reason to assume that other highly relevant elements entered into the decision-making process, too. Responsibility for war crimes must have been in Horthy's mind as the German military situation continued to deteriorate rapidly, and then there was that air raid against a military installation in Budapest. True, a military location had been bombed before, but in connection with the pleas by the Pope and the King of Sweden and of the German retreat, that recent bombing might have been a threat of what would happen if they did not stop deporting.

Threats had been issued recently by the BBC, though not, however, specifically relating to Budapest. Yet, Horthy certainly was not going to have his beautiful Budapest destroyed by saturation bombing the way the German cities of Berlin, Hamburg, Cologne and so many others were destroyed.

Most likely, the actual bombing of Budapest would not have been necessary. A threat that, if the sending to their death of Jews did not stop, Budapest would be bombed, would probably have stopped the deportations much earlier, maybe even while the Jews were being rounded up.

Besides bombing of Budapest, the bombing of the deportation rail lines to Auschwitz would have saved at least a part of those who were being shipped for annihilation, as that would have certainly delayed the killing machinery, if not stopped it entirely. Several first urgent, soon panicky, requests were received by the Allies. These pleas provided quite specific data. The transports had to use the Kosice-Presov railroad. Both these cities were important junctions for German military transports, too. The line between Kosice and Presow was one track only and therefore a particularly vulnerable link in the Auschwitz human supply system.

Most important, the pleas asked for the destruction of the murder facility itself, the crematoria and the gas chambers. On May 16, 1944, Rabbi Weissmandel of Bratislava dispatched to Switzerland a coded plea for bombing. This action, as all actions involving writing, sending, and smuggling of messages abroad would have resulted in torture and death if found out. A second message, also in code, was sent on May 24. The pleas arrived in Switzerland and were handed to the representative there of the World Union of Orthodox Rabbis, who, in turn, without using diplomatic channels cabled them to his headquarters in New York. There, the President of the organization, Jacob Rosenheim, sent them on June 18 to the War Refugee Board. Its chairman, John Pehle, took the report to the War Department where, according to existing government orders, he could expect to find full cooperation regarding the bombing requests. Unfortunately, he found there obstruction and collusion to prevent military action on behalf of those destined for annihilation.

The legal situation was clear enough. Executive Order 9417 had been issued in January 1944 following the revelations by the Treasury Department that the State Department was practicing "acquiescence of the government in the murder of Jews." To prevent any such or similar actions in the future, Executive Order 9417 had made it undisputably clear that full rescue efforts were the duty of the War Department as well as of the Departments of State and of the Treasury.

Mr. Pehle, therefore, in bringing the bombing requests to the War Department, was addressing an agency that had been specifically named as duty-bound to take all measures within its power to help in a situation exactly like the one he was presenting.

Pehle's visit to the War Department was a total failure. Instead of the assistance prescribed by the law, he encountered determination to interdict any rescue effort by the military. The Assistant Secretary of War, whom Mr. Pehle went to see, was in collusion with certain elements in the War Department's Operation Division to scuttle any rescue action such as the bombing of Auschwitz and its supply lines. In fact, any planned rescue action by the military was ruled out. In doing so, those sabotaging the bombing request invented military reasons for their refusal and a civilian like Mr. Pehle was, of course, unable to stand up against alleged military necessity in a bitterly fought war. In the following pages we will demonstrate how contrary to the truth the "military" reasons were, which were named as the cause of the refusal to help. We will, in particular, point out that targets within 5 and 13 miles of Auschwitz were repeatedly precision bombed by large fleets of U.S. planes while Auschwitz, amidst those places, was precisely avoided.

Let us now look closely at what happened to Mr. Pehle's request and to a request handed over to the State Department at the same time by Mr. Jacob Rosenheim, Chairman of the World Organization of Orthodox Rabbis.

Offices do not make decisions; people do. So let us have a look at the people who decided to let Auschwitz continue its operation. The Assistant Secretary of War, Mr. John J. McCloy, had been approached by Mr. Pehle right after the War Refugee Board was created and Executive Order 9417 issued. At that time, Pehle had asked McCloy to send a copy of that Executive Order to the military commanders in the military theaters, so that they could plan, and/or suggest in accordance with that order, what actions, consistent with the successful prosecution of the war, could be effected. Such coordination demanded by the Order was immediately counteracted by McCloy. He forwarded the proposal to inform the Theater Commanders to the Chiefs of Staff, but not without a disparaging note:

"I am very chary to get the army involved in this while the war is on."

This comment, in direct contradiction of the Executive Order, was hardly less than an invitation to reject the suggestion. The Chiefs of Staff obliged, and the Theater Commanders were never informed about the Government's determination to "take all measures within its power to rescue the victims of enemy oppression..." Mr. McCloy ordered his Executive Assistant Harrison Gerhardt "to kill" the

Pehle request for bombing.[5] This "killing" was done by forwarding it to the Operations Division where a "friendly" man was waiting for this request. On Saturday afternoon, June 24, 1944, the request for a "study" of the situation arrived at the Operations Division. On Monday June 26, the "study" had already been completed and forwarded to McCloy. No commanders in the field were asked their opinions. An issue which involved the lives of hundreds of thousands of human beings was decided at a desk, in the confines of the Pentagon. Who were these decision makers? We do not know whether there were several, but such requests landed on the desk of a Colonel Thomas Davis who handled them—to his fullest satisfaction. From his comment when he learned of the request we can guess what kind of "study" he conducted between that fatal Saturday afternoon and Monday. He said: "I cannot see why the army has to do anything whatsoever."[6] He added later in a conversation with McCloy's representative, "We are over there to win the war and not to take care of the refugees... Obviously there will be continuing pressure from some quarters to enlarge the sphere of this thing. I think that we should make our stand quite inelastic."[7] He certainly stood up against "this thing." Backed by his findings, and therefore supported by the Logistics Group of the War Department's Operation Devision, the request to bomb, as expressly wished by McCloy, was "killed".

For reasons of completeness we note that the operations of the 15th Air Force in Italy were undertaken without support of air forces stationed in England and that no drain on the fighting in Western Europe was associated with the plea to bomb Auschwitz.

Actually, the War Department proved to be quite "inelastic" anyhow. In countering the demands of Order 9417, the War Department had determined its future policy towards rescue action. It was decided that:

> It is not contemplated that units of the armed forces will be employed for the purpose of rescuing victims of enemy oppression unless such rescues are the direct result of military operations conducted with the objective of defeating the armed forces of the enemy.[8]

In other words: no rescue action whatsoever by the military was to be planned. If it should happen that in the course of other actions lives were saved, this must have happened entirely coincidentally.

But there was at least one case in which the War Department's order not to go out of the way for rescue actions was not applied. The Germans had evacuated from Vienna the famous dancing White Stallions, the Lipizzaner Horses. The little village soon became threatened by warfare, too. General Patton, a horse enthusiast, had a daring, behind the enemy line operation executed. As reported in the History of the Second US Cavalry[9], Captain T.M. Stewart, himself a horseman, was assigned to head the rescue action and to bring the horses safely into American held territory. Accompanied only by a German guide, moving at night and evading an SS unit he reached the location at which the horses were kept and persuaded the German commander of that unit not to resist when he, Stewart, would return in force. This way the horses would not suffer by combat. Captain Stewart returned with a heavily armed task force and the horses were saved and liberated.

Poor people in Auschwitz, on the way there or awaiting their deportation. Poor fools who had risked their lives to let America know what was going on.

Thus, when John Pehle met with McCloy, the War Department's policy was already fixed: no separate action whatsoever on behalf of the "victims of enemy oppression" was a foregone conclusion. McCloy who was, of course, the expert on warfare in relation to Pehle, succeeded even in making Pehle doubt whether he was asking for the right thing. The reply from the Operations Division which had come back to McCloy stated, contrary to facts, that the bombing requested was

> impracticable... it could be executed
> only by diversion of considerable air
> support essential to the success of our
> forces now engaged in decisive
> operations.[10]

McCloy was now backed by the Operations Division. In his reply to the plea to bomb the deportation route of the railroad and Auschwitz itself, he repeated the statement of the Operations Division to which he referred as a "study" and added that such action

> would in any case be of such doubtful
> efficacy that it would not warrant the
> use of our resources. There has been
> considerable opinion to the effect that
> such an effort even if practicable,

might provoke more vindictive action by the Germans.[11]

None of the Air Commanders in the field—not the one of the 8th Air Force in England, not the Commander of the 15 Air Force in Italy, not even the Supreme Commander of European Forces, General Eisenhower, was given a chance to express his opinion. This was in stark contrast to the broad spectrum of decision-making that the War Department generally left in the hands of the commanders in the field, especially General Eisenhower. The same applied to later decisions that dealt with issues of rescue. This Saturday-to-Monday "study" determined the fate of hundreds of thousands of humans as if it were a decision of very minor consequence. That was done because it was not at all a military decision; it was political. They did not want to carry out a rescue; therefore, they used all kinds of subterfuges.

The hypocrisy of wanting to avoid "more vindictive action" was compounded by "concern" about the killing of innocent victims. Such concern was not exhibited when German factories were bombed in which mainly foreign slave workers were employed—and killed.

However, the prisoners of Auschwitz, as well as those of other concentration camps, were united in their urgent desire to see the Allies unload bombs on their tormentors. To die in such a raid instead of being murdered had, at least, some purpose. Only to see that *someone* cared for them, would have made them happy. All those interviewed who were asked how they felt about a raid in which they would have perished themselves agreed as to that. One such concentration camp survivor puts it like that: "When we saw American or British planes fly overhead we prayed with consuming fervor: 'Please, please drop at least one bomb on our camp. Destroy it if you can.' How beautiful a death it would be to know: I die because somebody cares, not because everybody hates us. How we would have blessed the moment of dying in combat against that bestial enemy."[12]

Impracticable? Diversion of forces impossible? How did the reality look?

To the eternal shame of the United States, while her responsible officials refused, on the basis of deceitful excuses to destroy the death factory and its supply lines, a factory almost adjoining Auschwitz, less than 5 miles away, one that had at that time 30,000 slave workers from Auschwitz was bombed four times.

Other factories, located within 17 and 45 miles, were bombed on several more occasions.

Twenty-two missions were flown from Foggia to much farther Warsaw to aid the encircled Polish guerilla fighters there. These latter missions were performed by British planes, manned by British and Polish volunteers, but they proved that targets much farther away than Auschwitz could be reached from Foggia; and at all these missions, the prisoners at Auschwitz could to their horror hear the drone of the planes and often see them passing by.

Yet, the American policy remained that is was "impracticable" to bomb gas chambers and the crematoria, which with their high chimneys, could serve as orientation points for flying to points farther away. What hypocrisy! What a poor attempt to cover up what was the truth behind the unconditional decision to keep Auschwitz operating.

When we investigate the validity of the reasons given by the U.S. War Department for letting Auschwitz continue its bestial mission, we should be aware that by the time the bombing requests were made, the Luftwaffe had been decisively defeated, a fact that has been officially acknowledged. The official historians of the U.S. Air Force have stated that "by 1 April 1944, the GAF (German Air Force) was a defeated force... wrecked by the spring of 1944. After this... U.S. bombers were never deterred to bomb a target because of probable losses."[13]

When in June, McCloy excluded Auschwitz as a bombing target because, besides other reasons, it would be "impracticable," the chemical factory at Monowitz had already been studied and chosen as a target. It had been decided to be hit first, after the much larger complex at Blechhammer 45 miles away, where just as in Monowitz, synthetic oil was produced. Blechhammer was repeatedly attacked by huge fleets of heavy bombers of the 15th Air Force, flying from Foggia, first in July, and the last raid on November 20. The smallest of the fleet consisted of 102 heavy bombers, the largest of as many as 357. As Blechhammer was located northwest of Auschwitz, a little farther from Foggia than the annihilation complex, the planes flying to Blechhammer had, every time, to fly either right over Auschwitz or near by.

On August 7, 1944 Trzebinia was struck, only 13 miles from Auschwitz. On August 29, Moravska Ostrava as well as Bohumin were bombed, both within 45 miles of the place at which the assembling of groups of 2,000 for immediate gassing proceeded without any interference. At none of these numerous bombing missions was Auschwitz given even as an alternate target, if weather conditions prevented a strike on the primary objective. To their despair, the prisoners at Auschwitz could see the planes which flew at 26,000 to 29,000 feet; they could hear their drone.

Finally on August 20: they are not going to bomb nearby, they are bombing here! The sky was clear in the morning as the 227 American planes, 127 heavy bombers, all of them Flying Fortresses, accompanied by 100 fighter planes came flying straight towards Auschwitz. One could hear them from a distance already, and soon one could see them in the brilliant sunshine. And now! The first heavy explosions could be heard—and felt as the ground shook. They have come! They are here!

But they were not. They were precision bombing the Monowitz factory, less than five miles from the gas chambers. The planes hit in five runs. Maybe the next one will hit the crematoria and gas chambers. None of them did. The towering chimneys and adjoining chambers of mass murder were precisely avoided. Bombing them would have been "impracticable" and would have meant a "diversion of forces."

One thousand three hundred and sixty-six 500-pound bombs were dropped at the Monowitz bombing August 20, 1944. Two or three dozen of them could have annihilated the murder factory towards which, at the same hour, unimpeded, more trains were rolling in with human, disposable cargo.

The shameful act was repeated on three more occasions. American bombers struck again at the Monowitz plant on September 13, on December 16, and December 18. In the September raid, two stray bombs fell even near the murder installations. But it just reminded "the victims of enemy oppression" how close the true bombing target was. To bomb the chemical factory was all right. It was taboo to strike the adjacent factory, the one that produced death.

And while all this bombing was centered on the area, on August 14, the plotters in the War Department put it down in writing! Bombing Auschwitz would divert American air power from operations elsewhere. Auschwitz was not only not bombed; it was avoided. Those in Washington who knew better had conspired in that evil decision and covered their devilish act by statements that were in blatant contradiction to the facts.

The rail lines supplying Auschwitz remained just as untouched by bombs as the facility itself. On at least five occasions, Allied fliers had to cross these tracks and on at least one, the American planes flew along the track that was used to bring the victims to their death.

During all that period of concentrated bombing right around Auschwitz, the crematoria worked at full capacity. Hungary was, of course, only one of the sources of supplies. From all over Europe trains came rolling in. The Germans had massed 60,000 Jews into the Ghetto of Lodz; and, at the time of the Monowitz bombing and that of the surrounding area, the time for the Jews in Lodz had come, too. Trains from there were loaded in the familiar way and arrived in Auschwitz on August 15, 16, 21, 22, 23 and 24. There—what a busy railroad center—arrived also on August 16, the Jews deported from the lovely Mediterranean island of Rhodes. They had been on the way for the better part of a month and it is not known how many had perished during the voyage. It is known that 1,802 arrived in living condition—for their slaughter.[14]

The British did not behave better than their American allies. Mr. Hubert Ripka, the Acting Minister for Foreign Affairs of the Czechoslovakian Government in Exile, located then in London, forwarded an eight page summary of the Vrba-Wetzler report, combined with corroborating information, to the Foreign Office. There it arrived on July 4. This document provides also the information that 12,000 Jews from Ruthenia, Transylvania and Kosice district were in the process of being deported. It recommends bombing of the rail lines and of Auschwitz and makes the Foreign Office aware that the crematoria are easy targets because of their watch towers and high chimneys.

Mr. Sidney Silverman, a member of the House of Commons, asked the day after the Foreign Office had received this report what the British Government intended to do about it. Mr. Eden said that nothing would be done. He formulated it in diplomatic verbiage though: "the speedy victory of the Allies would be the answer to the problem."[15] This was essentially the same answer that his partner McCloy in Washington gave: let Auschwitz go on operating. If at the end of the war there are survivors, that speedy end will have saved them. But what if there were no speedy end or a few million less survivors, if the Allies let Auschwitz continue its operation?

The day after these futile diplomatic attempts, on July 6, 1,180 Jews from Pecs in southern Hungary were deported to Auschwitz. Also on July 6, Eden met with Chaim Weizman and his right-hand man, Moshe Shertok. The German offer to trade Jews for trucks was discussed and also the plea for bombing Auschwitz and its Birkenau section, as well as the rail lines. Eden reported to the Prime Minister about that meeting, and Churchill's reaction to the bombing plea was such a definite "yes" that an order should have gone out to the RAF to do everything in its power to bomb, as had been so fervently pleaded for. It should have—if what amounted practically to an order by Churchill, had not been deviously counteracted.

Immediately upon learning of the request to bomb the death factory and the rail lines supplying it, Churchill told Eden:

Get anything out of the Air Force you
can and invoke me if necessary.[16]

But this was not at all what Eden transmitted.

He inquired in a letter to the Secretary for Air, Sir Archibald Sinclair, about the "feasibility" of such bombing, and even that he did only after stating that Weizmann had thought that only little could be done and that a previous bombing request had been rejected.[17]

The draft of his letter to the Secretary of Air was prepared by Mr. Walker of Eden's office, and it is interesting the reducing element that this letter contains, in stark deviation from Churchill's order.

This draft reads "… Dr. Weizmann admitted that there seemed to be little that we could do to stop these horrors but he suggested *and both the Prime Minister and I are in agreement with this suggestion*[18] that something might be done to stop the operation of the death camps by

1. bombing the railway lines leading to Birkenaus (and to any other similar camps if we get to hear of them) and

2. bombing the camps themselves with the object of destroying the plant used for gassing and burning.
I should add that I told Weizmann that as you may know, we had already considered his suggestion (1) above, that I would reexamine it and also the further suggestion of bombing the camps themselves. Could you let me know *sometime soon*[19] how the Air Ministry view the feasibility of these proposals. I very much hope that it will be possible to do something. I have the authority of the Prime Minister to say that he agrees."[20]

What a far cry this letter of Eden's requesting view of feasibility after first minimizing the issue from the Churchill words: "Get anything out of the Air Force you can and invoke me if necessary!"

No wonder, getting the spirit of Eden's letter, Sir Archibald wrote to Eden on July 15th "... I am not clear that it would really help the victims... The distance of Silesia from our bases entirely rules out doing anything of that kind."[21] Yet only the day before, July 14, the British determined that Monowitz would be a potential target for British bombing, and by that date four photographic missions had already been flown over the target.

Furthermore, within two weeks the Air Ministry organized British planes to fly from Foggia the much larger distance to Warsaw to bring supplies to the encircled Polish guerillas there. The flights to Warsaw were made by volunteer flyers, both British and Polish. Using the U.S. base at Foggia, 22 RAF flights flew from that Italian location to Warsaw and back between August 8 and 17. Their flight path brought them right over Auschwitz or close by. The distance to Auschwitz of which the Secretary of Air had stated that it "entirely rules out anything of that kind" had suddenly shrunk. It had become bridgeable as a part of a much more distant target. Could it be that aid to the Poles was something entirely different from "a thing of that kind?"

Why on both sides of the Atlantic the claim that military reasons prevented a rescue action regarding Auschwitz although facts blatantly belied the validity of these reasons? Of course military reasons were sacrosanct during the war; no civilian, even if he knew better, could argue against them. Their use also contains an element of "moral enforcement." Arguing against a decision made for military reasons made one appear unpatriotic and thereby certainly stopped many a potential critic. Yet the facts prove the military reasons given both by Britain and the United States to have had no validity.

And *why did Mr. Eden's letter* to the Air Ministry so obviously *whittle down what had really happened* in his talk with Churchill? *Why did he delete from his letter the words "some time soon"?* Was the matter not urgent? He did know that each day of delay meant the massacre of thousands of additional human beings.

All during that time, between July 6th and the last bombing mission to Warsaw on August 17, and beyond that day, trains crammed with thousands of victims arrived at the death factory from all over Europe. As the true reason was not military, was it political? What kind of politics were being followed?

Decision-making is not done by objective facts only. Psychological elements inevitably enter into the process. Let us have a look at some psychological factors that might have played a part in the maneuvers resulting in the respective operations.

Proof exists that overt anti-Semitism was a strong motivating feeling in some of the decision-makers. Covert anti-Semitism in others is a conclusion that is hard to avoid in viewing the unbelievable fact that leading figures made themselves collaborators with the Germans in details of the Final Solution activities.

The British Foreign Minister, Eden was an avid anti-Semite. He did not just dislike Jews; he hated them.[22] His Jew-hatred was known to his staff.

As to whether we are correct in concluding from the facts that anti-Semitism entered decision making, we refer to nobody less knowledgeable of what was going on in British officialdom than Winston Churchill.

After the outbreak of World War II, Zionist leaders had offered a Jewish Legion to be formed and to fight as an integral part of the Allied military. The request was resubmitted in spring of 1942. The British War Office, as well as the Colonial Office, firmly opposed it. But, according to Churchill, who favored this proposition, that decision was influenced by anti-Semitism. In a minute to the Colonial Secretary Lord Cranborne, dated July 5, 1942 expressing his favoring the proposition of a separate Jewish unit, and commenting on the opposition to it, Churchill wrote:

> Now that these people are in direct danger, we should certainly give them the chance to defend themselves...[23]

In the same year, writing to a personal friend of his, Churchill stresses that anti-Semitism is "customary" and warned of the influence it exercises to the disadvantage of Britain. He writes in a note to Sir Edward Spears, then British Government representative in Syria, warning him

> "against drifting into the usual anti-Zionist and anti-Semitic channel which it is customary for British officers to follow."[24]

To cite a particularly cynical example of anti-Semitism in Mr. Eden's Foreign Office, as brutal as unabashed: On September 7, 1944, well after the time that the horrors of deportations to Auschwitz had become known to the Foreign Office, the Secretary of the Board of Deputies of British Jews, Mr. A.C. Brotman requested the Foreign Office that, in view of the fact that the Soviet Army was liberating areas in the East where Jews had been or still were under German control, cooperation with the Soviets regarding help to those Jews be established. Mr. A.R. Dew of the Foreign Office wrote down his reaction to this visit:

> In my opinion a disproportionate amount of time of the Office is wasted on dealing with these wailing Jews.[25]

No wonder that with an attitude like that no help for bombing Auschwitz or the rail lines, nor any help for "these wailing Jews" could be expected from the Foreign Office.

As to the United States, not to be surprised by the fact that brutal anti-Semitism evolves as the most likely and explainable cause of the described maneuvers, let us recall what polls of the period showed. We will not wonder by finding that logical conclusion if we recall that polls showing, when America was already deeply in the war after Pearl Harbor's "Day of Infamy," Americans by a majority of 3 to 1 considered Jews in America more dangerous to the country than Japanese. Neither was anti-Semitism just a fleeting prejudice. Studies conducted in the 1960s by Charles Glock and Rodney Stark polling both Protestant and Catholic laymen, as well as clergy, resulted in the finding that about half of them thought all Jews were responsible for the crucifixion of Christ, that this was an act for which they could not be forgiven until they converted. And as for their suffering, they believed that the Jews themselves or God was responsible for it.[26]

Such attitudes, deeply imbedded in the psyches of mainstream Christians, illustrate very clearly the persistence of these, and similar hate-filled fallacies in the teachings from both Protestant and Catholic pulpits. The strength of these destructive myths was unbelievable at the time.

We have previously mentioned Assistant Secretary of War John McCloy and his staff, particularly his assistant, as the ones who formulated the policy of no specific rescue action whatsoever. By this and by keeping the decision regarding Auschwitz entirely within the Pentagon under exclusion of the commanders in the field, they assured the continuing operation of the Final Solution. But they must have known that their superior, Secretary of War Henry Stimson would, to say the least, not find such policy objectionable. He did not. For Stimson's motives the evidence is not as clear as that regarding Eden. For Americans, anti-Semitism is officially not acceptable and high officials would not be expected to express such prejudice openly in front of their staff. We may, however, draw conclusions from such acts as his referring to the German murder complexes as "Semitic grievances."[27]

A telling combination of human interest and anti-Semitism just at the time the public learned details about Auschwitz comes to the fore in correspondence between the War Refugee Board and the editors of the Army magazine *Yank*. The editors asked the War Refugee Board for an article on atrocities. When Yank received the Auschwitz report, the editors decided that they could not use it. For their readers, it was "too Semitic." They asked for a story which was "less Jewish." This one would stir up "latent anti-Semitism in the Army."[28]

For those who close their eyes to the width and strength of anti-Semitism, this incident might seem an odd happening. Actually, it is, in its blunt naivete, quite characteristic. Human interest yes, but Jews are excluded from it. Learning of their agony would only increase Jew hatred in such a cross section of the population as the war-time army. A backfiring of guilt feelings about one's anti-Semitism?

As we pointed out at the beginning of this chapter, 500,000 humans were murdered in Auschwitz after the Allies had gained the military capacity to destroy it. From Hungary, alone, 437,000 Jews had been brought to their death after the Allied forces had become able to bomb the murder factory out of existence. This figure is so enormous, its full meaning so hard to assimilate, that to permit it to sink in we are citing the number of Americans killed in World War

II: killed in battle 291,557; died while on active duty from other causes, e.g. accidents, natural causes, 113,842. That is, altogether battlefield losses and other amounted to 405,399.[29] Those who lost their lives fighting for their country could feel that they knew what they were fighting and dying for. The lives of those murdered at Auschwitz were utterly wasted.

It speaks for the unbelievable efficiency of the German murder and transportation for murder machinery that they succeeded in destroying in about 8 months in one place alone about as many lives as the United States lost in 3 years and 8 months of a ferociously fought war conducted on two fronts with millions of men involved. It is also a sad monument to the inhumanity of those who could have prevented it but left the factory of death operating and supplies coming in.

[1] Riegner to Wise World Jewish Congress 269/8.

[2] Harrison (the U.S. Ambassador to Switzerland) to Secretary of State, 7/6, 44 War Refugee Board Box 56, Jews in Europe; Morgenthau Diaries, June 27, 1944 p. 4, June 28, 1944 p. 8.

[3] *The New York Times*, June 29, 1944 p. 51.

[4] *Manchester Guardian*, June 27, 1944 p. 4, June 28, 1944 p. 8

[5] Commentary Vol 65 #5 N.Y. May 1978 p. 19 as quoted by Wyman, "Why Auschwitz was never bombed."

[6] Gerhardt, memo for Subcommittee 2/11/44, meeting held at 4:00, ASW 5, as quoted by Wyman, Abandonment. p. 293.

[7] Ibid.

[8] FR 1944 V. I 987-90 MD 699/22 TRH Memo for record (6/26/44) RG 165 (1) Pasco to Gailey, 2/7/44. Handy to Chief of Staff 2/8/44,. JHC Memo for record (nd) RG 165 OPD 334.8 WRB Sec. 1 case 1 as quoted by Wyman, Abandonment, 291. 407.

[9] The Ghosts of Patton's Third Army. A History of the Second US Cavalry. p. 293.

[10] McCloy to Kubowitzki, 8/14/44, ASW 1 as quoted by Wyman, Abandonment, 296, 408.

[11] FDR Library, Papers of the War Refugee Board, June 24, 1944, McCloy to Pehle.

[12] Interview with Annemarie Tiele-Rosenberg, survivor of Ravensbruch Concentration Camp.

[13] National Archives; U.S. 15th Air Force, Daily Operations 1944, as cited by Wyman. op. cit., p. 298.

[14] As cited by Gilbert, op. cit. 302.

[15] House of Commons debate 7/5/1944 as cited by Gilbert, Auschwitz 265.

[16] Prime Minister's Personal Minute PM 44.501 Premier Papers 4/51/10, folios 1365-67 as cited by Gilbert, op. cit. p. 270.

[17] Draft in FO papers 371/42809 folio 141 as quoted by Gilbert, op. cit. 285, 272.

[18] Words in italics omitted by Mr. Eden in the final draft.

[19] Words in italics omitted by Mr. Eden ibid.

[20] Air Ministry papers 19/218. Draft in Foreign Office paper 371-42809 WR 276-10-9 folio 141 as quoted by Gilbert op. cit. 272, 285

[21] Air Ministry papers 19/218 as cited by Gilbert, op. cit. 272, 285.

[22] Diaries and Papers of Oliver Harvey (Lord Harvey of Tasburgh) Diary for April 25, 1943 as cited by Bernard Wasserstein, Britain and the Jews, 1979 p. 34.

[23] Premier Papers 4/51/9 as cited by Gilbert, official Churchill biographer, p. 49, op. cit.

[24] Prime Minister's Personal Minutes D.M. 1/2 Premier Papers 4/52/5 as cited by Gilbert, op. cit. p. 76.

[25] Foreign Office papers 371/42817 WR 993 Dew minutes, Sept. 1, 1944, Chetham minute 7 Sept. 1944, as cited by Gilbert, op. cit. p. 312.

[26] Charles Glock and Rodney Stark table 24, Christian Beliefs and Anti-Semitism p. 62.

[27] Stimson Diary, Sept. 3, 1944, Oct. 3, 1944, pp. 73, 117, 118, as quoted by Bradley Smith, Road to Nuremberg, New York, 1981, pp. 29-31, 44.

[28] As quoted by Wyman, Abandonment, op. cit. 324, 325n.

[29] Department of Defense History Reference Division.

Chapter 7
THE OTHER AMERICAS
LATIN AMERICA - CANADA

LATIN AMERICA

Prior to the Evian Conference, it had been widely assumed that Latin America, with its huge land mass and thinly populated countries, would play a major part in easing the refugee crisis. Latin America seemed to stand just at the beginning of development. Brazil, alone, with its 3,806,410 square miles and, next to the Soviet Union and Canada, the third largest country in the world—yet with a population of only 40 million—presented almost unlimited possibilities. In the 50 years preceding Hitler's ascent to power, it had admitted 4 million immigrants, an average of 80,000 a year. And Argentina, with its 1,072,637 square miles almost two and a half times the combined size of France, Italy, Great Britain and Northern Ireland, was populated by only 13 million. Most of the smaller countries were similarly empty of people and, as their history showed, most ready to admit newcomers.

To look at more recent times, since 1921 Brazil had admitted 840,000 newcomers. It was outdone by Argentina, even more eager than Brazil to attract immigrants. Though smaller in size, since 1920 it had admitted 1,406,000, exceeding its average of 100,000 a year for the preceding decades.

These substantial figures formed the basis for the expectation that Latin America could take care of whatever number of refugees there would be and that it would provide a new home for many hundreds of thousands. In 1930, due to the collapse of coffee prices on the world market, Brazil had experienced a brief unemployment crisis, but it was recovering rapidly. The shock of the Depression of 1929 had sent some waves all the way south, but by the mid-1930's this was an episode that had passed. Expectations of possible mass immigration into Latin America were, therefore, justified.

However, such hopes did not take into consideration anti-Semitism. Particularly among the uneducated, lower classes, among the masses who had never even seen a Jew, the medieval Catholic teachings and the associated superstitions were a force counteracting the admission of "too many" Jews. This tendency found an echo in the attitudes of the upper class—there was no middle class in Latin America in those days. Altogether, anti-Semitism, though not in such vehement form as in some parts of Europe, was quite prevalent in Latin America.

With the advent of Nazism in 1933, the number of Jewish immigrants increased, and the Brazilian Government aimed to curb the "too Jewish" influx. On April 16, 1936 a decree was issued which limited the number of annual immigrants, yet kept it at about the previous average. A total of 84,186 for each year were to be granted entrance permits. Also enacted was the American pattern of a quota system according to national origin. The national quotas were frozen to the percentage of immigrants in the last fifty years. In line with that principle, the Italian quota was fixed at 27,475 per year, the Spanish one at 11,562, and the Portugese at 22,991. The German quota was established at 3,118, the Austrian with even less: 1,679. The Japanese quota, in contrast, was higher than the German quota—3,480 and remained higher than the one for German Jews, even while Brazil was at war with Japan. Thus an easy and, on the surface, defensible way to keep out "too many Jews" had been found and copied.

The Latin American delegations in Evian had come with the expectation of American example-setting and pressure and they were determined to do only a minimum but to go along with the principle of rescue. The first speech of the American delegate and the exclusion of Palestine from the debate, which had everybody gasping, changed the Latin American hesitancy into an openly expressed attitude: the United States and Britain want to unload on us, while doing nothing themselves. We will not be the suckers. Brazil which, according to plans was to hold the vice-chairmanship of the committee to be created at the conference, declined that position and soon stopped coming to committee meetings. If conditions for admission to Latin America were bad prior to Evian, they became overtly biased against Jewish immigration after the Conference. Plotting to counter attempts to use Latin America as a haven for those who had to flee for their lives started right away. Conspiracies to block the escape route to Latin America developed not only on the intra-governmental level. They were conducted even intergovernmentally.

A typical example of such international conspiracy is the agreement signed in February 1939, days only after Hitler's announcement of the planned "annihilation of the Jewish race in Europe." *Argentina, Uruguay and Paraguay* agreed to cooperate in the endeavor to keep out "undesirables" and of course we know who these undesirables were.

Besides more obvious measures to keep the Jews locked up in Europe, there were also more devious methods. Thus, *Uruguay* demanded from an applicant for immigration a certificate from the authority of his residence that he or she was not a communist. Such a document was next to impossible for Jews to obtain, while a Nazi could easily produce it. To make even more certain that those who wanted to flee could not reach Uruguay, that country as well as *Bolivia* withdrew from all their diplomatic representatives abroad the right to issue visas. Every entrance permit had to be granted directly by the government in Montevideo or La Paz, respectively.

Chile and Guatemala who had been the first ones in 1935 to attack the issue from the point of work permit, declared that no alien was permitted to work unless he had obtained a special work permit. Applicants for immigration were then turned down because they would be unable to earn a livelihood. And all that happened in a continent in which it was usual to subsidize immigration by paying part of the expense of the ship's ticket.

Peru required, in addition to the other conditions, a bond of 2,000 soles ($360) to cover deportation expenses if the immigrant had not established a means of livelihood within 90 days. Peru was especially successful in its plot to block escape to its shores. During the entire Hitler era, from 1933 to 1945, a total of 600 Jews—an average of 50 a year—made it to that country.

So badly did anti-Jewish hysteria rule the actions of Latin American immigration officials that the prestigious *Inter-American Quarterly* reported that authorities subjected even United States citizens to special questioning when they had what the officials considered to be a Jewish name.

Often the excuse for refusing a visa was that the applicant was not an "agriculturist." Yet people with agricultural occupations could, while certainly having a much better chance, not count on a visa either if they were Jewish. None of the Latin American countries was entirely closed to Jewish immigration, but the difficulties which were raised were part of a system, and those lands which were previously used to accept immigrants by the hundreds of thousands devised complex schemes—and applied them—to keep as many Jews out as they could without openly declaring such intentions. There was space enough anyhow for agricultural workers, as well as for most of the occupations fleeing Jews had previously practiced. An old established Jewish organization, (ORT), which had for decades been dedicated to training Jews for agricultural work and all kinds of handicrafts, offered its services for retraining immigrants.

The whole idea of a preference for agricultural workers was proven by later developments to be entirely out of step with the needs of the time. Late in 1940, the *Inter-American Quarterly* published an in-depth research study on the subject of immigration and politics in Latin America. It arrived at the conclusion that an economically serious mistake was being committed by keeping out enterprising, hard-working people, persons experienced in so many fields of human endeavor which Latin America, at that point in its development, would urgently need. This study stressed that the refugees could contribute so much more than agricultural labor. Yet they would be happy to work the land, too. There "are thousands of desperate fugitives, formerly useful, hard working citizens to whom the hardships of settlement in Latin America would be nothing compared with the nightmare of terror that Hitler has spread over their native lands."[1] This study concluded that anti-Semitism played a major part in the handling of the refugee problem, quite in contrast to the economic needs of the various countries.

That anti-Semitism damaged the true developmental needs of Latin America was also cited in three very detailed reports by the International Labor Office. In its old, established, *International Labor Review* it stressed that, for progress, Brazil did not need to have more of its vast land reserve made arable but that it needed diversification of its products, away from coffee and cocoa as almost its sole export goods. Marketability, more mechanization, and altogether more modern methods of agriculture and good sales organization to trade its products at better prices than presently achieved were the great needs.[2] Thus, the reason most often used to deny the entrance for those few who would have otherwise qualified, on the basis that they were not agricultural laborers, is shown not to be a valid one. This lack of validity was exposed by an independent, international source, the International Labor Bulletin which wrote regarding the founding of new colonies with the methods used so far, "... their establishment in Brazil in such primitive conditions would contribute nothing to the economic prosperity of the country—on the contrary, it would act as a deadweight hampering the social progress which every organized community must promote... There must be a chance of selling part of the produce of the land." Transportation, domestic and export marketing were more needed than a few more primitive settlements in which the settlers, even by hard work, could hardly make a living. One commercial activity that had just started but begged development was rooted in the reversal of seasons as far as Europe was concerned. Vegetables and oranges from South America had, in small quantities, begun to appear in Europe and had become serious competitors to oranges and fruit from Spain and Palestine. The same was true of grapefruit, of which 5,000 boxes had been exported in 1933 and 35,700 in 1934. Tangerines exported in 1933 amounted to 364,000 boxes; in 1934 to 834,000 boxes. Economic development had just started, and there was a need for experienced, enterprising persons to make use of the large potential which Brazil and, actually, the whole Latin American continent represented. Conditions for shoe manufacturing were ideal, and some of the top European experts in shoe manufacturing were among those who were perishing because a cruel and economically foolish plot kept them locked up in Europe. Most of the clothing was then imported into Latin America, as were textiles of all kinds, because what little industry the area produced served entirely the home markets. What Latin America did was not only inhuman. It pushed those people into the German death machine who could have contributed greatly to Latin American developments.

How those who were given a chance did not present a burden to their new home, but provided new jobs by creating new economic units, is shown in a report of the Hebrew Immigrants' Aid Society (HIAS)[3] compiled in 1944 about the first 10 years of Jewish refugee activities in Colombia (1933-43). In that period, altogether 3,971 Jews made it to that country. Although most of them had not arrived before the end of the 1930s, they had by 1943 already established and were working in the following enterprises: a clothing factory, the manufacture of ladies' underwear, a factory for chemical products, production of shades and curtains, leather goods manufacture, furniture making, a toy factory, car repair, production of cosmetic articles, and the production of dairy products. Previously most of those goods had to be imported into Colombia. Now some of them were sold for export.

Immigration was not made easier following the nationwide pogrom of Crystal Night in November 1938. It was tightened. By late 1939, most Latin American countries had adopted sharply restrictive immigration measures. How uniform that compact was to keep the Jews locked up in Europe became dramatically clear during the tragedy of the SS St. Louis. That happening attracted wide publicity when it occurred, as well as in 1967 following the publication of Arthur Morse's book *While Six Million Died*.

On May 27, 1939, flying the swastika flag, the German luxury liner SS St. Louis docked in Havana, Cuba. On board were 936 German Jews, most of whom had sold their last possessions to pay for the transoceanic voyage, plus an average of $150 for a Cuban landing certificate, issued and signed by the Director General of Immigration, Colonel Manuel Benite himself. The 936 escaped from hell and were sailing to safety and freedom. Seven hundred thirty-four of them had obtained a U.S. immigration quota number, but, due to the restrictive American system, they would have to wait from three months to three years for actual admission to the United States. For that interim period, they had found an officially approved haven.

As the ship approached Cuba, the passengers learned that their entrance permits had been invalidated, but that all endeavors would be made to reverse that decision.

Only 22 out of the 936 were permitted to land. They had not been left without means after paying for the visa and the passage, and had taken the precaution to hire, from Germany, a lawyer in Cuba who had managed to buy for $500 a person entrance permits issued by the newly appointed exclusive visa issuing authority in Havana. Panic gripped the others. They could see in front of them the land of newly won freedom, yet it had become unreachable. The Cuban president was obviously determined not to admit them.

Telegrams went out to all countries in the western hemisphere pleading that those whom Germany had in fact sent out be shown compassion and not be forced to return to their death. All countries refused admission to the damned, including those whose admission quotas were well below their own established numbers.

From New York, representatives of JOINT, the major Jewish organization dealing with immigration problems, came flying in. They soon learned that the name of the game was blackmail and bribery. A lawyer who had been chairman of the American Cuban Chamber of Commerce was to conduct the negotiations in Havana. He had in his favor the additional factor of being a personal friend of Fulgencio Batista, then chief of staff of the Cuban army. The use of the seemingly valuable Batista connection appears to have been a grave mistake. Unknown to the Americans, Batista was aspiring for President Bru's position. His interest was to see Bru discredited and certainly not to obtain a large amount of money which had been demanded for Bru's "election fund." The JOINT, whose funds were strained by worldwide needs, finally transferred $500,000 to a bank in Havana, but to no avail. More people showed up demanding bribes. The press and radio waged an anti-Semitic campaign—whether in the hope to come in on the big bonanza is not clear. Speakers in Congress demanded that the ship be sent away immediately. The JOINT agreed in addition to the cash payment of $500,000, to be responsible for the care and maintenance of the refugees and to guarantee that none would become a financial burden to Cuba. But it was not enough. On June 6, 1939, after eleven days of fruitless negotiations, 914 Jews who had arrived on a German ship in the Western hemisphere were being returned to Europe, most of them sailing to their death.

Of the Latin American countries, not one was ready to accept even a single one of those unfortunates. Some had given negative answers, others had not even bothered to reply. Special intervention with the governments of Colombia, Paraguay, and Argentina was to no avail. The U.S. State Department, asked to intervene with the Latin American countries, answered that it saw no prospect of admission to any of them. It intervened with Cuba though. The effect was, of course, nil. How could such intervention be taken seriously when the United States herself refused to accept a single one, not ex quota, not on one of the more than 70,000 unused annual British quota spaces, not by mortgaging the quota for the coming year. Victims of inhumanity to the extreme and of human greed, these desperate humans were being pushed back into Europe in what amounted to complicity between German and western inhumanity.

Greed and bribery played altogether too often a major part in obtaining a visa to a Latin American country. In 1944, Paraguay dismissed its consul in Switzerland because he had issued visas to Jews in danger of being deported. A real problem developed with passports of various Latin American countries issued by consuls mainly in Switzerland and usually paid for by relatives in the United States. When the Germans threatened to deport holders of such doubtful Latin American passports, pressure by the U.S. State Department and also by the Vatican, which had at that very late hour become active in the rescue of Hungarian Jews, caused 13 Latin American countries to inform the Germans that they were honoring these passports, and in this way were able to prevent deportation where that information had not come too late. Several thousand persons were thus saved, the exact number of such passport holders never became known.

Concluding: here are some figures regarding Jewish immigration to Latin America during the Holocaust. To put them into perspective, we have to recall that during the 50 years preceding Nazi rule in Germany, Argentina alone saw 5 million immigrate and that during the last 10 years, the average had exceeded 100,000 a year; that Brazil alone received during the same period 4 million immigrants and had only in 1936 determined to admit 84,000 a year. Yet, during the Nazi catastrophe that hit the nine million Jews of Europe, the combined total of admission of Jews into all Latin American countries, for the entire period of 12 years, is 103,000 Jews. In other words the total admitted by these countries, of which several are larger than Germany, averaged 5,150 annually. All that in the worst refugee crisis mankind ever experienced. How many lives unnecessarily lost, how many that could have contributed economically, scientifically, to the arts or other human endeavors, to the growth of these countries that instead blocked the escape and threw the masses that wanted to come back into the claws of the monster.

CANADA

With its 3,851,000 square miles, Canada is, after the Soviet Union, the second largest country in the world. Its population in the late 1930's amounted to only fifteen million. Even when one considers the most northern parts as uninhabitable, it still was and remains one of the most thinly populated countries on the globe. When the first plans for the Evian Conference were developed, Canada was therefore viewed hopefully as a country of substantial possibilities for mass refuge. This hope was the more justified as Canada was rightfully seen as a sleeping giant, a land of tremendous opportunities for development and growth. It was rich in economic potential due to its wealth of only rudimentarily exploited mineral deposits, of immense possibilities for industrialized agriculture, and for chemical and lumber utilization. Its tourist industry was in its beginnings, in spite of the beauty of the country. It was, altogether, a land in dire need of talented, hard working people, eager to advance themselves and, with it, the country.

Yet, of all the major countries, Canada has the most miserable record as far as rescue actions during the Holocaust was concerned. It has, to the contrary of rescue, a record of unabashed support of the Final Solution program by deliberately and carefully plugging the escape possibilities to its shores.

Those deciding and executing this immigration policy in Canada acted rather openly as conspirators, often with incredible, clearly expressed cruelty. So determined was Canada in its exclusionary policy that it did not mind hurting its own interests, as long as Jews could be kept out of the country. Understandingly, William Birks of the Canadian Chamber of Commerce wrote to Thomas Crerar, the Minister of Mines and Resources under whom the immigration branch was placed, that he felt that as a Canadian he had to "hang his head in shame" at the way Canada was handling the problem of the refugees and that "Canada should have sent trade missionaries to beg such people to come and not to wait for them to seek and beg us."[4] Differently from the United States and other countries that used subterfuges for their actions assuring that the German supply lines for the Final Solution remained flowing freely, Canada was consistently brutally blunt in its anti-Semitism as it followed its exclusionary policy.

This is an interesting phenomenon because it belies the anti-Semitic claim that it is the presence of Jews, especially of "too many of them", that causes anti-Semitism. Canada, the country with the most overt anti-Semitic immigration policy, had only 1.5 percent of Jews among its population, and its anti-Jewish racism was most rampant in rural areas where no Jews lived. This, by the way, is a phenomenon well known to Jews. In Austria, where almost all Jews lived in Vienna, anti-Semitism was strongest in the mountain valleys of Tyrol, Styria and Carinthia, and least in Vienna. Similarly, in

Poland, Rumania and Hungary, in areas where there were fewer Jews, anti-Semitism was stronger than in areas of stronger Jewish concentration. It was much less widely spread in Budapest than in outlying Hungarian provinces, less in Bucharest than in the Rumanian countryside. In Canada, it was most massive in the rural areas of Quebec where there were hardly any Jews.

When, early in 1945, a senior Canadian official was asked as Canada did not now admit Jews, how many he thought should be admitted after the war, he answered: "None is too many,"[5] a sentence which became the title of Abella's and Troper's meticulously researched book regarding Canada's actions during the Holocaust. This principle, so sharply formulated by that official, was the one that directed Canadian policy towards rescue actions during the entire time of Nazi rule, and to a good degree also applied to the few survivors of the Holocaust.

There are always exceptions to principles, but during the entire twelve years of the Nazi regime, actually from January 1933 to December 1945, this second largest country in the world admitted in the face of a catastrophe that brought torture and murder to millions, fewer than 5,000 Jews, an average of less than 385 per year. Yet when one was not Jewish, an entirely different treatment applied. When the Sudeten area of Czechoslovakia was occupied by the Germans in the fall of 1938, besides the hundreds of thousands of Jews who had to flee Czechoslovakia for their lives, there were also German Christians who wanted to leave or had to flee because they had been opposed to German incorporation. Three thousand refugees from the Sudeten were admitted into Canada, a drop in the bucket for a country that big. But this is not the entire story. *Among the 3,000 refugees admitted were only six Jewish families.*[6]

Nobody had to twist the Canadian Government's arm to adopt and execute such anti-Jewish policies. William Mackenzie King was Prime Minister during the time of highest need for rescue, but he was more than just a Prime Minister and was often referred to as Mr. Canada. A leader in the liberal movement, he was Prime Minister from 1923 to 1930, with only a short interruption in 1926. Again appointed Prime Minister in 1935, he kept that position for another 13 years, until his resignation in 1948. Mackenzie King was a Canadian institution. He was also an admirer of Hitler.

In Mr. King's view, Hitler was a "very sincere man." He even described that monster as "sweet."[7]

No less praise for Hitler than in the just-mentioned interview is to be found in the Canadian Prime Minister's diary. "Hitler and Mussolini, while dictators" he writes, "have really sought to give the masses of people some opportunity for enjoyment, taste of arts and the like." His justification of what Hitler did is couched in rhetoric that Hitler used for explaining why he robbed the Jews. Dictatorship is excused in that diary entry by "it may have been needed to wrest the opportunity from the privileged interests that have previously monopolized it."[8]

The following sentence of King's also sounds like a speech of Hitler's: "We must keep this part of the continent free from... too much an intermixture of foreign strains of blood."[9] The overall assessment of Hitler by King appears to be formulated in the following entry in his diary, "He might come to be thought of as one of the saviors of the world."[10]

This is what the top looked like in matters relating to the Holocaust. The actual work of exclusion was entrusted to a man who, in Canadian government machinery, occupied a position paralleling the one held in the United States by Breckinridge Long. His name was Frederick Charles Blair. He headed the Immigration Branch and was a key figure in the conspiracy to keep Jews out of that vast, rich country and did thus contribute to the success of the German Final Solution. Blair too was an overt anti-Semite. He tried to rationalize his anti-Semitic prejudice with what he calls "unpopularity" of Jews, not realizing that he tried to excuse anti-Semitism with anti-Semitism. As if there were not a most valid reason for Jews to plead for a haven in Canada, he writes on September 13, 1938: "Pressure on the part of Jewish people to get into Canada has never been greater than it is now and I am glad to be able to add, after 35 years of experience that it was never so well controlled."[11] He assured his superior, Thomas Crerar, Minister of Mines and Resources, that he knew that the country was in danger of "being flooded with Jewish people" but that he understood it to be his function to prevent that.[12]

He disliked in the Jews "certain of the habits," and mentioned as one of them that "they are utterly selfish in their attempts to force through a permit for the admission of relatives or friends."[13] Mr. Blair does not explain though, why endeavoring to save the life of a relative or friend is so selfish. He does however have another weighty complaint against the Jews: They are dangerous people "who can organize their affairs better than other people do.[14] This, in the eyes of an official of the ministry in charge of resources, is certainly a valid reason to keep those people out.

In his dealings with pleas for admission, he used, as a rule, less diplomatic subterfuge than his American colleague, Breckinridge Long. For his rejections he gave usually the same "reason." There was no need for that applicant in Canada. That the world, that Canada could do something for the petitioners' "need" to live seems to have been out of his sight. The reason given for refusing to save was mostly that the applicants were not agriculturally oriented—no Jews ever were in his opinion—and therefore not needed. Yet in some regions of Europe, Jews had been farmers and landowners. They were rejected just as those whose different talents Canada could have used very much to its advantage.

The Windsor Times, in its issue of January 27, 1939, pointed out how prejudiced the government's attitude against Jewish farmers was '"... a glance at what has taken place in Palestine has shown that Jewish farmers can succeed since the Jewish colonists in Palestine have made that country a garden and the products of Jewish farms are being widely distributed throughout the world." Even before that article in the *Windsor Times*, one had been published in the country's leading financial journal, the *Financial Post*, which took the government to task for not making use of the manifold talent that had become available. "If Canada really wants desirable immigrants from Europe, now is the time to get them. The opportunity is not likely to be repeated."

And talent from which Canada could have profited was offered in thousands of applications—and rejected. In the Baltic countries, farming had been an occupation in which Jews too, engaged and those who did were mostly highly successful. Mark Sorensen was a Canadian Christian of Danish descent. As the representative in Copenhagen for the Canadian Pacific Railroad for Scandinavian and the Baltic countries, and quite familiar with conditions in the Baltic, Sorensen kept records of those from the Baltic region who applied for entrance and transportation to Canada. He confirms that hundreds of experienced Jewish farmers, many of them with substantial capital, applied for immigration to Canada, and he reports how, to his amazement, though they constituted exactly the kind of element Canada said it wanted, they were all rejected just because they were Jewish. Some of them had funds in excess of a hundred thousand dollars, still: entrance denied. Most of these applicants were murdered as the Germans conquered the Baltic area.[15] Sorensen notes that the Immigration Branch was "entirely out of tune with the needs of the times and the desires of the Canadian people."

Similarly critical of the performance of the Immigration Branch was the European Colonization Manager of the Canadian Pacific Railroad, H.C.P. Cresswell. Among other cases, he reports the one of a Czechoslovakian Jew who had deposited $100,000 in a London bank, a very large amount at that time and who wanted to invest that money in Canada. Entrance denied. And the reason given in that case was that "this money could be used to advantage in Britain" by the applicant.[16]

The Canadian garment market was entirely dominated by New York, yet successful European garment manufacturers with sufficient capital—as much as $170,000—to start a manufacturing enterprise in Canada were denied entrance. They were Jewish. The reason given in that case was that these applicants would have to compete with others.[17] Just to mention one more case of denial to applicants who were able to contribute to the industrial growth of Canada and to create new jobs: from France came the applications of three Polish Jews who had successfully operated a tannery and had a capital of $120,000, with access to another $100,000. They intended to build a tannery in Canada. Denied. Reason given: Canada does not need another tannery.[18]

Agriculturists as supposedly desired, industrialists, name the occupation, if you were Jewish you were—with the exception of a very few who had some quite special pull in Ottawa—all rejected. Skilled craftsmen, scientists, mechanics, even an experienced aircraft repairman, an occupation at a premium at that time, were all denied entrance when they were Jewish.[19]

The rejection of the application by the aircraft repairman, who was also experienced in the manufacture of diesel machines, infuriated Mr. Sorensen. He writes: "At a time when the services of a skilled aeroplane fitter is at a premium, when stirring appeals are sent out over the empire for more and still more aeroplanes because it is a matter of life and death, is Ottawa capable of turning such applications down?"[20] This Canadian patriot could not accept the fact that descent and not qualification was the issue. He was not aware that the Prime Minister had written in his diary: "We must keep this part of the continent free from unrest and from *too great an intermixture of foreign blood.*"[21]

The applications were processed in Canada by the Jewish Immigration Aid Society, and that organization's reply was always the same. They stated that they were sorry but were unable to help because presently Jews were not being admitted into Canada.

But this was the policy of those who conspired to let the Jews perish rather than to admit them to their vast, empty country that needed their services. Mr. Blair could be quite blunt in the expression of his anti-Semitism. He was, after all, backed by his co-conspirators: the Prime Minister as well as the leader of the opposition, Maurice Duplessie, who represented Quebec, a province in which anti-Semitism was deeply rooted. They watched that there should be no deviation from the established immigration policy. Bluntness, including a good measure of cruelty and hubris considering the power position from which he spoke, is recorded by Blair in the description of a meeting with a group of Jews. He does not say whether they were a delegation pleading for the life of their brethren, only that he was well acquainted with the three. This is how he described what happened at that meeting. "I suggested that it might be a very good thing if they would call a conference and have a day of humiliation and prayer which might be profitably extended for a week or more, where they would honestly try to answer the question why they were so unpopular..."[22]

Of course, with such offensive behavior practiced at the top, similar arrogance and cruelty could be found farther down on the bureaucratic scale. One such case is reported to have happened at the Canadian consulate in Holland. A woman applied for admission of her family to Canada and pointed out that they had available what was then the substantial amount of $50,000 in foreign currency— more than the sum required. The official said, "Wonderful", and had the woman, who did not have a Jewish sounding name, fill out a form. When she handed it to him he noticed the name of the family: "Rapaport?" he said. "They are Jewish, I am sorry we have no visa." Then, in her face, he tore up the application. The brutality of this case would be unbelievable would we not know of the attitude and behavior at the top of the hierarchy.[23]

In his treatment of those who were pleading for rescue, King went even so far as to make remarks that might have indicated that it was unpatriotic to ask for the admission of Jewish refugees. When, following the wide publicity that the horrors of the Kristallnacht created, he agreed to meet with a group representing Canadian

Jewry, he not only told them that the Kristallnacht might turn out to have been a blessing, because of the reaction it created in the world; he also told them his own reaction to that blessing. He could not do anything because he had to "keep up the views of those supporting the government."[24] For people used to listening to hints of anti-Semitism, this certainly indicated that those pleading for rescue action were acting against their government.

Many of the applications were not even for permanent residence. They came from Jews who had applied for immigration to the United States, had supplied the required affidavits of support by relatives or friends in the United States, and had been registered for immigration. They had been given a "quota number", which meant that they would be considered for immigration to the United States when their number came up. Due to the so restrictive American quota system, the waiting time might have been very long, maybe several years, but often the expected time was just a few months. The problem for such people was to survive that interim period. These applications for temporary admittance were not treated any better than those for immigration. In fact, Canada adopted a policy of "no visa for persons en route to the United States." Thus even those whose expected waiting time might have only been a few weeks were often condemned to perish. Each of these weeks was fateful because any day, any hour, they stayed in German-held lands, they could—and often were—picked up and deported.

The interrelationship between the restrictive American quota system and the Canadian exclusion system is probably best demonstrated by the frustration that a young official at the Canadian legation in Washington experienced. Escot Reid was a brilliant man, a Rhodes scholar. He had, prior to joining the External Affairs Department, been Secretary General of the Canadian Institute of International Affairs. In his papers is recorded a case in which Supreme Court Judge Felix Frankfurter tried to get two elderly aunts of his into Canada. Judge Frankfurter had taken upon himself the obligation to take care of them for the rest of their lives. That request was rejected. A few weeks later Mr. Reid describes in a letter to his wife another experience which was haunting him:

> A terribly sad and good looking Jew
> came in to me this morning about
> getting his parents out of Vienna.
> They are too frightened even to go to

the consulate. His father had already
been attacked on the street by some
young hooligans. Every time one of
them comes in it leaves me shaken
and ashamed of Canada. I can't see a
reason why we can't let these old
people in when they are not going to
work and their children in the States
are willing and able to support them.
*It is like being a bystander at an especially
cruel and long drawn-out murder.*[25]

An important role in the machinations to keep Jews out of
Canada wherever possible was played by Canada's highest diplo-
matic representative in Europe, Vincent Massey, Canada's High
Commissioner in London. Massey belonged to the circle that had
formed about Lord and Lady Astor, the great admirers of Hitler,
Germanophiles and vehement anti-Semites. One such chance to
keep Jewish victims of the Nazi era out of Canada is suggested by
Massey to King at the time of the German occupation of the Sudeten.
Massey saw here the chance of using the situation to bar—in the
future, too—entrance to more Jews. He wrote to King: "Would it not
be a wonderful tactic to admit as many as possible Aryan Sudeten
Germans... if we could take a substantial number of them it would
put us in a much stronger position in relation to later appeals from
and on behalf of non-Aryans."[26] He pressed his point further by
urging "these refugees are of a superior type to certain other categories of refugees who are engaging our attention."[27]

When, during the height of the Hungarian Jewish catastrophe in
April 1944, the issue of possible rescue came up, Massey rejected the
idea as a cheap political plot by President Roosevelt. The Democrats,
he said, just "want the Jewish vote without taking in more Jews,
because if they allow more Jews they would lose the Roman Catholic
vote."[28] Interestingly, Massey was made Canadian representative to
the Intergovernment Committee for Refugees. Just the right man to
take care of refugee interests.

Particularly clear in the case of Canada is the evolution of the
planned and active cooperation among those who devised, upheld,
and executed the country's immigration policy: their conspiracy to
bar entrance to those who wanted to flee for their lives. A bluntly
anti-Semitic man in charge of the immigration branch found coop-

eration by the Prime Minister who had viewed Hitler as "sweet" and a "very sincere man" and who saw Hitler as a person who might one day be seen "as one of the saviors of the world." Occasional doubts on the part of King as an accessory to the murder policy his government had adopted did not change his full support of the existing and expanding policy of Jew-hatred.

Vincent Massey fed anti-Semitic comments and suggestions for the exclusion of Jews to Blair. Their cooperation in that matter was smooth and undisturbed. The representatives of the French opposition in Canada, Ernest Lapointe and Maurice Duplessis, were also fully in the game. They watched that there should be no relaxation of the exclusionary role and fully supported the blocking of any of the several suggested major rescue actions.

And the worst in this situation is that these people were, in their actions, supported by the media and the population, though the latter two do not have to carry the direct responsibility which historically burdens the policy makers. Seeing all the facts, one can hardly avoid sympathizing with the Canadian Pacific Railway executive, Mr. Mark Sorensen, who saw the death sentence handed out to hundreds of persons who he knew could make valuable contributions to his country. Filled with moral indignation, he writes "one day those responsible for this inhumane policy will be brought to the bar of justice."[29]

Well, they were not. But they have to stand before the bar of historical judgment for having been, to say the least, to some part, cold-bloodedly co-responsible for the murder of tens of thousands of their fellow human beings, whom they threw back into the jaws of the devouring moloch.

[1] E.W.H. Lumsden. "Immigration and Politics," *Inter-American Quarterly*, October 1940, Vol. 2, No. 4, p. 72.

[2] International Labor Review, February 1937, Vol. XXXV, No. 2, p. 224 ff.

[3] Association Filantropica Israelita, 1944, *Diez Anos De Obra Constructiva En America Del Sud*, p. 256.

[4].Birks to Manion, June 12, 1939 as cited by Irving Abella and Harold Troper, None Is Too Many, 1982, p. 65.

[5] Abella and Troper, op. cit. 1982, Preface, p. V.

[6] Abella and Troper, op. cit. 1982, p. 298 n. 83.

[7] National Archives, RG 84 File 842.00 PR Refugees. Memorandum of interview, July 23, 1938.

[8] 1 King Diary, May 10, 1938, as quoted in Abella and Troper, op. cit., p. 36.

[9] King Diary, March 29, 1938 as cited by Abella and Troper, op. cit., p. 17.

[10] King Diary, September 15, 1938, as cited by Abella and Troper, op. cit., p. 37.

[11] Blair to F.N. Sclanders, September 13, 1938 IR File 54782, as cited by Abella and Troper, op. cit., p. 8.

[12] Ibid. Blair to Crerar, October 12, 1938.

[13] Blair to Crerar, March 28, 1938, IR File 644452, Blair to H.R.I. Henry, January 30, 1939 as cited by Abella and Troper, op. cit., p. 8.

[14] Blair to F.N. Sclanders, October 9, 1938, ibid.

[15] Mark B. Sorensen Papers, Interview with Mark Sorensen, as cited by Abella and Troper, op. cit., p. 73.

[16] Mark B. Sorensen Papers, Notes on Gustav Barth family application 1940, as cited by Abella and Troper, op. cit., p. 73.

[17] JIAS File 21130 Solkin to JEAS Warsaw November-7, 1938; HIAS Solkin to HICEM August 1, 1939.

[18] JIAS Solkin to Kraizer December 13, 1939. Mark B. Sorensen Papers, Otto Sygall File 1940, as cited by Abella and Troper, op. cit., p. 74.

[19] Ibid.

[20] Ibid.

[21] King Diary March 29, 1938 as cited by Abella and Troper, op. cit., p. 17. Emphasis added.

[22] IR File 54782/5 Blair to F.N. Sclanders, September 13, 1938 as cited by Abella and Troper, op. cit., p. 9.

[23] Quoted by Abella and Troper, op. cit., p. 29 from E. Barzel "Zita's Odyssey", Jewish Life, December 1979, 14, 26.

[24] King Diary November 24, 1938 as cited by Abella and Troper, op. cit., p. 43.

[25] Escot Reid Papers, E. Reid to R. Reid January 28, 1939 as quoted by Abella and Troper, op. cit., p. 39.

[26] Massey to King, October 18. November 29, 1938, 828, DCER VI, Ottawa, 1972 as quoted in Abella and Troper, 48, 296.

[27] Department of External Affairs Records Box 779, File 382, Massey to King, December 2, 1938; Department of External Affairs Records Box 1870, File 327-11, Massey to King December 2, 1938 as quoted by Abella and Troper, op. cit., pp. 48, 49.

[28] Public Records Office, London, Dominions Office Records File 121/14 High Commissioners Meeting, August 10, 1944 as quoted by Abella and Troper, op. cit., p. 178.

[29] Mark B. Sorensen Papers. Notes on the application of the Edward Pree family 1940 as quoted by Abella and Troper, op. cit., p. 72.

Chapter 8
MORAL POWERS IN SUPPORT
OF EVIL

THE VATICAN

The sixth commandment, THOU SHALT NOT KILL[1] was, in the course of the Holocaust, broken millions of times by tens of thousands of Christians who were otherwise practicing their religion. For Catholics, violating the sixth commandment constitutes a mortal sin, and almost half of greater Germany's population, 41.3%, were Catholic. Of the SS, 22.7% were Catholic.[2] The murder of the millions who perished in the Holocaust demanded the services of tens of thousands, not only for the actual killing, but for the preparation of it: locating the Jews, assembling and bringing them to the collection places, transporting the victims, guarding those who were to be killed so that there should be no escapes, the physical and logistical work of running the murder factories, and in many other ways as the situation demanded. Much of that auxiliary work was performed by volunteers of various nationalities, Poles, Ukranians, Baltics, Hungarians and other ethnic groups. The countries that supplied these helpers were populated by Roman Catholics. This is particularly true of Poland, Hungary, the Baltic countries, and the states created by the Germans: Croatia and Slovakia. The latter two are among the most devout Roman Catholic countries in Europe, yet they established their own SS type of organization, the Hlinka Guards in Slovakia and the Ustaschi in Croatia. These national organizations were often more feared than the German SS because, in many instances, they outdid the SS in cruelty, and they were certainly more efficient in providing the victims for slaughter. They knew local conditions and were better able than their German partners-in-crime to locate Jews in hiding and to prevent escapes.

During the entire time they engaged in torture and murder, those committing these heinous acts were able to perceive themselves as good Christians. They could receive absolution and could take part in their religious services without being told that what they were doing constituted a major sin.

In formally independent Slovakia, the German-appointed ruler who was, as such, in charge of the Hlinka Guards, was a priest, Father Tiso. Neither he nor any of his Hlinka Guards, nor the Ustaschi in Croatia, nor the Arrow Cross in Hungary, were ever excommunicated or even threatened with excommunication. Nor were those who pulled the wires in Germany. Excommunication—especially of the leaders—would have been a highly visible reminder to the populations of what they owed to their dignity as humans, as well as to the precepts of Christianity. Hitler was born to Catholic parents, was baptized, went to school and lived for two years in a monastery, in Lambach, Austria. Goebbels, too was Catholic, as were Eichmann—who orchestrated the Final Solution—and numerous other top war criminals. Excommunication would have served as a signal to the masses of perpetrators to reevaluate their actions. It would also have brought home to the leaders of the free countries what they were doing when they made themselves accomplices to the Holocaust.

It was then, as it is today, strictly forbidden by the Catholic Church to be a member of a Free Masons Lodge, but it was not prohibited to belong to the SS, the Hlinka Guards, the Ustaschi or the Arrow Cross.

To say that membership in these organizations and the partaking in their actions was not interdicted amounts to an understatement, because the Church assumes the function of moral leadership for its adherents. That this moral leadership responded with silence to those horrendous activities was therefore bound to be interpreted as condoning them. This way masses of probably well-meaning Catholic laymen and thousands of priests were left without the moral leadership which they were entitled to obtain. The church leaders failed to provide leadership and never spoke out unequivocally. Especially German Catholics could hardly doubt that the Church condoned the anti-Jewish measures. Catholic leadership in Germany was not simply passively reacting to the actions taken against the Jews. In numerous announcements, it heaped hatred against the Jews in a situation which was already loaded with German hate propaganda. To mention just a few representative cases of spewing oil into the anti-Semitic conflagration, we want to point out that even before the National Socialists assumed governmental power on January 30, 1933, their rapidly growing popularity received valuable "moral" support by prominent churchmen.

As early as 1923, the Franciscan Father Erhard Schlund wrote and published a book that justifies anti-Semitism. It agrees with the Nazi program of fighting the Jews' "destructive influence in religion, morality, literature, art and political and social life." Also, like the Nazis, it says that the "hegemony in finance" allegedly exercised by "the Jews should be fought."[3] In these days many Catholics in Germany looked for advice from their church on how to react to the vehement anti-Semitism preached by the Nazis, and such statements helped them to establish their attitude. Of special help in this confusing time were guidance books. One such early book, edited by Bishop Michael Buchberger of Regensburg, contains an article by the Jesuit Gustav Gundlach that speaks of the "exaggerated and harmful influence of the Jews."[4]

The growing Nazi party could also find encouragement by such statements as those made and published as early as 1923, by Curate Joseph Roth. He calls the Jews a morally inferior race of whom public life has to be cleansed. If in the course of such elimination "some good and harmless Jews *with whom immorality because of their race is latent*[5] will have to suffer together with the guilty ones, this is not a violation of Christian love of one's neighbor... "[6] Catholics who looked for guidance in that confusing time found also an answer in the Vicar General of Mainz, Dr. Mayer's assertion, that Hitler in *Mein Kampf* had "appropriately described" the harmful influence the Jews had on German intellectual life.[7]

In the same vein, Father Philipp Haeuser of Augsburg, in a book, agreed with the Nazi claim that the Jews were largely responsible for Germany's having lost the war. He described the Jews as a people disowned by God, a people under a curse, and refers to them as the cross of Germany.[8]

In no case did the anti-Semitism spread by representatives of the German Catholic Church reach or even approach the hate level and brutality espoused by the Nazis, who were at that time singing "When the Jews blood squirts from the knife everything goes much better." Most of the Catholic justifications of anti-Semitism are tempered with the pious suggestion to apply Christian love and the boundaries of Christian morals when anti-Semitism is practiced. While these pronouncements by Catholic clerics did not demand specific actions, they were sparks in a powder keg. There were numerous such still relatively mild incitements to Jew hatred in these early days of growing National Socialist sentiment. With Hitler's coming to power, anti-Semitic statements and actions on the part of the Catholic Church in Germany grew in intensity and number.

Most impressively was the support of Nazism expressed by Cardinal Innitzer of Vienna and by the Austrian bishops. Austria's population was 94.4% Catholic. Traditionally church and state policies were closely interwoven. For many years Austria's most prominent politician had been a cleric. Besides other government functions, Monsignor Seipel had been twice Chancellor (Prime Minister). The Austrian Cardinal Innitzer was a decisive political power, and many Austrians expected guidance from him as to how to relate to Nazism after it had taken over. They did not have to wait long for that guidance. When on the morning of March 19, 1938, the Viennese, after a week of arrests, murders and cruel persecution entered the streets, they found the city swamped with huge placards. From a distance of 25-30 feet already they could recognize on the placards' bottom the cardinal's familiar signature. On top of it, also in his handwriting he had written the words and the exclamation mark of the salute with which Nazis greeted each other: *Heil Hitler*!

The placard was a giant reproduction of a letter which accompanied a "Solemn Statement" by the bishops of Austria expressing their satisfaction with what Nazism had done for the German people, particularly for the poor, and exhorting the faithful to fulfill their duty towards their German nation.

The accompanying cardinal's letter is addressed to the newly appointed governor of the province of Austria and is written in an almost subservient style. It concludes with a deferential phrase: "With the expression of most outstanding respect". To make the submission absolutely clear, the words Heil Hitler had been added in large lettering by the cardinal's own hand.

Two happenings symbolize clearer than anything else the close collaboration between the new government, what it stood for, and the Catholic Church.

Shortly after Hitler came to power, Archbishop Konrad Groeber of Freiburg, one of the most prominent members of the Catholic hierarchy in Germany, joined the SS as a "promoting member" (foerderndes Mitglied)[9]. And Bishop Wilhelm Berning of Osnabrueck, who had shortly before in Berlin presided over a conference of German church provinces, was appointed a member of the Prussian Council of State. As may be expected in a dictatorship, the State Council wielded little power; decisions were made by Hitler and his cronies, but the position was a highly visible one and testified publicly to the unity of Nazi leadership with the Church. For the Church this appointment was one of principal importance, and it had been approved by Pope Pius XI.[10]

So close was the cooperation that Bishop Berning was permitted to visit "a number of concentration camps." He was reported in the press to have addressed the inmates and to have exhorted them to fulfill their religious duty of obedience and loyalty to the German people and the government. The report also states that the Bishop, in a talk to the camp guards of the Aschendorfer Moor concentration camp, praised their work and ended that speech with three *Sieg Heil* for the Fuehrer and the fatherland. The *Koelnische Volkszeitung* reported that he had even found the furnishings of the concentration camps visited to be praiseworthy. The Jesuit Father Friedrich Muck-ermann, who published a weekly in Holland, often critical of the policy practiced by the Church in Germany, verified the visit by checking with Bishop Berning's diocesan chancery in Osnabrueck.[11]

Catholics who might have felt guilty about the murder of Jews could find, in an official church publication, a rationalization for hating Jews "murderously". In a pastoral letter of the archdiocese Freiburg on January 30, 1939, Archbishop Groeber wrote that the Jews hated Christ "murderously" and that their "murderous hatred" continued "through centuries."[12] This inciting statement was made in times in which murder of Jews was an ongoing occurrence, well after the Crystal Night. It is difficult to see no connection whatsoever between the Archbishop's promotional membership in the SS and this inflaming announcement.

Neither was Groeber alone among leading Catholic churchmen to fan the fires of anti-Semitism. Theologians supported Jew-hatred by their theories. In a book published shortly after the above statements by Archbishop Groeber regarding the ongoing "murderous hatred" of the Jews, the theologian Theodor Bogler OSB writes that the Jews not only killed Jesus but that in their unending hatred of Christianity they were still out to destroy the Church.[13] Couched in academic language, as may be expected from a leading theoretician, Bishop Alois Hudal puts at ease those who wonder how the treatment of the Jews can be sanctioned in a society that is built upon the principle of justice and legality. Never mind, he says. Jews are outside the legal system, they are not protected by it.[14]

The instances we have cited here are just some of the most blatant occasions at which representatives of the Catholic Church in Germany not only omitted to provide the moral guidance in regards to the persecution of Jews one might have expected, but, to the contrary, stoked the conflagration which was intended to consume all Jews of Europe.

How about those high-ranking Catholic churchmen who dared to stand up against the policies of National Socialism? Did not Cardinal Faulhaber of Munich go so far in condemnation of Nazism that his palace was set afire? Cardinal Faulhaber did in fact speak up for the rights of the Catholic Church. He even defended the Old Testament. But he did not miss that occasion of feeding the hatred of Jews; the moral beauty of the Old Testament, he claimed, has nothing to do with the spirit of the Jews of today nor with the ones of olden days. In the same statement in which Cardinal Faulhaber defends the Old Testament, he accuses the Jews of being usurious, land grabbers, and oppressors of the farmer. As to the Old Testament's moral standards, he announces "People of Israel, this did not grow in your own garden, of your own planning. This condemnation of usurious land grabbing, this was against the oppression of the farmer by debt, this prohibition of usury is not the product of your spirit."[15]

Not only regarding Jew-hatred did the Catholic Church in Germany in fact support the main theme of the National Socialist credo; it did so in every possible way in regards to the military attack on Germany's neighbors. When Catholic Poland succumbed to the German invasion that resulted in the death of tens of thousands of pious Catholic Poles, all the churches were ringing their bells in hailing the victory. The same triumphant ringing of the bells was practiced when Catholic France collapsed under the German onslaught, and thus the philosophy and the power of Germany was imposed upon still another area. When the war was long lost already, the bishops as well as lower level priests admonished the German soldiers not to give up and presented it to them as their religious duty to fight to the very end for that criminal system that ruled Germany. So strong was the identification with the official German doctrines that in some churches Christians who had a Jewish ancestor (up to one of the four grandparents) were required to sit on separate benches during the church service. At least one cardinal counselled against such procedure and suggested instead, truly in the spirit of charity, separate services for "Jewish" Christians.

Next to Cardinal Faulhaber, the other leading churchman often named by those who endeavor to prove that the Catholic Church in Germany stood up against Nazism, is the Bishop of Muenster, August von Galen. He publicly denounced the German program of killing the mentally retarded and severely disturbed. This barbaric action had already resulted in the killing of 70,000 mentally handicapped persons. It was stopped as a result of the protests that demanded the end of these "mercy killings." The success of that protest shows that public resistance against killings could be successful. Unfortunately, no such public resistance did ever develop in Germany that would have been directed specifically against the massacres of those who were the prime targets of official German bestiality, the Jews. Bishop von Galen did not speak up publicly against the murder of Jews as he did—so successfully—against the "euthanasia" program. He spoke for "the fundamental rights of man."[16] Yet defending the "rights of man", as well as any other statement that did not mention the *Jews* specifically, did entirely miss the purpose—if help for the Jews was the purpose—because it could at best just serve as an alibi for the uninformed. The issue was that, based upon nearly fifteen hundred years of Christian teaching, sharply formulated by German propaganda, the Jews had been described as satanic, devilish, as children of the Devil. The powerfully impressive German propaganda machine, building upon ancient, very active prejudices painted the Jews as not really human. They did not kill Jews, they *exterminated* them, like vermin. The important word to be spoken by a leading churchman in Germany was never spoken. It would have been an unequivocal reminder that the *Jews*, like anybody else, were children of God and that everything that applies to the right and dignity of man has to be applied to Jews, too.

Typical of such vagueness that seems to provide an alibi of having spoken up in behalf of the victims of the ongoing industrialized mass murder was, as the war neared its end, a decision by the annual conference of German Catholic bishops in 1943 in the city of Fulda. The bishops decided that a letter should be read from all pulpits expressing charity for those who are protected by the ten commandments and though innocent, cannot help themselves. It specified those groups as "innocent hostages, disarmed prisoners of war and... other prisoners, people of foreign races or origin." Also mentioned as worthy of Christian love are "foreign workers," the large numbers of slave workers who had been brought from the conquered territories and were forced to work for the German war machine. By specifying these various groups yet blatantly omitting the group that was the prime target of persecution—the Jews—the Bishops seemed to imply the view that the Jews did not deserve such aid. The mentioning of "foreign races and origin" could and was meant to be interpreted as referring to other nationalities. Germans claimed to be the master race, and all Slavs, Poles, Russians, Yugoslavs, etc. in fact, all others were inferior to the Germans and referring to other races and foreign blood without naming the Jews, just as prisoners of war and foreign workers were specifically named, showed that the Jews were not included in the demand for Christian love. After all they had "murdered" Christ. Were they not cursed? This vague formulation did not and could not work to the good of the Jews.

Among the thousands of churchmen in Germany and Austria, there were only a few who felt and expressed openly the moral duty to protest what was being done to those fellow humans, the Jews. Bernhard Lichtenberg, Canon of St. Hedwig church in Berlin was a shining exception. After he had witnessed the horror of the Crystal Night, he prayed publicly for that outrage's victims. Following what he felt to be a call for morality, he did even more than pray. He hid three Jews in a friend's house. The authorities found out about it. They burst into this friend's home. The Jews were killed right away. Lichtenberg was arrested. After serving a two year sentence in a penitentiary, he was sent to Dachau but never made it to the concentration camp. He "died" on the way. And during all that time relations between the representatives of the Vatican and the German authorities continued to be smooth—no major disturbance.

Outside the influence of the German Catholic Church and away from the influence of the papal envoy in Berlin, Catholic clerics in much larger numbers spoke up against the persecution and deportation of the Jews. In Holland, the Catholic Church acted quite independently from the example given by the Vatican. In 1943, it forbade Catholic policemen to take part in the hunting down of Jews. In Fiano, Italy Don Aldo Mei, a young priest found it his duty to hide a Jewish family. The authorities found out about these Jews being hidden in the mortuary. They shot and killed the Jews in their hiding place and arrested Don Mei. He was tortured by the Gestapo because he refused to name the location of six more Jews who were hidden elsewhere. Abandoned by the Vatican, which did not take any firm stand on his behalf in order not to disturb its relations with the Germans, he withstood the torture and wrote into his breviary, shortly before being killed: "I die with sealed lips and serene in God's peace." In Vidukie, Lithuania, the village priest put the Vatican to shame. Father Jonas hid there thirty Jewish children whose parents had been deported. An informer had told the Germans about this hiding place, and when the Gestapo arrived, Father Jonas blocked their way and shouted: "If you kill the children, you will have to kill me first." A burst of fire from a submachine gun killed him; a few more bursts and the children were dead, too.[17]

While the national leadership of churches outside Germany were not unaware of their duties, it was hard to fight both, the Germans and one's own leaders at the same time. In July 1942, all the bishops and cardinals of occupied France sent a declaration to Marshal Petain, the puppet ruler of France, in which they stated:

> Profoundly shocked by the mass arrests and the inhumane treatment meted out to the Jews, we cannot stifle the outcry of our conscience. In the name of humanity and of Christian principles we raise our protest in favor of the inalienable rights of the human being... We ask you to comply with this appeal so that justice and charity be respected.[18]

This was strong language, but the protest was directed to the wrong person. Petain was hopelessly enmeshed in doing as ordered by his German bosses. A protest directed to the Germans would have made more sense but would still have had little effect as long as the Germans could figure that no major action would be forthcoming from the Vatican. The Pope with his power to influence the so pious Catholics in the occupied eastern territories—Poles, Baltics, Croatians, Slovaks, etc.—was the one whose voice counted.

More moving examples of individual courage were set by a few ranking Catholic clerics outside Germany, in contrast to their supreme authority's inaction and missing guidelines. On Sunday, August 22, 1942, Jules Gerard Saliege, Archbishop of Toulouse, had read from all pulpits under his command a statement that unequivocally condemned the deportations of the Jews as cruel inhumanity and sin. It also accuses the Catholic hierarchy of having surrendered.

> Children, women and fathers have been treated like animals. That the members of one family can be severed and shipped like cattle to unknown destinations is a sad spectacle reserved for our days. Why does the right of asylum no longer exist in our churches? Why have we surrendered? Lord, take pity with us.[19]

The Prefect of Toulouse had learned of the impending reading of that message and ordered the Archbishop to withdraw it. Saliege refused in words that should have been used by the Pope.

> It is my duty to teach morals to the members of the diocese and when it is necessary to teach them also to government officials.[20]

And the message was read from the pulpits of 400 churches.

What was the Pope's reaction to the courageous stand which those bishops took in defense of what they felt to be their moral responsibility? He did promote Archbishop Saliege to the rank of Cardinal. He did that in 1946, well after the Germans' unconditional surrender.

And how about the Germans? Did they arrest and kill the Archbishop? They did neither; he was too popular a figure. Archbishop Saliege's standing up against the German horror was not a lone occurrence among leading French clerics. Monsignor F. W. Theas, Bishop of Montauban had from the pulpits under his jurisdiction the following message and condemnation read:

> ... Scenes of undescribable suffering and horror are occurring in our land. In Paris, tens of thousands of Jews are being subjected to the most barbaric treatment. In our diocese we are witnesses to the most heartbreaking happenings of similar uprooting of

men and women being treated like beasts.

In the name of Christian conscience, I am protesting and I proclaim that all men are brothers created by one God. The current anti-Semitic measures constitute a violation of human dignity and of the sacred rights of the individual and the family. May God comfort those who are persecuted and may He give them strength.[21]

In Holland, the first deportation of Dutch Jews was denounced by the Bishops in strong, condemning terms,[22] and in Belgium, the local priests were active—with the support of their Bishops, in hiding Jewish children.[23]

These condemnations by locally influential clergymen did not, however, cause the Germans to abstain or in any way change the measures they took. They knew that the Vatican would back them up whatever the locals said, and the cooperation they received in Poland, the Baltic countries—in fact wherever Catholics worked with them on the extermination plan—was not endangered. Only a firm announcement by the Holy Father could have influenced Germany's partners in the annihilation process.

The only too few, but energetic, local protests helped to create a climate in the population that resulted in the saving of hundreds of children whose parents were murdered. In private homes, as well as in monasteries, they were hidden to the end of the war. The exact number cannot be established because in so many cases, there were, after the German collapse, no relatives left to claim the child, who then grew up as a Catholic.

The protests by some courageous Catholic clerics against what they saw happening all around them did apparently not give the Pope the feeling that in regards to the Holocaust he was out of step with the main body of the Catholic hierarchy. He had been in Germany from 1917, when he was appointed Papal Nuncio in Bavaria, until 1929, and he knew what the National Socialist Workers Party and their leader stood for. In 1930, he was made Secretary of State for the Vatican—and he had never condemned what happened in Germany as far as Hitler's program to murder all Jews went. His position was well known to the conclave that in 1939 elevated him to the papacy. Of all those eligible, the cardinals elected the one who had since its birth observed the National Socialist party and knew Hitler's and the party's determination to solve the "Jewish problem" in the way Hitler had promised. In electing him to be the new Pope, the cardinals were aware that they were putting into St. Peter's chair a man who would not take a stand against the plan to kill all the Jews of Europe. Certainly most of the cardinals assembled for the conclave were ready to take the German annihilation plan into their stride. The question may be asked to what degree this cardinals assembly made itself co-responsible with Pius XII when he continued to act in regards to the Holocaust after the election as he had done before as Secretary of State.

Dutch and Belgian Catholic clerics stand out the more with their courageous acts as they knew that this position was not backed by the Holy See. When the French puppet government of Marchall Petain introduced special "Jewish statutes" and the cardinals and bishops of France announced their disapproval of these measures, the Vichy ambassador to the Holy See, M. Leon Berard informed Petain that the Vatican did not consider such legislation to be conflicting with Catholic teachings. No principal conflict, it was just asked that the new statutes be applied with "charity" and "justice."[24]

In the case of the Vatican, silence was a conspiracy of moral support of the Holocaust because it was a main function of the Pope and his staff to provide moral leadership to the 400 million Catholics. Silence in the face of the annihilation process could only mean that this carnage ongoing without a respite, did not offend the principles of morality. Not only the Catholics actively involved in the slaughtering process were bound to interpret the papal nonintervention as approval. Plotters in countries not under German control were encouraged to continue actions of which they might have abstained if the issue of morality would have been raised by the Vatican. It seems that notwithstanding an individual intervention here and there, the Vatican did not think that morality was involved. In an English language broadcast in September 1940, the Vatican defended its policy of "neutrality" but assured at the same time that where morality was involved, no neutrality was possible.[25] Thus the silence amounted to "there is no moral question involved in these mass murders."

In all these activities and purposeful abstaining from public announcement, the Vatican acted as one conspiratorial unit. As one would expect, not one of the numerous members of the Church's world government is known to have ever even hinted that he did not share the Pontiff's attitude of not standing up publicly against the abomination. Yet the men in the Vatican were better informed than anybody else about what was happening in the lands held by the Germans, as, in addition to the sources available to others, they received reports from hundreds of clerics located right on the various spots. In variation of Luke 23:34, *They did know what they were doing.* In the Pope's own city of Rome, in the night of October 15 to 16th, 1942, the Germans hammered at the doors of homes in which Jews lived and assembled them for deportation. Even then, when Jews were arrested "right under the Pope's windows" and led away, the Pope did not stand up publicly against it. This being a time at which the Germans were already highly vulnerable, Germany's Ambassador to the Holy See, Ernst von Weizsaecker, was very concerned with the possibility that this outrage against the Jews of the city of which Pius XII was the bishop might make him openly condemn the entire program. But von Weizsaecker could report that the Pope continued to shy away from overt action, and he negotiated through emissaries. Without a public stance by the Vatican on October 16, 1,007 Roman Jews, the majority of them women and children, were deported. They included Enrico Fermi's father-in-law and Admiral Augusto Capon, a war hero in World War I. Also pressed into one of the freight cars was a Catholic nurse who had been attending a young epileptic Jewish boy and refused to let him go alone. The sealed train's destination was Auschwitz. It was seven days en route. No facilities whatsoever were provided.

A terse entry in the Auschwitz log book dated October 23 records:

> RSHA transport Jews from Rome. After the selection of 149 men registered with numbers 158451-158639 and 47 women registered with numbers 66172-66218 (sic) have been admitted to the detention camp. The rest were gassed.

Those "admitted to the detention camp" were to be worked in a way which resulted in a survival time of 3 months. Only 16 of the 1,007 survived.

The Vatican knew in detail what was waiting for the deported. The procedure varied. Often there was no selection, dependent on the availability of work places. Among the reports available to the Vatican was even one from a German source. SS First Lieutenant Kurt Gerstein had been active in church matters, and he felt that, notwithstanding the risk of being tortured to death if found out, he had to let the Vatican know about the horror which he had eyewitnessed. He handed a report to R. Winter, the coadjutor for Cardinal Count Preysing of Berlin.

Early in the morning of August 18, 1942, Lieutenant Gerstein witnessed the arrival of a death train. There were 6,700 Jews packed into the freight cars. Of them 1,500 were dead on arrival. As soon as the train stopped, 200 Ukrainian guards, equipped with leather whips, unsealed the cars, cursing and yelling at the Jews that they should hurry up; they pushed and pulled them out. Immediately when they touched the ground outside, they were severely beaten, many to the ground, while loudspeakers blared the command to undress for "disinfection". Dazed and stunned, the Jews obeyed. With a few brutal motions, the hair was shorn off the women's heads. And as now ordered by the loudspeakers and enforced by the guards the deportees, all naked, started marching towards the nearby "disinfection-bathhouse".

Three weeks prior to the deportation from Rome, the Germans had launched what might well have been a trial balloon to find out whether serious Vatican action should be expected in case of deportation from Rome. On September 25, they informed the Roman Jewish community that it had to deliver within 36 hours, 50 kilograms of gold, otherwise 200 Jews would be deported. In their despair, the Jews asked the Vatican to help, but no public protest against that cruel blackmail ensued. Instead the Pope promised a loan from the Vatican treasury of the difference between gold collected by the Jews and the quantity demanded. It was moving to see Jews standing in line with wedding rings, little gold chains, with everything they owned in gold to avert the deportation of the 200. They obtained from the Germans an extension for the delivery, and in the end the Vatican's loan was not needed. The gold was delivered on September 28. And the Germans now knew that the Vatican did not loudly protest and condemn a major crime committed against the Jews of its city.

The Vatican's involvement in this deportation went even farther than permitting the roundup and deportation right in its view without public protest and without telling Catholics not to take part in it. Everything points to the fact that the Pope knew in advance of the surprise raid and deportation plan, yet did not warn the targeted victims. With the Italian population set against the annihilation policy, most of the 1,007 could have fled and hidden in Italian homes had the Vatican not catered to the German need for secrecy. The acting German ambassador to Rome, Eitel Friedrich Moellhausen,[26] informed the German ambassador to the Holy See, Baron Ernst von Weizsaecker, a devout Catholic, of the impending action. Von Weizsaecker, according to Moellhausen, communicated this knowledge to Vatican officials. But even without information stemming from the Germans, the Vatican must have known. It had informers everywhere, loyal Catholics who for years had been reporting unusual occurrences. The census bureau had been requested by the Germans to supply names and addresses of Jews, and from other locations, this was known to precede deportation. Some Italian police were involved too, in the preparation of the raid, and the Vatican received regularly reports from Catholic police sources.

That many would have been saved had the raid not been a surprise, may be inferred from the fact that everywhere in Italy, Jews were in hiding with the help of the population, but they considered Rome a safe place because of the Pope's presence.

Rufino Salvatore Niccacci was the Father Guardian and the head of the St. Damiano Seminary in Assisi, central seat of the Holy Order of St. Francis. His detailed account of a locally initiated and locally conducted rescue action is recorded in a book tellingly titled *While The Pope Kept Silent.*[27] He and the area's bishop, Giuseppe Placido Niccolini, were the main figures in that rescue action, for which they obtained the cooperation of the city's mayor, Arnoldo Fortini.

There were no Jews in Assisi, but it was learned that in nearby Perugia some thirty Jews were in imminent danger of roundup and deportation as a Gestapo raid was upcoming. As advised by the bishop, Father Rufino went to the convent of Quirico and asked the mother abbess to hide the Jews in the cloister. Because the presence of any male in the cloister was inexorably interdicted, those hidden there would be most likely safe from German raiding parties. The abbess was horrified at the suggestion. For seven hundred years, she protested, no male had entered the cloister. She had taken a vow to protect that seclusion, and nobody except the pope or the cardinal in charge of the Franciscan order could lift that vow. Father Rufino returned with the bishop, who falsely announced that in ordering admission of those fleeing for their lives to the cloister he acted on orders of the pope. At that, the abbess unlocked the gate and opened the double grill which separated the cloister from the rest of the world, and the Jews survived the Holocaust.

Similar actions were initiated and conducted all through Italy. 4,236 Jews are known to have been saved in various monasteries, in houses of the orders and in private places all through Italy. This includes 477 of them hidden in Vatican City, the latter fact undoubtedly known to the pope. This is, by the way, not such a large number considering the size of the sprawling buildings.

But the thousands saved were not the issue. The issue was the condemnation of the murder of millions at a time when often in one day ten thousand and even twelve thousand were slaughtered in Auschwitz alone.

Ten days after the deportation from Rome, when most of the deported had been reduced to ashes, the Vatican newspaper Osservatore Romano printed an article which in a vague way and as if dealing with an abstract matter expressed disagreement with what had happened. It stated that "the eternal charity of the Supreme Pontiff knows neither boundaries nor nationality, neither religion nor race".[28] In a letter to his Foreign Office, Von Weizsaecker, knowing that this article constituted all the public reaction forthcoming from the Vatican, expresses his satisfaction as he writes:

> ... only very few people will recognize in it a special allusion to the Jewish problem.

The question may be raised why this book discusses attitudes and actions of only the Catholic Church and does not make the Protestant churches equally a subject of the inquiry. While the horror of the Holocaust would have demanded an incomparably stronger reaction, the Protestant churches did not conspire to act in such a way that in fact they would have provided active support to the Final Solution plan. Protestants are not monolithically organized. They do not have one supreme head who is responsible for the church as such. Yet occasionally, one or the other Protestant section did speak up quite specifically and quite powerfully. So did the Archbishop of Canterbury, head of the Anglican Church on several occasions. In

December 1942, he, in conjunction with the Anglican archbishops of York and of Wales, issued a proclamation which far from being merely a protest against the German actions, did direct specific demands to their own and to other governments.

> The bishops of the Church of England state that the number of victims of the cold blooded policy go into the hundreds of thousands, that Hitler himself revealed that he plans to annihilate the Jews which means the end of six million Jewish humans. The bishops of England declare that the suffering of these millions of Jews and the announced plan to kill them place upon humanity an obligation which nobody can shirk.

> There must be no delay in saving them. The bishops believe that it is the duty of the civilized nations, whether Allied or neutral, to provide havens to these victims. Therefore they appeal to the British government to take the leadership for the whole world by declaring its readiness together with the dominions and all Allied and neutral governments to provide havens within the British empire and elsewhere for all those who are threatened with annihilation and can escape from the Axis countries, as well as for those who already have escaped so as to provide space to those who so far could not escape.[29]

As to the Roman Catholic Church, one would not expect that the Pope needed to be asked by anybody to intervene but that, constituting the moral power that he was, he would have intervened on his own. But as he did not, there were appeals to the Pope to raise his voice as so many hoped and expected he would. As the Vatican did not speak up, requests to do so reached it from various sources.

In October 1941, Mr. Harold H. Tittman, the Assistant Chief of the U.S. delegation to the Vatican, did on behalf of the United States ask the Vatican to condemn the atrocities. He was told that the Vatican could not do so as it would have a negative influence on the Catholics in German-held lands. Contrary to the previously mentioned Catholic clerics in the field—and to the many more who remain unnamed, the Holy See wanted to remain "neutral." Apparently the Pope considered "neutrality" between mass murder and the right to live a moral attitude.

A second plea was made when in December 1942, Myron Taylor, who headed the United States delegation to the Holy See, pleaded for a papal condemnation of the mass murders. Again the need for neutrality was cited. That "neutrality" of the Vatican and its maintenance were very desired by the Germans. The Reich's delegate to the Holy See shows in his reports to the German Foreign Office again and again that concern, and the replies by the Foreign Office confirm that very understandable desire.

Actually, there was much more than neutrality in the policy of the Vatican. The Pope was not only silent; he cooperated with the Germans in issues regarding the Jews—not by physical involvement, of course, but by speaking up in support of some anti-Jewish matters. Thus finding no objection to the anti-Jewish measures introduced by the German puppet regime in Vichy France was just part of the overall set of actions followed and the set of values applied. There was much more than silence on the part of the Vatican. The Jesuit magazine *Civita Cattolica* announced that there was no Catholic objection to German anti-Semitism, except that it did not stem from religious conviction but was race oriented (according to which principle, Jesus would have wound up in a cattle car being shipped out for "extermination").

Added to this announcement is just the routine requirement that anti-Semitic measures should be applied without hatred in a spirit of Christian charity. We could understand them and "even *praise* them[30] if their policy were restricted within acceptable bounds of defense against Jewish organizations and institutions." Added to it is the routine exhortation that when one practices anti-Jewish measures to do this "without hatred... in a spirit of Christian charity."[31] Notice that this announcement does not specify what "acceptable bounds" in the practice of anti-Semitism are and thus leaves it to each practitioner of anti-Semitism to determine what these bounds are. The same Catholic mouthpiece declares it to be legitimate to confine Jews into a ghetto, as the Christians have to "defend" themselves against the threat posed to them by Jews.[32]

Myron Taylor had reminded the Pope that not only was the question of Jews at issue but the reputation of the Pope's office and thereby the trust in Catholicism as a moral power. After the seemingly invincible German military had run into serious difficulty in the initially successful battles against the Russians, it became known in informed circles that a papal statement regarding the Final Solution would be forthcoming.

At that time, in 1942, some of Germany's allies started wavering and the Germans could hardly afford energetic steps against the Holy Father. Expectations of a sharply worded condemnation of the Final Solution abomination were high. What was expected by many and urgently needed was a communication of the type of a special encyclical Pro Judaeos or an equivalent to it. Soon the informed learned that no such encyclical could be expected, but that year's Christmas message would take care of the issue.

From the point of condemnation, it was a complete failure and disappointment. It did not even mention the Jews—as the clerics in occupied countries, in Holland, France, and in Belgium, had done. Neither did it speak of the Final Solution program a year after its adoption at Wannsee, in full operation by then. Towards the end of a lengthy sociological discourse, by pointedly omitting to mention the Jews and the extermination program, this Christmas message refers in a vague way to it. It pleaded for a more humane conduct of hostilities and in its last part mentions the "hundreds of thousands who, without personal guilt, sometimes for no other reason but on account of their nationality or descent were doomed to death or exposed to a progressive deterioration of their condition."[33]

Mussolini commented on that much expected papal announcement:

> This is a speech of platitudes which might better be made by the parish priest of Predapio (Mussolini's native village).[34]

And the British Minister to the Holy See stated in a similar vein

> ... the condemnation is inferential and not specific and comes at the end of a long dissertation on social problems.[35]

When it was pointed out by those who were badly disappointed by the Christmas message's total failure to be specific, the Vatican used the argument that it could criticize in general terms only and that it was not its role to condemn specific actions. Yet where the issue concerned other matters,not the ongoing mass murder of Jews, the Vatican was specific again and again as, for example, when it protested just a few weeks before that vague and veiled message the Allied bombing of allegedly non-military objects in Genoa and Milan.[36]

This papal Christmas message only proved to the Germans that, notwithstanding energetic efforts on the part of the Allies, and in spite of the open stand taken by Catholic churchmen, the Vatican was "safe" for Germany. Even in view of the fact that the murder was by then going on in full blast, the Vatican did not dare to even mention the Jews.

After the monumental loss of the battle for Stalingrad, it had become clear that the collapse of Germany, which was by then all over on the defensive, was unavoidable. Now Pius XII, still hesitating and still not coming out with anything like an encyclical condemning the Holocaust, did take a few steps. The result they had only shows how influential the papacy was and how many it could have saved had it earlier asserted the moral leadership it assumed. Still it was not an all out effort, another case of too little and too late— a few million lives too late.

Acting in the later stages of the war, Pius XII in a personal message, the King of Sweden, and other neutrals appealed to Hungary's puppet leader Miklas Horthy, to stop the deportations. Horthy complied with the plea.

Also, in conjunction with others, as the war's end approached, Pius XII could be persuaded to intervene with several Latin American governments to acknowledge as valid—until the end of the war—the "emergency passport" which several thousand Jews had succeeded in obtaining. But even then there was no condemnation of the mass murder that was daily committed. The "extermination" according to plan to annihilate an entire people went on. Never were any of the persons excommunicated who committed millions of times that mortal sin. Thou Shalt Not Murder.

* * *

Forty-one years after the surrender of Germany, on April 13, 1986, speaking in the synagogue of Rome's Jews, Pope John Paul II referred to the Jewish people as "our dearly beloved brothers and in a certain way could be said our elder brothers." He deplored "the hatred, persecution and the display of anti-Semitism directed against the Jews any time and by anyone. I repeat by anyone" which was seen as reference to the Church itself.

Switzerland and the International Committee of the Red Cross

For more than 400 years, Switzerland has been priding itself—and has been known all over Europe—to be the center of humanitarianism and as the land that offers asylum to the religiously as well as to the politically persecuted. This role reaches back to the 16th and 17th century wars of the Reformation and Counter Reformation which pitted Catholics against Protestants. In the wake of the St. Bartholomew's day massacre in August 1573, French Protestant families, commonly referred to as Huguenots—2,360 according to official records—fled to Switzerland and were hospitably received. A second wave of religiously persecuted Protestants arrived in 1685 when the Edict of Nantes, which had granted religious freedom, was revoked. Even before the cancellation of the Edict, more Huguenot families had come to Switzerland. Between 1675 and 1700, an estimated 140,000 French Protestants came to the country that continued to prove herself a haven for the persecuted. Many of them stayed only temporarily and finally emigrated to Holland, Germany and England. Swiss history books stress the gain for that country as the newcomers brought new talent, and later famous Swiss were descendents of the Huguenots.

Towards the end of the 17th century, Switzerland again proved itself a haven for the religiously persecuted when it offered asylum to the Waldenses, a Protestant splinter group persecuted by Catholics as well as Protestants. In 1870, an entire French Army Corps fleeing from the Germans was given asylum. In 1887, France and Switzerland almost went to war when the French demanded the extradition of Napoleon III, and Switzerland refused to give up its position as a sanctuary for the politically threatened.

After the revolutions that swept Europe in 1848, many of the revolutionaries found asylum in Switzerland, notwithstanding the accusation that she thereby made herself a center of destructive revolution. In the second half of the 19th century, Switzerland provided a shelter for anarchists, communists and other left-wing extremists whose stay in Switzerland was only conditioned by the demand that during their stay they abstain from actions hostile to any other country. This tradition continued into the 20th century, and among the more famous revolutionaries who enjoyed the right of asylum in Switzerland were Lenin and his followers. During World War I, numerous deserters from both camps found safety in Switzerland, and when the war ended there were 25,894[37] foreign deserters and conscientious objectors registered there.

Yet right from the beginning of the severe persecution conducted by Germany against the Jews, Switzerland, as we reported in Chapter 1, became the originator of the "Jew passport" by suggesting that the Germans mark the passports of all Jews whether they traveled to Switzerland or not. It amounted to a sign of Cain, and thus made arrival at any border one of special treatment and hopelessness. The "J" in the passport came to constitute for hundreds of thousands a death sentence.

The anti-Semitic remarks made by the Swiss to the Germans in the course of the negotiations about Jewish refugees added to the shamefulness of this loss of humanitarianism. How was it possible that with a tradition of humanitarianism declared and practiced for 400 years, the representatives of Switzerland could become the initiators of the deadly "Jew passport?"

Many thousands, including a large percentage of families with their small children, trying to escape almost certain death, reached the supposedly rescuing Swiss border, where they were apprehended and handed over to the German slaughterers. Many who had made it past the border area to some location deeper inside the country were, when found, arrested and brought back to the German border. It was well known to the Swiss that those brought back were immediately arrested by the Germans. Men were separated from their wives and children. They were all kept in jail until they could be placed on the next train to an annihilation camp.

To give the reader an idea of what such "Zurueckweisung" (return order) meant, let us cite a case typical of thousands of others.

On August 24, 1942, Herman Boeschenstein, who headed the Berne office of the prestigious Basler *National Zeitung* filed the following report with his newspaper:

> The caretaker of the Jewish cemetery
> in Berne discovered among the grave-
> stones one early morning a couple

that had spent the night there. Husband and wife, both young, they were Belgians of Jewish origin who had been secretly slipped over the Swiss border and brought to Berne after a dramatic escape from Belgium and through occupied France, in order to avoid deportation to the east. In Berne, they went immediately to the Belgian Embassy, which gave them money and directed them to the organization for refugee assistance. Afraid lest they find no effective help there they then spent the night in the Jewish cemetery. It was also to be their last night of freedom. The cemetery caretaker informed the refugee relief office, whose staff immediately took over the couple and, in the belief that this was the proper thing to do, notified the police without delay. The policemen who were completely sympathetic took them to the police station, with every evidence of good will, had to hold them until appropriate orders were received.

The orders from the Police Section were explicit: The two refugees were to be deported at once to the occupied territory from which they had come.

This launched a battle between Police Section officials and representatives of the refugee organization who, assisted by outstanding personalities outside the Jewish community, waged a last ditch fight to save the couple from eviction, inevitable separation and death.

... we must confine ourselves here to the painful statement that all efforts were unsuccessful and the Federal Police Section uttered its fateful word of command. The Berne police were authorized and ordered immediately to proceed to remove the couple...

Since then the refugee organization have had no further word of these two persons who were thrown back into the vast ocean of monstrous suffering. Are we to keep silent? Do the Swiss people approve of such practice?

The journalist, Mr. Boeschenstein repeated the accusation. The Jewish community investigated what had become of the couple, 19 and 21 years of age. They had been captured shortly after their "removal" from Swiss territory. The man was reported to have been shot on the spot, the girl deported.[38]

This experience must be multiplied by many thousands. There were thousands of cases in which those who believed that they had saved themselves by reaching the "saving" Swiss border—and often by having crossed it—were apprehended and handed to their assassins. The number of those unfortunate ones increased as the Final Solution advanced.

In 1942 there were, according to the Police reports, 1,056 such cases.[39] In 1943, the number of humans forced back into the power of the devouring Moloch tripled. It amounted to 3,344.[40]

In 1944, the figure of the previous year was topped by 642. The police reported 3,986 persons returned.[41] How could a country with Switzerland's glorious past of asylum to the persecuted act in such ways?

The most important posts regarding immigration were held in the United States by Mr. Breckinridge Long, a firm enemy of rescue actions, and in Canada by Mr. Blair, who had a comparably hostile attitude towards the refugees. Similarly, in Switzerland, the corresponding position was held by a man who was determined to prevent what he called "judaization" of Switzerland. Dr. Heinrich Rothmund was the Chief of the Swiss Federal Police, and this included being the chief of specifically the Alien Police, a force he had created. In 1936, two years prior to the great influx of refugees that followed the annexation of Austria, he reported on the naturalization procedures:

> Towards Jewish applicants the utmost reluctance is practiced *even if they were born and brought up in Switzerland*[42]... Intellectuals whose activities might extend their influence over their immediate or more distant environments, must be subject to much stricter requirements to assimilation than for instance an ordinary worker, who, as a rule, is very quickly made to adapt by the influence of his environment.[43]

Dr. Rothmund was a supporter of the nationalist Fatherland Front and, due to the power he wielded, its most important one.

Rothmund's claim that he acted to prevent "judaization" of Switzerland should be seen in connection with the relevant statistics. They show that in 1910, the Jews constituted 4.9% of the population and that figure had by 1950 been reduced to 4%. Even prior to the war a formidable percentage of that small number of Jewish residents of Switzerland were foreigners, as it was quite common among well-to-do European Jews to retire to Switzerland. Here are the relevant figures:[44]

Year	% of Jews	Total	Swiss Citizens	Foreigners
1910	4.9	18,462	6,275	12,187
1920	5.4	20,979	9,428	11,551
1930	4.4	17,973	9,803	8,170
1941	4.6	19,429	10,279	9,150
1950	4.0	19,048	10,753	8,313

While the Federal Office that dealt with immigration was headed by a person whose attitude towards rescue was comparable to his colleagues in the United States and Canada, Dr. Rothmund's position was more difficult to maintain than the one of either Mr. Breckinridge Long or of Mr. Blair. We have reported in preceding chapters that the mood of the population in the United States as well as in Canada supported an exclusionary policy. This was not so in Switzerland. The press, as well as interpellation in Parliament, often criticized the harsh measures practiced by the Alien Police and by the Justice and Police Department. Switzerland is a Federal republic with its cantons, each of which was similar in its constitutional position to a state in the United States. Several of the cantons were particularly dissatisfied with the severity of the Federal Government's immigration policy and especially with the "Ruecksendungen," the forcing back to Germany of those who had succeeded in reaching the Swiss border. Yet Rothmund was firmly entrenched. While the refugee issue was not of the utmost importance for those who made the inquiries in the parliament or who otherwise protested, it was for Rothmund and his allies in the Fatherland Front. He, and particularly Federal counselman Eduard von Steiger, his associate in the endeavor to keep as many refugees as possible on the other side of the border, used the following argument to defend their measures. "If we let too many refugees in, we Swiss will not have enough to eat as we have no access to the sea and are surrounded by warring nations who themselves have problems in assuring for their own use sufficient food." Although this argument could carry little weight prior to the war, it was used in the period right after the German annexation of Austria in March 1938 to the outbreak of war in September 1939. It hit home with many who felt quite uncomfortable to see the right of asylum—of which the Swiss were so proud—so grossly violated. To counter their critics, the exclusionists used a sophisticated and, for the most part, confusing argument. The asylum policy of Switzerland had always been applied to the politically as well as to the religiously persecuted. The Jews, that argument claimed, were neither. They were not religiously persecuted as many had not or hardly at all practiced their religion. And, since, according to the same argument, the great majority had not been politically active, they were not political refugees. They were "racially" persecuted, a special category that had not been protected by the Swiss asylum principle. To claim that the Jews were not political refugees was of course absurd. The elimination of Jews was a major principle of German politics. This limitation of the concept of "political refugee" confounded many of those who did not want the traditional principle of asylum violated. Often the border guards, in disregard of the exhortations by the Federal police, did not return those who tried to save their lives but let them slip through. For this reason, the Police Section had to issue repeatedly the order to turn back all those people who were unable to present proper papers. The following is a timetable of orders to the authorities on the border.

1938

April 8. The Federal Justice and Police Department urged the cantons to be extremely cautious in decisions to admit refugees.

August 18. The Federal Council (Federal government of the Swiss Confederation) issued an order to seal all borders. *Refugees who have no visa must be sent back without exception.*[45] Swiss who had the chance to see the tragic scenes which the orders to be sent back created, protested the cruelty that order constituted.

September 7. The Police Section issues new orders to the border authorities: "Emigrants holding German passports are to be turned back. Whether the persons are emigrants is to be determined as much as possible by the border police."[46] Those carrying German passports were most probably Jews. They must be sent back and entry to this effect must be entered in the passport. Note the viciousness of entering in the passport that this person was already sent back by Switzerland. If he then tried for example the Dutch or Belgian border, this note in the passport just invited still another rejection. The numerous tragic happenings at the borders which this order caused—no exception, watch out particularly for Jews, and the obligatory entry in the passport—created much comment in the press, and on December 7, a debate in the Parliament ensued.

1939

September 19. In the Parliament again there was severe criticism of the Police Department's refugee policy. But Dr. Rothmund and the

Fatherland Front had plotted the campaign well. Their policy won out. The argument that "we might ourselves not have enough to eat" proved too powerful to be overcome. Many Swiss remained in opposition to the Government's refugee policy as they could not see their country so grossly deviating from its tradition of providing a haven for the persecuted. The Police Section, supported by the Fatherland Front, countered such feelings by stressing that refugees would be covered by the asylum principle only if they were personally involved in political activities and were persecuted for that reason.

October 17. The Federal Council, in accepting the above definition, decreed that, with the exception of deserters and political fugitives, all foreigners who entered Switzerland illegally be immediately expelled to the countries from which they came. Definition of "political refugee" was stressed.

The number of cases in which border guards could not make themselves enforce the tragedies which they had to witness grew. More refugees arrived illegally in the larger cities where they expected it would be easier to remain unnoticed.

1940

June 18. The Federal Justice and Police Department instructed the cantonal police departments that all civilian refugees were to be turned back, with the exception of invalids and women and children up to the age of 16.

June 19. As France collapsed under the German onslaught, the French 45th Corps, including a Polish division, crossed into Switzerland to avoid becoming prisoners of war in Germany. To the end of the month more than 40,000 French military personnel—of course without visas—and close to 7,500 French civilians entered Switzerland. But by the end of July, most of them had returned to France.

1942

August 4. The country seemed divided in its attitude towards admission of refugees, and the Federal Council clarified that it was fully aware that refusal of admittance was equivalent to a death sentence. All orders regarding the admissions must be followed "even if the foreigners thereby affected may incur the gravest perils (danger to life and limb)."[47]

August 13. As the Germans were rounding up all Jews in France for deportation and annihilation, a new wave of fugitives arrived at the Swiss border. Again there were cases of guards who found themselves unable to enforce the demanded cruelty and Dr. Rothmund therefore issued orders which repeated that all civilian refugees must be returned right at the border.

August 28. Demonstrating that the Federal Government's orders of August 13 were fully accepted on the canton level the Police Commissioners' Conference in Lausanne, in which each canton was represented, expressed its approval of the Federal Government's guidelines of August 4 and 13 and urged strict adherence to them.

September 26. As some refugees successfully convinced the guards that they were political refugees, the Federal Police Section issued by telephone still another clarification: "Under current practice, refugees on the ground of race alone are not political refugees."[48]

October 3. Von Steiger asked for military support in handling the border controls. Six days later the army erected barbed wire emplacements on border points that had been used for unauthorized entries.

November. The Fatherland Front publicized its exclusionary demands in a lengthy statement that contains several anti-Semitic passages.

December 29. The Federal Police Section instructed the border guards in an even more stringent move that "in every case care must be taken that the refugees who must be turned back receive no opportunity to communicate directly or indirectly (specifically by telephone) with... anyone."[49]

1944

As the war neared its end, with the Germans in full retreat in the East and with the Allies in the West having successfully invaded Normandy, Switzerland tried to establish an alibi. So did the Germans and this combination, together with cleverly conducted negotiations, led to a last minute liberation and admission to Switzerland of thousands of Jews who would have almost certainly otherwise perished.

July 9. The stringent order of December 29, 1942 which since had governed the Swiss admission procedures, was rescinded. While the position that Jews were not political prisoners was formally maintained, the new order of the Police Section informed the Swiss border guards that "for the present refugees whose lives are actually in danger for political *or other reasons*[50] and who have no alternative but flight into Switzerland in order to escape this danger" were to be admitted.[51]

August 21. Three hundred eighteen Hungarian Jews arrived from Bergen Belsen in Switzerland and were admitted without complicated formalities. This was a result of negotiations conducted by Saly Mayer, the head of the Swiss Jewish community with the SS contact man Kurt Becher.

August 25. Completing the turnabout, Dr. Rothmund asked the Swiss embassy in Berlin to protest the deportations. He also announced that Switzerland was ready to admit more Jews.

November. By that time, Paris had been liberated and the Americans were advancing into Germany, while Russian troops were outside Budapest. Hitler issued an order that no Jews must survive German retreat. Before the surrender of any concentration camp all Jews had to be killed.

The Union of Orthodox Rabbis in New York had two most efficient representatives in Switzerland, Isaac and Recha Sternbuch whose home town was St. Gallen. As early as 1939, the two with the aid of fictitious visas, had achieved the release of several hundred Jews from Dachau and aided by the humane police chief of St. Gallen, Paul Grueninger, had smuggled them into Switzerland. They also had been active in obtaining life-saving Paraguayan passports for Jews whose lives were saved by this device. They had later joined forces with Dr. Rueben Hecht, the European representa-

218

tive of the Irgun, the Jewish underground organization in Palestine. Dr. Hecht, an imaginative, brilliant young man, was a native and citizen of Switzerland. This helped him to understand the Swiss and to anticipate their actions. In addition, the fact that he came from a well-known Swiss family opened doors for him which others might have found shut. He was not hampered by thinking in conventional terms only, and his working with the Sternbuch couple created a group which saw possibilities—and followed them up—that were not seen by others. In 1944, the Sternbuch-Hecht group developed a plan that was anathema to the Jewish establishment.

Jean Maria Musy, a former President of the Federal Counsel, was a Fatherland Front man, a hardliner. He had attended several of the annual party gatherings at Nuremburg and was sometimes referred to as the Swiss Quisling. Musy was rumored to be a friend of Heinrich Himmler, and the leaders of Swiss Jewry kept away from him. The Sternbuch couple and Dr. Hecht figured that Musy's position made him a man through whom the Germans could be approached. Musy, who wanted his reputation restored, was contacted by them, and he was found ready to appeal to Himmler, whom he described as a casual acquaintance. He agreed to go to Berlin and speak with Himmler regarding the release of Recha Sternbuch's two brothers and to bring up the issue of release of *all* Jews which at that late date (October 1944) was obviously in the interest of Himmler and other Germans who wanted to establish an alibi.

November 2. Musy went to Germany and the two met in Himmler's personal railroad car in Silesia. In a two-hour conversation, he convinced his host that the previous demand for trucks could not be met but that cash compensation should be substituted for it. The two-hour meeting ended with Himmler agreeing to have all 600,000 Jews who, according to him, were in German camps, released against a not yet determined sum of foreign currency to be given to the German Red Cross for medical supplies and aid to German victims of Allied bombings. Hitler's orders stood in the way of such a release, but Himmler thought he could take care of that. Himmler demanded that as part of the deal American and British newspapers comment favorably on his "change of mind." In the middle of February 1945, this time in a hotel in the Black Forest, a second meeting between Musy and Himmler ended with the latter's order to release first 1,699. It was to be followed by another group of 1,600, once the favorable action in Allied papers was proven. After this there should be mass releases with the amount of payment to be settled with Himmler's representative in that matter, Walter Schellenberg, a high SS official.

December 6. 1,355 Orthodox Jews arrive in Basel, Switzerland. Both Saly Mayer and, pointing to the Musy-Himmler meetings, the Sternbuch group, claim credit. Probably the German decision was reached under the influence of both the Mayer-Becher and the Musy-Himmler negotiations. The Swiss admitted the 1,355 without causing any problems.

1945

February 5. Eichmann was ordered from Hungary to Germany to meet Himmler. Eichmann had commanded the evacuation of Jews in camps that were threatened by the Allies. He had ordered the inmates to march often hundreds of miles to various camps in Germany. Whoever fell behind on those marches, and many of the near-skeletons did, was killed. He was now ordered by Himmler to stop these death marches.

As a result of the Musy-Himmler agreement, a train with 1,210 Jews, including 58 children freed from the Theresienstadt camp, arrived in Switzerland. The Jews in the train experienced a comfort that increased the feeling that the ride was a dream. No cattle car, they came in regular third class passenger carriages, had been well fed, and were given vitamins.

Dr. Hecht met with Swiss Conferderate President Eduard von Steiger and obtained assurance of admission to Switzerland of any Jew who arrives at the Swiss border. Hecht visited the Swiss press to assure a positive attitude towards Steiger's decision.

May 9. Germany formally surrenders unconditionally.

These releases into Switzerland point out what the British and the Americans did by their earlier refusals to even negotiate about the German offer to release a million Jews.

The cruelty of the Swiss attitude of "fighting judaization" is expressed in figures not only by the numbers of Jews living in Switzerland before the Nazis, formally the National Socialist Workers Party, were put into power (a figure of between 4.4% and 5.4% of the population) but also by looking at the figures of the Jewish refugees admitted.

At the beginning of May 1945, in the days immediately preceding the German surrender, the total number of reported refugees in Switzerland amounted to 115,000.[52] There may have been a small number hidden by acquaintances whose presence was unknown to the authorities. No deportations had occurred for a year.[53] The total number of persons who during the war at one time or the other had sought protection in Switzerland was 295,381.[54] This included many Frenchmen and Italians who had stayed for a short time only. Of them:

103,869 were military personnel, escaped prisoners of war, deserters, soldiers wounded near the border who had come for medical treatment.

55,018 civilian refugees.

9,909 "emigrants," those who arrived seeking asylum prior to October 1939.

59,785 children who mostly had come from the neighboring region to escape warfare or who had entered to receive better food. Most of those children had been brought in by the Swiss Red Cross or other organized charitable groups and stayed for a limited time.

251 "political refugees."

66,549 border population. Residents of the areas bordering Switzerland who at one time or another had crossed over, in general, to avoid the perils of warfare. All of them returned home after a short stay.

In the beginning, most refugees were Jews. Later, as it became known among the Jews that Switzerland returned refugees to the Germans, and as more and more Jews were in concentration camps or already deported, the majority of those seeking asylum were no longer Jewish.

Of the 9,909 "emigrants," 6,654 were Jewish. Of 55,018 classified as "civilians" 21,858 were Jewish. Thus, although nobody's life was so endangered as the lives of Jews, many more non-Jews had been admitted than Jews.[55]

To gain an overall perspective: in the years of the Holocaust, Switzerland had a population of roughly 6,000,000. The 115,000 refugees who were in her borders at the time of the German collapse constituted less than 2% of her population. The 28,512 Jews amounted to less than half of 1% of the Swiss population.

And it was much easier to be admitted if one was not a Jew, thus not in an obvious danger of being murdered. And whether somebody was Jewish or not was clearly marked on his passport—if he had any—with a large red "J" and with the addition of the name Israel to his given name, Sarah if one was female.

* * *

The International Committee of the Red Cross (ICRC) is discussed here together with Switzerland because in its origin, in the composition of its leadership, and in the policies it follows it is as Swiss as Switzerland itself. The same is true of the direction of its actions during the Holocaust.

The Red Cross was founded by a Swiss, Henry Dunant, who after the battle of Solferino in 1861 was deeply moved by the sufferings to which the wounded and sick were exposed, particularly when they had fallen into enemy hands. Dunant wrote a book entitled *Un Souvenir de Solferino* which vividly describes the misery of those soldiers who were often left unattended. Dunant's book aroused all over Europe the strong feeling that the caring for the victims of warfare should be internationally supervised and handled by a neutral organization. The Swiss took a leading role in calling a conference to act upon this issue and in 1864 delegates from sixteen countries met in Geneva. This meeting resulted in the founding of the International Red Cross. Regional Red Cross organizations were soon established.

There were and still are several reasons which caused the International Red Cross to be dominated by the Swiss. They were the founders; the International Committee of the Red Cross was—and continues—to have its headquarters in Geneva; all members of its board are Swiss citizens. The Swiss dominance is symbolized by the fact that the flag of the Red Cross is almost identical with the flag of Switzerland. The only difference is the reversal of colors. The Swiss flag shows a white cross in a red field, the Red Cross flag and emblem shows a red cross in a white field.

For all these reasons, we cannot be surprised when we notice that the International Committee of the Red Cross, as far as the persecution of Jews and the Holocaust are concerned, followed the philosophy practiced by the Swiss government.

In the course of time, the ICRC widened the scope of its activities. In 1929, it called a conference which was to specify the duties of warring nations to their prisoners of war. The Geneva Convention of 1929 remains to this day the internationally recognized Magna Carta of the rights of prisoners of war.

Due to its lofty aims, the Red Cross rose during World War I to even higher esteem as a neutral power which protects in emergency situations the rights of the underdog. By 1938, the time the persecution of Jews by Germany assumed harsh forms, the moral power of the Red Cross had been well established. This moral power, however, was not put to use. This was not by neglect of the issue. The ICRC was repeatedly asked, by Jewish organizations as well as by the American War Refugee Board to use its prestigious position for help. But it refused. The reason: It might be interpreted by the Germans as lack of "neutrality." All over the world, the International Red Cross was viewed as *the* protector of prisoners, as the standard bearer of humanitarianism who would come to the aid of those in need whether this need was the result of war or of inner strife or of natural catastrophes like floods or earthquakes.

The original Geneva Convention of 1929 had covered military personnel only. It was planned to include protection of civilians but time was too short for a formal inclusion. The warring countries however had informally decided to extend ICRC functions to include civilians who had been caught by war in enemy territory. They were called "civilian internees." The ICRC assumed that role and practised it very actively. For all those in need, even for those who were not interned, like the Greek civilian population and the Yugoslavians, the ICRC organized a large scale shipment of food when the peoples were starving. Yes, the International Red Cross represented by the ICRC was quite active on behalf of those in need during World War II. They were of invaluable help to all. Except for Jews.

The main functions of the ICRC were inspecting camps in which the prisoners were held, checking on accommodations, food, general treatment, and making the captors aware of it if the ICRC found that the obligations which the countries had taken upon themselves were not fulfilled.

The ICRC had offered such services for the Jews, too, but the Germans refused to have them included in the category of those to be served. The Jews, according to the Germans, were not civilian internees; they were common criminals, stateless, and thereby excluded from the category to be helped.

The ICRC did not protest such exclusion of those who needed its help most. It de facto accepted the German version of the cause for the treatment of Jews.

Red Cross officials insisted that they could not force the Germans to accept its services. There was no firm protest, no threat not to serve the German prisoners and interned civilians if the reciprocity was not granted to all those who were held captive. The ICRC was afraid to make demands of the Germans, but they needed the ICRC just as the ICRC needed the cooperation of the Germans.

Even if one accepts the ICRC version that it could not force acceptance of services for Jews, too, there were other ways in which this humanitarian institution could and should have acted. No institution with the exception of the Vatican was as well informed about what was going on. The ICRC officials moved in German-held territories with more freedom than any other group or organization. The moral power they represented should have caused them to cry out loudly and publicly in protest and condemnation of the worst crime history has known. But requests to condemn the treatment of the Jews, coming from Jewish groups, were rejected. Condemnation of the mass murders by such a prestigious body as the ICRC would have shown the Germans that somebody cared; it would have made many a German or henchman from a satellite country think over what he was doing. It would also have influenced those in the Allied camp who were either uninvolved or were active in supporting the supply line for the death camps.

Two female board members moved that an energetic protest be launched with the Germans against excluding Jews from ICRC services and the whole matter be made public. But the two were the only ones who voted for that motion. The board decided on a conspiracy of silence.

The brutal breaking of the rules of the Geneva International Convention was most evident in the case of Jewish Prisoners of War. Although both Poland and Germany were signatories to that convention which specifically forbids segregation by ethnic or religious differentiation, this is the story of the Jews who in the war between Germany and Poland had served in the Polish army: The Germans took in September 1939, 420,000 Polish soldiers as Prisoners of War. Of them, 61,000 were Jews, 15%. The enlisted men who were Jews were from the beginning separated from the others and assembled in separate camps where the food, rations as well as general conditions were far below those of their Christian fellow soldiers. In one of these camps, they were forced to wear a special triangle on their back. Early in 1940, they were "released." They had to turn in their uniforms and had thereby become "common Jews." As such, they were liable to persecution and deportation. The Germans had broken their pledge of the 1929 Geneva Convention to protect Prisoners of War. Some 700 Jewish POW's suffered a somewhat different fate. Early in 1941, they were brought to Lublin and there ordered on a "death march." In the icy Polish winter, not equipped in any way for it, they were made to march through Piaski, then through Lubartow, just to march on. More and more fell behind or just collapsed. The German rearguard shot those who could not make it any more.

In Lublin was a camp for Jewish Prisoners of War. Those who had survived the conditions there were "liquidated" in November 1943. Jewish officers who had become POW's stayed longer with their Polish comrades, but in some of those officers' camps separate ghettos were installed for the Jews. Unpredictable as to when it would happen, from time to time Jewish officers were taken from the camp and "liquidated."

It has not been established with certainty whether the ICRC knew what was happening to those POW's who were Jewish. If they did not, it was due to their not being concerned with the fate of the Jews. Two years after the end of the war, the ICRC published a brochure *Inter Arma-Charitas*. A year later in 1948, the ICRC published a 3-volume work reporting in much detail its activities during that period. It defends the ICRC record and points out many undertakings by the ICRC on behalf of Jews. A major part of this attempt to clear itself deals with the aid given to the Jews of Hungary, especially an urgent appeal to Hungary's ruler Miklos Horthy to stop the deportations. He did, but was later overthrown, and the deportations started again. Let us look at the dates of the ICRC actions. Hitler had been in power since 1933. As long as the Germans seemed to be winning the war, we see even in the ICRC's own account how little it did for those who were more than anybody else in need of rescue. Once the Germans, before so victorious, were in retreat after the Stalingrad debacle, all those who had previously kept away from rescuing actions became busy, establishing an alibi. But even then the ICRC limped behind. Let us look at action regarding Hungary. The relevant dates tell the story of the involvement of the ICRC. When the Jewish organizations early in 1944 learned that Eichmann had ordered Hungarian Jews to assembly places and that a blitz deportation was planned, they appealed to the ICRC to send a special envoy to Hungary and to intervene directly with the Hungarian government. The request was rejected. By June 17, 1944, 326,000 Jews, almost one-half of Hungary's 800,000 had been deported to Auschwitz.

The Pope wrote to Horthy on June 25 and again on June 30. King Gustav of Sweden wrote a letter to Horthy which was strongly formulated. The ICRC joined in appealing to Horthy on July 6th only. Max Huber, the ICRC representative relayed an appeal to Horthy. It urged him to take the steps necessary to refute the rumors and accusations "and to prevent the repetition of events which gave rise to such terrible rumors." Following this, the ICRC became quite active; at this very last stage, it provided real help to those to be deported and by following the death march from Budapest to Austria and aiding the marchers.

Some ICRC workers individually, just as a number of Catholic clerics, acted in the most unselfish, heroic way. But this was personal commitment, not action initiated by the institution to which they belonged.

Most of the Jews of Europe who ended up in the death camps were citizens of countries at war with Germany: Polish, French, Belgian and Dutch Jews, Czechoslovakians and Baltics. As they were civilians, the agreement to respect and to protect civilians under the enemy's rule applied to them. Firm ICRC condemnation of the mass murders and appeal to the German leadership, as well as to the Allied leaders, would have given, considering the great weight the ICRC carried, the entire Final Solution program a different slant. In fact if early action had been taken, the Wannsee decision might not have been made, and an appeal to the Allied leaders to discontinue the actual support of the annihilation plan would have broken the conspiracy of silence and have saved a good percentage of those who, with the moral power of the ICRC standing by, were massacred.

In summary, there can be no doubt that much of the catastrophe of the Holocaust could have been prevented had the ICRC lived up to its own standard.

[1] In the original King James version of 1638, the command reads THOU SHALT NOT MURDER, a formulation that even more sharply defines what so many were committing.

[2] As of December 31, 1939.

[3] Erhard Schlund Katholizismus und Vaterland, Munich 1923, 32-33 as quoted by Gunter Lewy, *Pius XII, the Jews and the German Catholic Church*, Commentary February 1964, p. 23.

[4] Gustav Grundlach, *Anti-Semitism in Lexicon fuer Theologie und Kirche* I 504, 1930 ed. by Bishop Michael Buchberger, as quoted by Lewy op. cit. p. 23.

[5] Emphasis added.

[6] Joseph Roth *Katholizismus und Judenfrage* Munich 1923 p. 5 as quoted by Lewy *The Catholic Church and Nazi Germany*, p. 272.

[7] Dr. Mayer Alfons Wild, ed. *Kann ein Katholik Nationalsozialist sein Augsburg 1930* p. 12, as quoted by Lewy, *The Catholic Church* op. cit. 271.

[8] Philipp Haeuser *Jud und Christ oder Wem gebuehrt die Weltherrschaft*, Regensburg 1923 p. 5 as quoted by Lewy, *The Catholic Church* op. cit p. 272.

[9] National Archive's Microcopy 580 rolls 40 and 42. Also correspondence Himmler-Pohl re Groeber, folders 243 I and 245 as quoted by Lewy, *Catholic Church* op. cit. 45-46 n. 72 355.

[10] Monsignor Georg Schreiber Zwischen Demokratie und Diktatur 1949 p. 22 n. 10 as quoted by Lewy *The Catholic Church* op. cit. p. 103 n. 34 p. 364.

[11] *Der Deutsche Weg* July 28, 1934, reprinted in Deutsche Briefe no. 97 July 31, 1936 p. 6 as quoted by Lewy, *The Catholic Church* op. cit p. 172 no. 90 p. 376.

[12] Amtsblatt fuer die Erzdioezese Freiburg no. 3 February 8, 1939 p. 15 as quoted by Lewy, *Pius XII* op. cit. p. 24 no. 11.

[13] Theodor Bogler *OSB Der Glaube von gestern und heute* Cologne 1939 p. 150 as quoted by Lewy, *Pius XII* op. cit. 25 n. 22 p. 34.

[14] Typical of his academic style Bishop Dr. Hudal formulates this as follows: "Certain extraordinary measures for members of the Jewish ethnic group should not be seriously objected to even if such measures do not comply with what one would expect from a modern state based upon the principle of law." Hudal Alois *Die Grundlagen des Nationlsozialismus* Leipzig and Vienna 1937, p: 88.

[15] Sermon of December 17, 1933 in Michael Faulhaber, *Judaism, Christianity and Germany* trans. George D. Smith, London p. 68, 69 as quoted by Lapide op. cit. 106 and Lewy *Pius XII* op. cit. p. 24.

[16] As quoted by Pinchas Lapide *Three Popes and the Jews*, New York, 1967 p. 253.

[17] As quoted by Lapide, op. cit. p. 213.

[18] As quoted by Lapide, op. cit. p. 191.

[19] Emile Maurice Guerry, *L'Eglise Catholique en France sous L'Occupation* (Paris 1947) pp. 33-65.

[20] Jules Gerrard Saliege *Fuerchtet Euch nicht: Hirtenbriefe und Ansprachen* (Offenberg 1949) pp. 150-51.

[21] Lapide, op. cit. p. 191.

[22] Victor Hooft ed. *Hollaendische Kirchendokumente* (Zollikon Zurich, 1944) pp. 58-60 as quoted by Lewy, *The Catholic Church* 398 n. 106.

[23] Leclef, ed. *Le Cardinal van Roey et. l'occupation Allemande en Belgique* as cited by Lewy, *The Catholic Church* p. 398 n. 108.

[24] Abetz to the German Foreign Ministry, August 28, 1942, PA Bonn, Staatssekretaer, Vatican, Vol 4, as quoted by Lewy, *The Catholic Church*, op. cit. p. 298.

[25] As cited by Lewy, *The Catholic Church*, op. cit. 248.

[26] Robert Katz, interview with Moellhausen, 134-139.

[27] Alexander Ramati, as told by Padre Rufino Niccacci.

[28] L. Osservatore Romano, October 25-26, 1943.

[29] As quoted in a report to the Swiss government by Ludwig., op. cit. p. 241.

[30] Emphasis added.

[31] Civita Catolica no. 2024, quoted in Dan Carpi *The Catholic Church and Italian Jews Under the Fascists*, Yad Vashem Studies IV 1960 51, 52 as quoted by Lewy *The Catholic Church* 297 and 399 n. 120, 121.

[32] Ibid.

[33] Carsten, *Koelneraktenstuecke* doc. 227, p. 280 as quoted by Lewy, *The Catholic Church*, op. cit. p. 299.

[34] As reported in the diary of Count Ciano, Italy's foreign minister and son-in-law of Mussolini's, Diary entry of December 24, 1942, p. 538.

[35] Osborn to Foreign Office, December 31, 1942 VAT vol. 9, p. 71 as quoted by Wasserstein, op. cit. p. 175.

[36] Harrison memo November 20, 1942, Bern folder 6 RG 226 National Archives, as quoted by Penkower, op. cit. p. 327, n. 96.

[37] The Refugee Policy of Switzerland 1933-45, Official Report by Professor Dr. Carl Ludwig, commissioned by the government of Switzerland, p. 21.

[38] As reported by Alfred A. Haesler in *The Life Boat is Full*, p. 5.

[39] The Refugee Policy of Switzerland 1933-45, Official Report by Professor Dr. Carl Ludwig, op. cit. p. 245.

[40] Ibid., p. 271.

[41] Ibid., p. 309.

[42] Emphasis added.

[43] Special publication at 50th anniversary of Swiss Jewish communities 1954, pp. 207ff as quoted by Haesler op. cit. p. 7.

[44] Report of the Swiss Government to the Swiss Parliament ZU 7347 *Die Fluechtingspolitik der Schweiz seit 1933 bis zur Gegenwart*, p. 60.

[45] Alfred A. Haesler, op. cit. p. 322. Emphasis added.

[46] Ibid., p. 323.

[47] Alfred Haesler, op. cit. p. 326.

[48] Ibid., p. 327.

[49] Ibid.

[50] Emphasis added.

[51] For details regarding the late-hour rescue to Switzerland, see The *Holocaust* ed. John Mendelsohn, Vol 16. An excellently clarifying introduction by Sybil Milton helps to understand the complex and often confusing situation. See also Penkower, op. cit. pp. 253ff.

[52] Alfred Haesler, op. cit., p. 331.

[53] Ibid., p. 331.

[54] Ibid., p. 332.

[55] Data from official report to the government, Ludwig op. cit. p. 318.

Chapter 9
CAN IT HAPPEN AGAIN?
Epilogue

To answer the question of whether it could happen again, we have to ask and to understand where "it" came from. And to understand fully where it came from, we must recognize where the past was heading. The two form a continuum which, to be truly comprehended, should be viewed from both sides.

In the mid-eighties of this century, the decision-makers of the world found the assumption that the world was essentially ruled by the two superpowers to be seriously challenged. A third—apparently major—force had shown up on the stage of world events. It had grown slowly but steadily into a disturbing defiance of the ways in which civilization moved. Although it had previously exhibited its symptoms, acts of unpredictable terroristic violence—and had done it often and dramatically—not until the middle of the eighties was it recognized as a serious threat to the existing social fibre of humanity. Blatantly defying values and rules which had developed during the course of many centuries, international terrorism challenged the hegemony of the world's ruling powers as it vied for a superpower role in the determination of international politics.

Its force was rooted in the ruthlessness and brutality of its methods which had compelled several legitimate governments to act as ordered by the terrorists.

It was furthermore strengthened by the sensitive interdependence of the cultures of this world. Society has become complex and intricate, a precarious balance keeps it working, and a disturbance in one spot may involve happenings far away. Most of all man knows that mankind's survival depends on the avoidance of nuclear warfare. The superpowers developed and practice a theory that the way to avoid the catastrophe is to maintain a balance of terror. Either side must know that a first strike could and would be answered with a counterattack which would leave no victors. To maintain this delicate balance, any development which includes a large amount of unpredictability must be avoided.

Here now enters international terrorism with the threat of creating alarming disturbances if its blackmailing demands are not met. Thus, while originally a threat only to those against whom it was specifically directed, it has grown into a risk even to the major powers, notwithstanding that one of them, the Soviet Union, endeavors to use it for its own special purposes.

Just as the actions of the German terrorists in the Thirties culminated in the Holocaust and in World War II, so now, in the later part of the century the terrorist's aggression has swelled from small, apparently minor acts into a global network of blackmail and fear. In the beginning most of those first on the terrorists' hostages list tried to save themselves by appeasement. "Spare me. If you must do it, do it to the others, and we will secretly support you." Yet the appeasers soon became targets themselves and then had to face an enemy which had grown stronger by annexations and by the image of invincibility. In a similar way, the small as well as the major powers are trying nowadays to save themselves by making some kind of a "deal" with the terrorists. And to varying degrees all countries are anxious to avoid anything that could interfere with the carefully watched balance of terror and bring closer the possibility of nuclear conflict. But the fanatics have much less to lose, and their threat to the existing order is therefore a very real one. Inclination to accommodate them is therefore ever present.

Fifty years ago the true German aim was not occupation of the Rhineland, not Austria nor the Sudeten and not the whole of Czechoslovakia. Not the Danzig corridor either. Those were just interim positions on the way to the true German goal—world domination—to which they felt entitled—seeing themselves as the master race. Similarly, what the Arabs call the West Bank and what Jews refer to as the ancient Jewish provinces of Judaea and Samaria is not the goal of Arab political striving. There are twenty-one Arab states, and to create a twenty-second one, a ministate on the narrow strip between Jordan and Israel, is not the purpose of their proclaimed demand. Nor is it the entirety of Israel. Just as half a century before the real German aim was world domination, so the real Arab objective is the recreation of the Arab empire, won in the seventh century and lost in the fifteenth, stretching from India to the Atlantic

Ocean. They strive for even more—an Islamic empire. It would include all countries inhabited by a substantial percentage of Muslims, large parts of Africa and of Southeast Asia. As those who gave Islam to the world, the Arab leaders see as their right and their destiny to rule them directly or by informal control.

In such a scheme, the Jewish state represents the advance post of Western civilization and is therefore target number one. In contrast to the Germans of the thirties and forties, the Arabs do not constitute a monolithic force but are weakened by rivalries among themselves. Terrorism is used to make up for the lack of power. The idea of controlling the world is gaining widespread support among the Arabs. According to the Muslim view, mankind is divided into the House of Islam (Dar al-Islam) and the House of War (Dar al-Harb). All the peoples and countries that are not under Islamic law belong to the Dar al-Harb. It is a religious duty to strive for a world that will accept Islam or submit to it. This ideology sees Christians as well as Jews, the "People of the Covenant", as inferior. They are called "Dhimmi" who have no right or any power, a point which is particularly stressed by the fundamentalists. According to the Koranic Sura, "Power belongs to Allah, his Apostle and believers." Striving for such a goal is the duty of every Muslim. The Panmuslims are striving for one political unit reaching from Jakarta to Rabat, ruled by the concept of *ummah*, the spiritual and political commonwealth of believers.

All this must be considered when one tries to answer the question whether what happened during the Holocaust could happen again. Hitler did not just fall down from the sky, nor did he suddenly arise from hell. And the actions against the Jews did not start from one day to the next. What were the circumstances that brought this man and his cohorts to the helm? The answer resulting from the study of the German preparations for the Holocaust and the comparison with what is happening today is frightening.

Another Holocaust is not only possible, it is being systematically prepared and in its preparation the means used by the Germans are being applied again, as if the Hitler era were still upon us. In a way, it still is. The intent of a "Final Solution," in fact concrete planning for it, did not stop with the collapse of Germany. It is only that the protagonists changed. And that the geographical target switched from Europe where there is only a remnant of Jews left, to Israel and its almost three and a half million Jews.

While fifty years ago, Germany, one country, planned the total destruction of Jewry, it is now an entire block of nations, those in the Arab League, which have solemnly vowed and have instituted measures to bring about the genocide. As Hitler vowed to annihilate the Jews in *Mein Kampf* and on numerous other occasions, so today, the Arabs call openly for the destruction of Israel and the annihilation of its Jews.

And precisely like half a century ago, the world acts as if it does not hear or know. Should Israel fall under one of the periodic Soviet-supported onslaughts, the horror committed there would quite possibly be used by the USSR to claim a Jewish revolt in their land. Some unrest by Jews in the Soviet Union in support of their brothers being tortured and slain in Israel could actually occur. Minor incidents would be exaggerated by the Soviets and taken as an excuse for a very major action. The two and a half million Jews in the USSR could be rounded up and disappear in the vast region of the Soviet Union's northeast, as happened to millions of others. With the victims in Israel, this would amount to six million, a figure that rouses most terrifying associations.

While it is relatively easy to visualize the Arabs, should they overcome the Israeli defenses, celebrating their victory by acting the way they have promised, it may be much harder to assume that the USSR would engage overtly in a genocidal activity. Certainly they would not act in the same open, triumphant way as victorious Arabs. But cultural genocide is now already being practiced by the Soviet Union against its Jews. The USSR is now trying to put an inglorious end to a history which reaches back four thousand years. It does so by interdicting any activity that would strengthen Jewish identification. The study of Jewish history, the teaching of the Hebrew language and other Jewish cultural activities are punished by prison or Gulag sentences of many years. Attacks of undisguised anti-Semitism occur in all the media so regularly that there can be no doubt of their being centrally directed. With their persistent and systematic assault, the Soviets have of course an aim in mind. Total disappearance of Jews from the Soviet scene might well be decided upon if an opportune moment develops.

As a by-product, it might even bring goodwill to the Soviets from their large Moslem population.

The invasion of Hungary in 1956, of Czechoslovakia in 1968, and of Afganistan in 1983 show that the USSR is ready to take any criticism in stride if it considers an action to be in its interest. Being the closed society it is, the rounding up of Jews and their disappearance could easily be decided upon and carried out.

Is this mere alarmist speculation, or is it a fact? With Saudi Arabia in the forefront, the Arabs have repeatedly called for the destruction of the Jewish state. They have proclaimed the Jihad, Holy War, against Israel, the war which according to the Koran must end with the enemy's total annihilation. In this endeavor the Arabs are making use of the methods applied by the Germans during the Holocaust as well as by directions resulting from their employment of former SS officials. The Arabs' demands and actions are supported by the USSR, which trains tens of thousands of terrorists and provides the weaponry.

As we have stated before in this chapter, history must be viewed as a continuum. Such an unfortunate continuum regarding the Holocaust exists in the continuing Nazi-Arab connection. The influence of these two groups upon each other is mutual. Too little attention is being paid to the way in which the Arabs contributed to the effectiveness of the Final Solution program. Haj Amin el Husseini, head of the Supreme Muslim Council and Grand Mufti of Jerusalem, a venomous Jew-hater, had prior to the war organized Arab terrorism against the Jews in Palestine. From 1941 on, he spent much of his time shuttling between Berlin and Rome. He met in Berlin with Ernst von Weizsaecker, State Secretary in the German Foreign Office, with Himmler, and on November 28, 1941 with Hitler. In his meeting, the Mufti tried to strengthen the Fuehrer's decision to "exterminate" all Jews, and both agreed that the Germans would fight the Jews mercilessly, in all of Europe "and beyond." Interestingly, the Wannsee Conference took place less than two months later. The Mufti had also met with Eichmann and visited Auschwitz. In Rome, he was received by the Italian Foreign Minister, Count Ciano, and by Mussolini himself. In his meetings with the German officials, the Mufti stressed the need to wipe out as many Jews as possible and to finally revoke the designation of Palestine as a Jewish National Home. He proposed that after the German victory, an Arab state—under his leadership—be created that would consist of Syria, Iraq, Transjordan and the Western, Jewish part of Palestine. In return the Mufti promised Arab revolts against the British who were then predominant in these areas. One such serious revolt against the British occurred in April 1941. It was led by Rashid Ali, who had been in touch with Husseini all the time. Fighting in Iraq lasted several weeks; during that time Rashid Ali declared on behalf of Iraq, controlled by him at that time, war against Great Britain. The Iraq revolt was put down by the British. Anyhow, Husseini's prestige grew in the eyes of Hitler and Mussolini.

The Germans had now an additional reason for their Final Solution. It assured them, they were told, of the cooperation by the Arabs, an element quite important for them as they had few allies. When at one point Romania and Bulgaria appeared ready to release large numbers of Jews and when there seemed to exist a possibility that in such a case many would reach Palestine, frantic lobbying in Berlin by the Mufti ensued, and the offer was finally withdrawn. When a trickle of Jews reached neutral Turkey, the German Ambassador von Papen, was ordered at the Mufti's urging to protest any relaxation of the rules preventing such escapes. The Mufti had overestimated the Allies' readiness to save any Jews, and the release from the Balkans would not have worked anyhow. As Richard Kidston Law (Lord Coleraine) the Parliamentary Undersecretary for Foreign Affairs stated bluntly, the Allies by admitting these Jews "would be relieving Hitler of an obligation to take care of these useless people."[1]

When Germany collapsed, many Germans who had held high positions in the government fled to Arab countries, which had exhibited a pro-German attitude. Some of those Germans, mostly high-ranking SS officers, assumed Arab names, and many entered the police, and others the public relations service, in their new homes. They trained the Arabs in terrorism, propaganda and the German type of police work. And they brought with them the unchanged desire to annihilate all Jews. Reported among these were:

Alois Moser SS Gruppenfuhrer (Major General). He became an advisor to the Egyptian government on anti-Israel activities. General Moser had been one of the leading SS officers in the Ukraine and had organized there massacres of Jews.

Erich Alten, Chief of the Gestapo's Jewish Department in Galicia, Poland, became supervisor of training an Egyptian "Army of Liberation," which was to invade Israel and to institute there the "Final Solution" program.

SS Standartenfuehrer (Colonel) Leopold Gleim, was head of the Gestapo in Poland. He became supervisor of the Egyptian Secret

Police and was in charge of a detention camp in the Western desert to which political prisoners were committed. Gleim was also put in control of Egyptian Jews.

Dr. Heinrich Willermann, camp physician at Dachau where he conducted sterilization, cold water and poisoning "experiments," was put in charge of the Egyptian Samara camp for political prisoners. Escaped inmates reported that he continued his "experiments" there.

SS Brigadefuehrer (Brigardier General) Oscar Dierlewanger. In Germany head of the infamous Brigade Dierlewanger which in Russia conducted punishment actions against the partisans and massacres of Jews. Gamal Abdal Nasser trusted him so much that he appointed Dierlewanger head of his bodyguard. This way Nasser could be assured that this position was held by someone removed from inter-Arab hatreds and politics. By his regular contact with Nasser, the SS General had easy access to the man who was then the central figure in anti-Israel planning.

Alois Brunner, Eichmann's right-hand man. Directly responsible for the murder of 125,000 Jews. A French court sentenced him in 1954 in absentia to death. He found a haven in Syria. There he became an advisor for Jewish affairs and for "security". Brunner does not deny but boasts of his murders. In an interview with the Chicago Sun-Times in October 1987 he announced "I have no regret and I would do it again... all of them... are human garbage".[2] President Assad of Syria refuses to extradite Brunner because he committed "no punishable crime".

The way Nazism, and in fact Hitler, are living on in "moderate" Egypt is shown in the Nazi-like attitude the leaders of Egypt have been displaying. Abdal Gamel Nasser, who had been working for a German victory during World War II and had been for that arrested by the British, remained a Jew-hater. His supposedly more moderate successor Anwar Sadat expressed his admiration for Hitler. More than eight years after the fall of the Third Reich, Sadat remained a loyal follower of Hitler's. When in September 1953, the rumor arose that Hitler was alive, living in Brazil, the Cairo weekly *al Msawar* asked several leading personalities what they would write if this rumor proved to be correct. Unashamedly Sadat wrote:

> I congratulate you with all my heart
> because though you appeared to have

been defeated you were the real victor... That you have become immortal
in Germany is enough reason for
pride. And we should not be surprised to see you again in Germany or
a new Hitler in your place

Anwar Sadat

The Germans had brought with them their methodology of
dealing with and promoting the Final Solution. Typical of their
systematic planning, they had tried to establish, for easier reception
of their propaganda, a common denominator, a meeting ground of
minds. Once they had reached their target emotionally, well
planned "logic" was used to make their actions acceptable. For
emotional access they used anti-Semitism, widespread anyhow and
fanned by them to a pitch. For making their anti-Jewish extreme
actions more acceptable, they used the principle of *delegitimizing* and
of *dehumanizing* the victims.

In trying to appear as if acting with legality, the Germans were
aided by the fact that Hitler had not come to power by a coup but by
the laws of the democratic Weimar republic. He represented the
largest German party when, in accordance with the constitution, he
was appointed Chancellor of Germany. To give his anti-Jewish
measures an appearance of legality, the Nuremberg laws were
introduced and soon followed by laws of increasing harshness. Jews
were systematically delegitimized until they finally stood outside
the protection of the law.

Typical of the way this delegalizing was accepted is the statement mentioned before by the eminent Catholic theoretician, Bishop
Alois Hudal, that anti-Jewish measures should not be objected to
"even if they do not comply with what one would expect from a
modern state based upon the principle of law." The delegalization
was complete. Jews were not and did not have to be protected by the
law.

Parallel with delegalizing, the Germans had systematically introduced the principle of *dehumanizing*. It made the subsequent
increase of brutality and finally bestiality more acceptable, particularly as it found a welcoming breeding ground in the simultaneously
growing vehemence of anti-Semitism.

Dehumanization was promoted by a steady stream of "news" items in the media. Reports of murders and rapes committed by Jews were concocted and widely reported. Torturing of German children, seduction of German girls, fraud and embezzlement of the modest life savings of widows and invalids—an unending chain of "data" were publicized on the radio, in the newspapers and in movies as well as in booklets, pamphlets and scientific sounding books.

Part of this dehumanization procedure is demonization. Jews are not only stripped of their human image; they are systematically portrayed as demonic, as Satan's representatives on this earth. Because the Devil is, of course, God's vicious antagonist, to kill those Jews becomes not just permissible; it becomes a religious demand. A venomous hate propaganda was thus directed towards painting the Jews as devilish. This is being done now by the Arabs, as it was done fifty years ago by the Germans. Let us have a look at the German media of these days and at the Arab ones of today. For the purpose of demonization, both use the impact which visual experience exercises, and both Arab media today and German media of then abound with cartoons that portray Jews as demonic. Hate propaganda is carried out, too, by words, of course, and here are some quotes from Arab sources.

The heightening of this demonization can be seen in the book published in 1986, widely distributed in Syria and Lebanon, entitled *After Liberation of Jerusalem*.[3] Muhammad Mustafa Tkhini writes that the Jews are *"enemies of God"* who constitute a *"cancer"* which should be uprooted. To *fight the Jews is a "religious duty"* sanctioned by Allah. Curses and tortures are the Jews' share and they will not succeed in removing them.[4]

The leader of the "New Umma" (Nation) party, Ahmed El Sabahi, writes

> ... The fighters among us were correct
> in stressing that there is no escape but
> to *destroy Israel and throw it into the sea*.[5]

Anti-Semites all over speak recently in their attacks more often of "Zionism" than of Jews. Zionism is, however, just a code word for them. Used instead of "Jews" and "Judaism", it seems to express a more objective approach. Yet the attacks are against Jews, Jewish synagogues, like those in Vienna and Istanbul, Jewish restaurants, or other places frequented by Jews. The most popular newspaper in Egypt, *Ahbar El-Yom*, admits that when they say "Zionism," they mean Jews, and when they attack "Zionism", they attack Judaism and Jewry. In its issue of January 11, 1986, Dr. Mustafa Mahmud, the well-known Egyptian writer and journalist writes:

> Zionism as an idea is just a political cover for Judaism.

In their March 1985 issue, *El Daawa*, published by the Islamic Cultural Center in Austria, writes:

> Jealousy prevented the children of Israel from believing in Muhammad... *Nothing will help them but swords which will cut their heads and bombs to explode their lives.*[6]

This statement is just one of many in which the Arabs express their intention to commit another Final Solution. Ahmed Abdal-Rahman, one of Yassir Arafat's closest confidants, for many years his spokesman, editor of the official PLO organ Palestine Al-Thwarta, announced in that paper on March 2, 1985:

> The armed struggle is the only way of liberating Palestine... there is no room in Palestine for a compromise solution based on two states, one Israeli and one Palestinian....The solution is the liquidation of Israel.

Next to delegalization and dehumanization, a third principle of German propaganda was the setting in motion of riots in the targeted area. This method had proven successful in the case of the Sudeten, against Czechoslovakia, against Danzig and Poland. The rioters, ethnic Germans and other supporters of the Nazi regime, demanded self-determination. When the respective government endeavored to keep control over order and law and to quell the disorders, it provided—as planned by the Germans—the organizers of the riots with a moral weapon: the charge of suppressing brutally the desire for freedom.

The next step the planners of the riots took should be of concern nowadays. Hitler threatened war, allegedly to protect his fellow nationals from savage persecution. At that point, Britain's Chamberlain and France's Daladier flew to Munich for a peace conference. Hitler solemnly asserted that the Sudeten were his last territorial demand in Europe, and against that promise the peace seekers agreed to forcing their Czechoslovak ally to surrender the Sudeten. They did. Six months later Germany invaded Czechoslovakia, using the newly acquired Sudeten as advance bases. Czechoslovakia, truncated, demoralized and left with indefensible borders, capitulated without a fight. Another six months and after having started riots there, the Germans invaded Danzig and Poland. World War II was on.

The German advisers to the Arabs had learned—and taught—their lesson well. In the early winter of 1987, instigated by agitators, riots were set in motion in Judaea, Samaria and the Ghaza strip. The Arabs improved on the German model by having the rampage initiated almost entirely by children, women and teenagers. To see them on the television screen pitted against police or the military created, from the beginning, sympathy for the rioters.

This reaction was strictly emotional. It did not consider that in trying to quell that violent challenge, Israel was fighting for its existence. The historical context, which led to the abuse of these youngsters by those who pulled the wires, was not considered, probably not even known.

As noted in chapter 2, in 1917, Britain pledged her endeavor to establish a Jewish national home in Palestine. In the League of Nations Mandate of 1920, it assumed the obligation to facilitate such an aim. The Jordan River bisected the Palestine of historical boundaries and of the Balfour Declaration, as well as of the Mandate. The British in 1922, complying with Arab demands, partitioned Palestine. The region east of the Jordan River, 77% of the Palestinian territory, was to become the Arab part. Only the remaining 23% was to continue as a Jewish National Home. Pressured to agree to this division, the Jews finally accepted it.

Palestine was then a badly neglected land, barren, desolate, underpopulated, riddled with disease and particularly rampant with malaria. Most of it was desert and marshes. Little had changed under Turkish rule since in 1869 Mark Twain had described its bleakness. At one point he wrote:

It is seven in the morning and as we
are in the country, the grass ought to
be sparkling with dew, the flowers
enriching the air with their fragrance
and the birds singing from the trees.
But alas, there is no dew here, nor
flowers nor birds nor trees. There is a
plain, an unshaded lake and beyond
them some unshaded, barren mountains.[7]

As soon as World War I ended, young Jewish pioneers in increasing numbers started to transform the land again into one of "milk
and honey." Deserts turned into orange groves, vineyards, and
gardens; and marshes became ponds and lakes stocked with fishes.
As the years went on, the pioneers brought with them industry and
science. They founded cities and universities. Scholars from the
western part of Palestine were among the leading scientists in
several fields of human endeavor. In the meanwhile, in 1946 eastern
Palestine, called Transjordan, was declared by the British to be
independent. This constituted in a greater part of Palestine, the
realization of the Arabs' claim for self-determination. It was the
more an achievement as in the long history of Palestine there had
never been an independent Arab state there. The only independent
state ever existing in Palestine had been the Jewish state. In assessing
the possibility of whether "it" could happen again, the issue of
Jordan being a Palestinian state is a crucial one. The support which
the allegation of "homelessness" finds on a world-wide scale makes
it quite likely that the Arabs, encouraged by it, will try again and
again the destruction of Israel. Israel can win many wars but it can
lose only one. To be at the mercy of victorious Arabs would auto-
matically trigger a Holocaust which would dwarf all the atrocities
and barbarism committed by the Germans.

When in 1948 the British ended their Mandate and withdrew
from western Palestine, armies of five Arab countries invaded the
infant state of Israel, the Jewish part of Palestine. They were beaten
back but succeeded in occupying in that western part of the country,
the area which in antiquity had been the Jewish provinces of Judaea
and Samaria and had been referred to as such in British documents.
After a bitter struggle, they also wrested from the Jews the walled

part of the city of Jerusalem and a strip of land in the Ghaza region. The sheikh of Transjordan had by then renamed the country ruled by him, Jordan, and elevated himself to the position of king. In 1967, again the armies of five countries invaded Israel. In a war that lasted six days, they were decidedly beaten. Judaea and Samaria, as well as the Ghaza strip and the ancient part of Jerusalem, were retaken by Israel.

While they clamor for the right to a Palestinian state at the expense of Israel, Arab spokesmen have on numerous occasions let the cat out of the bag and admitted that Jordan is the Arab Palestinian state.

The truth is that Jordan is Palestine and Palestine is Jordan.

> King Hussein in an interview for Al Nahar al-Arabi w'al Daouli Paris, December 26, 1981.

When the demand for a separate Palestinian state was first pushed into the foreground in 1977, it was admitted:

"The founding of a Palestinian state is only a tool in the continuing battle against Israel. After we have established our right in all of Palestine, we must not for a single moment delay the re-unification of Jordan and Palestine."

> Zuhar Muhsin, former head of the Military Operations of the PLO and member of the PLO Executive Council, in an interview with the Dutch Daily, TROUW, on March 31, 1977.

That the "West Bank" is only one phase of the demands is admitted by Arafat himself:

"The declaration of Palestinian Independence constitutes a beginning of the real confrontation of the Zionist project on the land of Palestine itself."

> Bagdad, Voice of Palestine, 3/21/89 FBIS 3-23

And the man designated as foreign minister of the state of Palestine, Farauk Kaddoumi, stated on April 4, 1989, on the BBC:

"The recovery of but a part of our soil will not cause us to forsake our Palestinian land — which will then form the base from which we will later pursue the next phase."

We all know, of course, what this next phase means: the annihilation, in German parlance "extermination," of the State of Israel.
This Palestinian state

"will escalate and grow. At first a small state and with Allah's help, it will be made large and expand to the East, West, North and South."

> Abu Iyad, Arafat's top deputy, head of the PLO's Unified Security Apparatus, Fatah Central Committee Member, in Al-Anbah, Kuwait, 12/18/88.

There are statistical data to confirm the admitted fact that Jordan is Arab Palestine and that Palestinian Arabs are thus not without a home. Dr. George Habash, the head of the Front for the Liberation of Palestine states in DER SPIEGEL of February 10, 1982, that as many as 70% of Jordan's population is of West Palestinian origin. This seems a conservative estimate. The Associated Press in a dispatch from Amman dated June 14, 1980, reports that 80% of Jordan's population originated in Western Palestine. It has been pointed out that as the distances are so small—about 45 miles from Nablus in Samaria to Amman, capital of Jordan—those who transferred to Jordan were certainly not uprooted but just moved a few miles. In Jordan, those who had come from Western Palestine were rapidly integrated. They control over 70% of Jordan's economy, according to Arab reports.[8] Palestinians from Western Palestine play an important part in Jordan's cultural life, the press, radio and television; and they supply the largest number of students and faculty to the institutions of higher learning. When every inch of the land labeled the West Bank was under Arab control, this did not promote peace. After exercising control for nineteen years without having created another Palestinian state, Jordan used the "West Bank" in 1967 as a forward base to attack the rest of Israel with the proclaimed aim of annihilating it. To provide—again—such a forward base is clearly not a way to prevent another Holocaust. From their own pronouncements, it would be used—again—for the same purpose.

To deliver arms to countries that have vowed to destroy Israel is to act not better but worse than the civilized world acted when faced with the German Final Solution plan. Then that plan was supported by making certain that the supply of humans for the death camps did not dry up. The poison gas was supplied by the Germans themselves. By now supplying arms to those who are determined to liquidate Israel, the nations of the world are taking a much more active part in the genocide the Arabs are preparing, than was taken in the nineteen thirties and forties by the world community.

Evil breeds evil. The powerful forces which are geared towards completing the not entirely completed genocide are gaining momentum and strength from two main sources. One is their actual involvement in planning a second phase of that Final Solution. The other is the acceptance which their crimes found even by the victors of World War II.

A basic requirement for counteracting of such plans is unequivocal condemnation of and punishment for what happened. Mere lip service to such an attitude is easily—and correctly—interpreted as just that. It encourages the plotters and induces the conclusion that the world does not really mind.

After the collapse of their reign of terror, the mass murderers of the Thirties and Forties expected to be held accountable. In fact most of the world assumed that this would be the case.

Winston Churchill had announced that "retribution for war crimes must henceforth take its place among the major purposes of the war." Similar statements had been made by President Roosevelt, as well as in the "St. James Declaration" of January 13, 1943, issued by the Governments (in exile) of Belgium, Czechoslovakia, Free French, Greece, Holland, Luxemburg, Poland and Yugoslavia.

The Allies had assembled a register of 33,810 war criminals partly as an outcome of their own intelligence, largely, however, from German files. The Germans, in their almost compulsive sense for order had kept punctilious records of every soldier and civilian. The personnel files thus showed who had belonged to the SS and during what period. They also contained data of what each SS unit had done and when. Yet only a minute part of those most actively involved were tried in a few showcases. To their surprise, the very great majority were not immediately called to justice. Most of the main actors had escaped from Europe to an overseas country. How did Eichmann, Mengele, Borman, Brunner, Klaus Barbie—how did those who should have headed the list of war criminals escape?

Soon after the German surrender, it became known in SS circles: if you made it to Rome, the Vatican will provide you with travel documents; all you have to do is claim that you are a Catholic. They do this in cooperation with the International Red Cross; and for those who assert to have been active anti-communists and know something of how to fight communism, entrance to the United States is assured, independent of what your background is regarding murders.

The unfortunate cooperation of the Roman Catholic clergy with the International Red Cross has been vividly described in a report by Benno Weiser Varon[9] and is fully supported by documentary evidence.

Anybody claiming to be a Catholic and anti-communist and bringing with him a "friend" who would confirm this and his "identity", could receive a referral from the Vatican to the International Red Cross office in Rome, which then supplied a travel document showing the often fictitious name.

The same U.S. State Department that had been charged by a government investigation team with "acquiescence of this government in the murder of Jews," was now making arrangements for the admission of war criminals who by law were excluded from entering the United States. Whatever crimes these people had committed, if they were anti-communists, they were now aided to enter. From the point of answering the question whether it could happen again, this aid to known war criminals is an important element that facilitates a second phase of the Final Solution. That one can remain unpunished after active, often leading participation in the massacres of the Thirties and Forties, certainly is an element favoring repetition. Illegal actions of a special secret unit in the State Department brought to the States altogether 10,000 war criminals. Those this way admitted to the United States include such leading figures as SS General Franz Kuschel whose troops in 1941 brought over 40,000 Jews to an execution ground; Stanislaw Stankievich, according to war crimes files, alleged to have directed the massacre of 7,000 Jews in one city alone; Emanual Jasuik, former mayor of Kletsk. He is charged of having supervised the assassination of 5,000 Jews as the work of just one day, etc. And of course, Klaus Barbie "the butcher of Lyon" charged with having had a leading hand in the massacre of many thousands of Jews in southern France and also of French partisans. Ladislaw Ostrowski, made by the Germans President of the puppet state of Byelorussia is the highest ranking of those who were excluded by law to from entering the United States but who immigrated with the help of American authorities and was even granted American citizenship. Would it be realistic to expect serious counteraction by United States' authorities if a group of states with numerous interests in America would initiate the often announced intention of completing the program of the Final Solution?

The escape from Europe with the help of the Vatican and the International Red Cross is recorded in the files of the U.S. State Department. In 1947, it became evident to the U.S. Embassy in Rome that there was an organization working in Italy that provided false documents to Nazis on the wanted list. The report was first classified Secret, but as the embarrassing involvement of the Vatican became clear, the report's classification was raised to Top Secret. In eleven single-spaced legal size pages, plus 26 pages of appendices documenting the findings of the report, it reveals in considerable detail how the Vatican and the International Red Cross cooperated in aiding the escape of those Nazis. To check on the exactness of the obtained data, the diplomat who consolidated the findings had two U.S. intelligence agents "run through the procedure" which others used, and they were able to obtain without any problems false travel papers.

In this operation of providing false travel documents, we meet again an old acquaintance. Bishop Alois Hudal who had previously announced that Jews were not entitled to the protection of the law, was one of the major figures in the operation of that document scheme.

* * *

The weapons which may be able to accomplish phase II of the Final Solution are lavishly supplied by the Soviet Union as well as by the Western nations, the United States, Britain and France, notwithstanding the fact that the receiving Arab nations are officially at war with Israel. The Western public on such occasions is assured that these weapons can and will not be used against Israel. As to that point, Tahir al-Maari, the Foreign Minister of Jordan stated on February 24, 1985

> ... arms will come to Jordan and immediately upon arrival they become Jordanian arms to which no conditions or other commitments are attached.

The genocide of Israel and its Jewish inhabitants has been proclaimed as a goal for many years. The intent has been announced and achieving this aim has been tried in each invasion of Israel. Here are some of the relevant statements:

> I want to tell Carter and Begin that when the Arabs set off their volcano, *there will be only Arabs in this part of the world*... Our people will continue to fuel the torch of the revolution with *rivers of blood* until the whole of the occupied homeland is liberated—*not just part of it.*[10]
>
> Yasser Arafat as quoted by
> AP Beirut, March 12, 1979

> The declared program of the PLO is to bring about the destruction of the Zionist entity of Israel.
>
> PLO. Information Office,
> Oslo, May 5, 1977

How such "destruction" of Israel would look was demonstrated in a grisly way by the Syrian Chief of Staff, General Mustafa Thias, when he recommended that medals be bestowed to Syrian soldiers who during the Yom Kippur War participated in the massacre of Israeli prisoners of war on Mount Hermon.

> There is the outstanding recruit from Aleppo who killed all by himself 28 Jewish soldiers. Singlehandedly he slaughtered them like sheep. This was witnessed by all his comrades.

Moreover, he killed three of them with an ax and decapitated them, in other words he did not use a military weapon to kill them but used an ax to chop their heads from their bodies. He fought with one of them face to face, laid down his ax, broke his neck and devoured his flesh.

Need I single him out for special honor? I will award the Medal of the Republic to any soldier who kills 28 Jews.

In a speech before the Syrian National Assembly as reported by Syria's official gazette, *Al Jarida Al Rasmiya*, No. 27, July 11, 1974.

Multiply the horror of the slaughter of these 28 prisoners of war by a hundred thousand, and you arrive at a picture of what would likely happen to the Jews of Israel if the Arabs were in one of their onslaughts to succeed in overwhelming Israeli defenses.

One may be inclined to say that the massacre described above happened in 1973 and that the Arabs might have changed or at least mellowed their attitude since. They have not. While more recently some Arab leaders have, as far as public utterances are concerned, become more restrained to avoid conclusions that "it could happen again," the trend remains unmistakable. Thus on March 8, 1986, President Assad of Syria talked openly about Syria's plan to commit another Holocaust. On February 27, 1986, he stated that in the future "the Golan will be located in the heart of Syria and not on its border," clearly indicating that his aim was not just the Golan Heights but the heartland of Israel. The sweep into Israel would wreak *"the apex of Israel's Holocaust."* [11] The Golan Heights are as little an aim for Arab actions as are Judaea, Samaria and Ghaza. They all are just a first demand for a forward base. The aim remains the totality of Israel. The Turkish daily *Gumhuriyet* reported on March 4, 1986 about the meeting of Turkish leaders with Syria's Prime Minister: "During the talks the Syrian Prime Minister criticized Israel in an extremely harsh manner and stated that they were opposed to the existence of this country."

Hitler, who lost his try for control of the world, succeeded largely in one of his aims. He and his cohorts had two out of three European Jews murdered. And with the end of the National Socialist regime in Germany, the danger of genocide has not disappeared. There is an uninterrupted chain of connections between the past and what happens nowadays regarding the fate of the Jews. Supported by SS experts, Arabs continued after the fall of the Third Reich to promote the Final Solution program by financing and backing the creation and functioning of neo-Nazi organizations, they keep their fingers in the European and American development of groups geared towards such an end.

Dr. Maarouf al Dawalibi, Senior Advisor to the Saudi king, at a U.N. Seminar on December 5, 1984, revived the Blood Libel. He was quoted by the Reuter news agency as claiming at that occasion that the Talmud says: "If a Jew does not drink the blood of a non-Jew every year, he will be damned for eternity." Thus the statement of an international representative of a "moderate" Arab country about the religion which in a world of utmost barbarity proclaimed to mankind the demand: "Thou shalt love thy neighbor as thyself" (Leviticus XIX, 18). And the occasion: a U.N. seminar on religious tolerance.[12] The stated purpose of this U.N. conference was "Encouragement of Understanding, Tolerance and Respect in Matters Relating to the Freedom of Religion or Belief."

The New Republic investigated this situation and reported the findings as follows on March 4, 1985.

> Readers may recall a Notebook item several weeks ago on a speech delivered at a U.N. conference on human rights in Geneva last December by the Saudi Arabian delegate, Dr. Maarouf al Dawalibi (TNR February 4). In this address, the Saudi human rights expert explained that anti-Semitism was a result of among other intrinsically Jewish characteristics, the obligation of Jews to drink non-Jewish blood at least once a year. Dr. al Dawalibi, it turns out, is no novice at

Jew-hating. In fact he had been at it for two generations and not just in the Arab world but as a servant to the Nazis. SS Obergruppenfuehrer Erwin Ettel described him in 1943 as "the Nazi Party's 'Arab confidence man in Paris.'" The scholar's evidence suggests that he was a critical link during the war years between officials of the Reich and the notoriously pro-Nazi Grand Mufti of Jerusalem. So the question is: Why would the Saudis send to the conference someone who was not merely an anti-Semite, tried and true, but actually a Nazi henchman? The answer is that it does not embarrass King Fahd to have such a man as his senior advisor.

This brings us back to the SS and its early links with terrorism and the Mufti's lobbying for a Holocaust.

CAN IT HAPPEN AGAIN?

It certainly can.

But it can never happen the same way it did in the Thirties and Forties.

The industrial nations are consuming energy so voraciously that exclusion from the mideastern energy sources would perilously destabilize their political, economic and military status and could bring about a breakdown of the laboriously maintained structure. The United States has made it clear on numerous occasions that exclusion from decisive influence in this area would not be "acceptable." President Carter, certainly not known for his militancy, found the issue of being pushed out of the oil rich region important enough to include the United States' reaction to such a situation in the State of the Union message of January 24, 1980.

Let our position be absolutely clear.
An attempt by outside forces to gain

control of the Persion Gulf region will
be regarded as an assault on vital interests of the United States and such
an assault will be repelled by any
means necessary, including military
force.

Yet, the Soviet Union continues to follow a policy which openly
aims at eliminating American influence from this region. Developments show a steady progress of this Soviet goal, as the West is being
ejected from one mideastern country after the other. With only a
short interruption in 1941, *Iraq* had been in the Western fold ever
since its creation after World War I. It was a leading member of the
Baghdad Pact, later the CENTRO defense treaty. In July, 1958,
General Abdul Karim Kassem staged a military coup and assumed
dictatorial power. The Western influence was substitutedfor by the
rule of the Arab Socialist Renaissance Party (Baath party). Agree-
ments with various communist countries were concluded. *Libya* had
been a central point in Western defense planning. The United States
built and maintained there the giant Wheelus Air Base, and the
British had a military base in Tobruk. King Idris, a national hero due
to his resistance to the Italian colonialism, seemed to be in control. He
was a friend of the western democracies but was overthrown in September 1969 by a coup led by Colonel Muammar al Qadafi. The new
government ordered the western powers to close their military
installations, and the American and British facilities were
"nationalized." *Iran* was a part of the Western defense system. It
looked back at a stormy history through much of the century. But
under its Shah Reza Pahlevi close ties with the Western powers had
been established as Iran endeavored to introduce Western economic
methods and the West, especially the United States, became a
partner in mutual undertakings. In December 1978, the Shah was
overthrown. Ayatolla Khoumeini established a strictly fundamen-
talist government, and bitter animosity towards the West took over
with known radical consequences. *Syria* and *Lebanon* had been cooperating with France in matters pertaining to defense. Nowadays, in
the second half of the Eighties, Syria is allied with the USSR.
Lebanon, with no functioning government, has been turned into a
hub of anti-Western scheming and of training for international terrorism. Egypt, Saudi Arabia, Jordan, Kuwait, North Yemen and the
Gulf Emirates tend rather to the West but are under heavy pressure

by fundamentalists to join the anti-Western forces. Their governments stand on shaky ground, and none of them permits the West to establish there a naval or air base, so urgently needed for strategic defense planning.

In summary, Western influence in the region has been steadily shrinking while Soviet power has been growing at alarming proportions.

United States policy tries to play a complex game: not antagonizing those Muslim countries in which it still maintains a foothold, yet not to undermine Israel's existence. There is no danger there of a coup that would turn the country towards the East. Being the only democracy in the region, Israel shares with the West many values, including the respect for human life, dignity and the regard for individual freedom. It has the most powerful military in the region and is scientifically highly developed. Scientific cooperation with the United States has proven itself fruitful and stimulating for both parties. Israel's existence is probably a main reason for keeping the Soviet Union from assuming the risk of occupying the entire area at a moment of American involvement somewhere else.

Aware of the cataclysmic effect a nuclear "first strike" would have, the superpowers are watching each other suspiciously with the most advanced methods on a 24-hour basis. The peril of a blowup, intended, by miscalculation or accident becomes multiplied by destabilization, and all this makes it likely that a Holocaust today would not engulf the Jews only, but mankind.

To obtain a correct picture of nowadays' slide towards another Holocaust, we must not underestimate the part which psychology plays in it and how it interlocks with the terrorist acts. The German terrorists could take over the German state after using psychological warfare against the German voter. Once they were put into control of the state machinery, they immediately adjusted their terrorism to the new format and the extended power. The German state became as a whole a terrorist state which employed blackmail on an international scale. The Holocaust was just the extreme symptom of the terrorist lawlessness. Equally, today's terrorism, especially the one which is aimed directly at the existence of Israel, employs psychological warfare to fit in with terrorist actions. Their combined purpose is to condition mankind gradually to the use of terrorist method to weaken morale and the will to resist, and raise the question of the *root cause* of all these actions.

The root cause, however, is not any political constellation. It is not for the Arabs, not for the Red Brigades of Italy, not for the German Red Army Faction and not for the Baader Meinhof group. Not either for the Turkish Gray Wolves, the Japanese Red Army, the Armenian ASALA, or the Puerto Rican FALN, or the Croatian, Malayan, or Basque separatists. Not for the IRA and other terrorist groups either. They all have different grievances. But the root cause for their terrorism is the same. It is, as Benjamin Netanyahu points out, the readiness to solve political problems by the use of extreme, utterly unrestrained violence without consideration for anybody or anything.[13]

It certainly does not have to happen, but to prevent it, the present trend has to be reversed.

Frank, pitiless examination as presented in this volume should hopefully stimulate other probes with a related focus and, particularly if this ties in with the existing rich literature, might serve as a potent element against mankind's sliding again into another Holocaust disaster.

[1] Breckinridge Long papers, Minutes of the Bermuda Conference April 20, 1943 as quoted by Feingold op. cit. 199, 337 n. 112

[2] Associated Press, October 31, 1987.

[3] Muhammad Mustafa Tkhini, After Liberation of Jerusalem, op. cit. p. 72-73, emphasis added.

[4] Ibid.

[5] *El Umma*. Egypt 10/19/85, emphasis added.

[6] Emphasis added.

[7] Mark Twain, *The Innocents Abroad*, p. 386, the Library of America edition, first printing.

[8] Al Ahram, Cairo, March 5, 1974.

[9] Midstream April 1984.

[10] Emphasis added.

[11] Assad's Recent Speeches; An Analysis. Israel Ministry of Foreign Affairs 142/23/3.1986/3.03.03.

[12] Reuters Ltd, North European Service, January 16, 1985, Wednesday AM Cycle.

[13] Benjamin Netanyahu, *Terrorism. How the West Can Win*, 204.

Index